Yesterday in Old Fall River

Yesterday in Old Fall River

A Lizzie Borden Companion

Paul Dennis Hoffman

Carolina Academic Press
Durham, North Carolina

Library of Congress Cataloging-in-Publication Data

Hoffman, Paul Dennis, 1945–
    Yesterday in old Fall River : a Lizzie Borden companion / Paul
    Dennis Hoffman.
        p.   cm.
    Includes bibliographical references and index.
    ISBN 0-89089-799-9
    1. Borden, Lizzie, 1860–1927. 2. Murder—Massachusetts—Fall
River—Case studies—Biography. I. Title.

HV6534.F2 H64 2000
364.15'23'292274485—dc21
[B]   00-040325

Carolina Academic Press
700 Kent Street
Durham, North Carolina
Telephone (919) 489-7486
Fax (919) 493-5668
E-mail: cap@cap-press.com
www.cap-press.com

Printed in the United States of America

To My Parents

Edwin Lester Hoffman
May Hoffman
They will live forever through the good they have done.

To My Family

Matthew Woodrow and his lovely wife Jami
their children Annabelle and Jacob
Leigh Ann
Brooke Elizabeth

Most of All to My Wife Christine

All we've gone through together was worth it.

and

In loving memory of
Frank X. O'Neil (1945-1999)

Contents

Illustrations

Foreword

The Borden legend is famous for its unanswered questions. The big one is, did she or didn't she? Paul Dennis Hoffman's book doesn't answer that one, but it does answer hundreds of other questions as well as provide cross-referenced data that gives anyone studying the case all the "connections" one needs. This text is rich in biographical information and simply puts together the factual history of the Borden story. Major players are given enough space to identify and define them as they relate to the Borden world. They are also given important added definition. For example, here we learn that Dr. David Williams Cheever (1831-1915) testified for the prosecution. He was a medical expert who, along with Dr. Frank Draper, testified as to the nature of the head wounds and the time of Abby and Andrew's deaths. In addition we learn that:

> Cheever enjoyed a brilliant career as a doctor and was the youngest senior surgeon at Boston City Hospital. He became a Professor of Surgery at Harvard in 1882, a post he held until made Professor Emeritus in 1893. He also kept a private practice during this time and received an honorary Doctor of Laws degree from Harvard in 1894. Cheever wrote several books and articles and frequently contributed to professional journals.

This is the significant trivia we need to enhance our love and awareness of a legend that has worked its way into American mythology and folklore. Isn't it wonderful to find out that defense attorney Melvin Adams' middle name was Ohio? Just look him up. He's right here, and so are his birthplace, his undergraduate college, his law school, the dates of both graduations, the staff he served on after law school and even the fact that he was "handsome and of medium build with a waxed moustache." Unless you are willing to devote thousands of hours to research and travel, you are not going to get the details and minutiae available in this book.

Paul Dennis Hoffman put in the thousands of hours, the travel and devotion necessary for filling many gaps within this famous murder case. His book is to the Borden legend what Webster's dictionary is to the English language. It is also the first (could there be a second?) encyclopedia of Lizzie Borden.

Anyone who knows the case knows that Adelaide Churchill was the next door neighbor to whom Lizzie was alleged to have said, "Do come over. Someone has killed Father." We also know that, along with Bridget Sullivan (You have to look her up!), she discovered the body of Abby on the second floor and called down, "There is another one." Did you know that her father was a popular mayor of Fall River in the mid-1800s and that her handyman was named Thomas Boulds?

Learning that John Ratcliffe "was a weaver from New Bedford; he was summoned to jury duty in the Borden trial, but was neither questioned nor selected for the jury" might tempt you to try a little prussic acid. But believe me, everything you want to know is here too. Most of us know that Lizzie burned a Bedford cord dress in her kitchen stove. Mary A. Raymond made that dress. She did other things too. Look her up. In fact, stop reading this introduction and do what this book asks you to do! Start flipping through the pages. If the Borden tale fascinates you as it does thousands of others, it will be a long time before you stop turning these pages.

Jules R. Rychebusch
Professor of English and Communications
Bristol Community College, Fall River
April 2000

Preface

I have always loved the historical era 1877-1901, named by writer Mark Twain the "Gilded Age." The 1890s, which I find the most mesmerizing decade of this time, is far enough away from the present so that its people lived in a world whose habits, morals and culture we will, sadly, I believe, never see again. On the other hand, it is also close enough to the present, or at least to the childhood of many who are middle-aged or older today, so that one may almost reach out and touch it.

Most people my age have grandparents or other relatives who were born in this era. Photographs and even old moving pictures exist that show how different the world looked then. As many before me have remarked, times seemed simpler then, even if they were not. No radio, television or computers existed. There were no automobiles, nuclear bombs or crack cocaine. No one knew of bio-terrorism, ozone depletion or high school students with guns. Instead there was horse-drawn transportation, bustles, old-fashioned American patriotism, and a blissful ignorance of what the twentieth century had in store for the world. It was a time of black and white photographs, ladies in prim waistshirts and long skirts and men with straw hats and starched collars.

I was born in 1945, but have traveled back to Gilded Age America many times. My birthplace was the Lower East Side of New York City, and I have always been captivated by old photographs of New York. My personal library contains several books that preserve old New York with wonderful pictures of buildings that have been torn down and people who have long since died. Yet all I have to do to walk down Fifth Avenue or Broadway and amble past the old Western Union Building or pass the arm of the Statue of Liberty on display in Madison Square is look at those pictures. I am there, smelling the air that reeked even then, although of horse droppings rather than industrial pollutants.

Similarly, I have been in "Old" Fall River and have walked down Second Street and Main and Weybossett. Although I can not be completely sure, I think I may have passed old Andrew Borden on his way "downstreet" to check his business interests. I might even have walked behind Lizzie herself on a stroll across town to see the fine houses on French Street and have some quiet time in Oak Grove Cemetery.

I have also learned little, yet important, things about everyday life in the 1890s, things such as how women managed with their menses before modern inventions made hygiene so much easier and the courtesy with which people addressed even their adversaries, as found in the transcripts of the Borden trial and the letters of District Attorney Hosea M. Knowlton. Where else could one get such a large portion of small-town American life than by studying the Borden episode?

Like most who study the Borden case today, the gruesome murders and their unanswered questions, the motives of Lizzie, ex-Massachusetts Governor George Dexter Robinson, reporter Edwin H. Porter and detective Edwin D. McHenry push me with the force of economist Adam Smith's "invisible hand" to investigate this case. But also, the knowledge that this is one of the few remaining doors to Lizzie Borden's lost time where my (and possibly your) ancestors breathed, and the world seemed fresh and full of hope, continues to beckon me to open the old books and relive that terrible, that wonderful crime and the now-faded world in which it happened.

One of the problems I confess to having in studying the Borden case is that of keeping all of the characters straight. Was Melvin Ohio Adams a lawyer for the prosecution or for the defense? Was it Chief Justice Albert C. Mason or Associate Justice Justin Dewey who was appointed to the bench by Governor Robinson, soon to be the leader of Lizzie's defense team? Who were William Medley, Dennis Desmond, Jonathan Clegg, Marthe Chagnon and Hyman Lubinsky and why were they called to testify at Lizzie's trial?

Whenever I read a book or article about the Borden murders, these and other questions inevitably entered my mind. Finally, I concluded that in order to keep the participants and their actions straight, I needed a program. So I began to list names and their relation to the murder or to the trial. Soon my list grew almost as fast as Fall River in the 1890s. I had more names than I ever expected; I was *totally* unaware of just how many people the Borden murders touched. Eventually I had the names of over 740 people.

I also believed that perhaps I was not the only student of the Borden murder case who was confused. Thus the idea for this book was born. These names, of course, were much more than just those of the participants in Fall River's greatest drama. They all had their own lives, personalities, successes and failures, most unrelated to the unfortunate deaths of Andrew and Abby Borden. For this reason, I felt it practical to include facts about their lives in my research when I could find those facts. I am glad I did. The background of many who were involved in the murders or the trial make interesting reading apart from the Borden saga and include a cross-section of late nineteenth century America.

Many of the physicians, lawyers and expert witnesses had Ivy League educations; several held Harvard degrees. The majority of those less formally educated were hard-working farmers and laborers toiling in nineteenth-century New England, living out the cycle of life near the place where they were born. Others had made their way to Fall River from Canada, Europe and beyond, living the American Dream as did millions of other immigrants in New York, Boston and similar cities as well as in towns large and small throughout the United States.

I believe that Lizzie Borden historian Howard Brody was right on the mark when he wrote in the April 1999 issue of *The Lizzie Borden Quarterly*, "the best way to become misinformed about the Borden case is to read a book about it." Virtually every book and magazine article ever written about America's most famous unresolved murder mystery contains some factual errors. Most are small and inconsequential. Others have been perpetuated over the decades and have resulted in puzzled expressions and frustrated sighs ever since their publication.

There are facts about the case on which all Borden scholars agree. Between 9:30 and 10:30 A.M. on Thursday, August 4, 1892, Lizzie Andrew Borden, or someone, attacked Lizzie's stepmother, Abby Durfee (Gray) Borden, and hacked her to death with a small ax or a hatchet

View of Second Street, Fall River, Massachusetts, c.1890.
Collection of the Fall River Historical Society.

in the second floor guest room of her 92 Second Street home in Fall River, Massachusetts. Approximately 90 minutes later, between 10:45 and 11:10 A.M., Lizzie Andrew Borden, or someone, similarly chopped Andrew Jackson Borden about the head and face with the same weapon, in the downstairs sitting room where he was taking a nap, until he was dead. Andrew and Abby Borden were the father and step-mother of Lizzie Borden and her sister Emma. One other person resided at the Second Street house: the Bordens' maid, Bridget Sullivan. Emma was in Fairhaven, Massachusetts visiting friends at the time of the murders, so only the two elderly Bordens, Lizzie and Bridget were known to be home when the murders were committed.

Within minutes of the discovery of Andrew's body, word began to circulate among the citizens of Fall River that something terrible had occurred at the Borden home. When Abby's body was discovered at approximately 11:30 A.M., many in the city began to fear that a crazed ax murderer was on the loose. Crowds of people began to gather on or near the Borden property, milling around, making their own inspection of the barn and the area around the house and quite possibly destroying evidence in the process.

Within the next five days, the police made numerous searches of the Borden house and found no clues, with the exception of what became known as the "handleless hatchet" that was found in the cellar and presented at Lizzie Borden's trial by the prosecution as the murder weapon. Lizzie Borden herself appeared in shock but calm the day of the murders. There was no physical evidence on her body that she had anything to do with the crime. Her skin, hair and dress were free of blood, and there was no indication that she had recently washed herself or changed her clothes. When the police interviewed Lizzie in her bedroom at about 11:40 A.M. that morning, she said that at the time her father died, she was in the barn eating pears while looking for fishing weights.

Because the crime was so brutal, almost no one thought that a female could commit such an act. Besides, the victims were members of her own family. The police immediately began looking elsewhere for the murderer. One prime suspect was Lizzie's uncle John Vinnicum Morse, an overnight house guest the night before the murders. Morse was soon cleared of suspicion, however, when he was able to prove that he was miles away from the house when the Bordens died.

Over the next few weeks, the police investigated scores of leads, conducted dozens of interviews and traveled hundreds of miles, both in and out of the Fall River area, in their attempts to find the killer. All of the investigations and clues led to dead ends.

Finally, as much as no one wanted to admit it, the finger of guilt continued to point at Lizzie Borden. Investigators felt that only she had the motive, the means and the opportunity to kill Andrew and Abby. Lizzie desired to live the "good life," one deserved of the daughter of one of the wealthiest men in town, even though Andrew, a miser and hard businessman, preferred living cheaply in a house on the poorer side of town with no modern amenities such as electricity and indoor plumbing. Since axes and hatches in nineteenth-century homes were as common as hammers and television sets are in today's houses, the murder weapon was easily accessible. And finally, Lizzie alone was in or near the rooms where the bodies were found when both murders occurred; Emma was out of town visiting friends in another town and Bridget Sullivan was asleep in her attic bedroom.

A formal inquest into the murders began on August 9, 1892 and two days later Lizzie was arrested and charged with the murder of her father. After a preliminary hearing and an investigation into the murders by a grand jury, Lizzie was indicted for the murders of both her father and her stepmother. The trial date was set for June, 5, 1893 in New Bedford, Massachusetts. By this time, the case had captured the imagination of the whole nation and Lizzie was famous from coast to coast.

The prosecution knew from the beginning that it would be almost impossible to convict a woman, and a relative of the victims at that, of such a heinous crime. All the arguments against Lizzie were circumstantial and two important pieces of damning evidence, her inquest testimony and the fact that she tried to buy a strong poison the day before the murders, were excluded from the trial. Public opinion favored Lizzie. The chief defense attorney was a popular ex-governor of Massachusetts and, to make matters worse for the prosecution, while governor, he had appointed one of the three judges presiding at the trial to his position on the bench.

It came as no surprise that when the verdict was announced on June 20, 1893, Lizzie was declared "not guilty." The local authorities were so sure that Lizzie Borden was the murderer that after the verdict, they never searched for another suspect. They unofficially closed the case and went on about their daily business.

Although most of Fall River and the United States in general felt relieved when Lizzie was exonerated, her life after the trial was not what she expected it to be. She and her sister did inherit Andrew Borden's considerable estate, and Lizzie did live the life of a wealthy woman. She bought a large house in the best part of town and was able to travel and enjoy many of the luxuries of turn-of-the-century America. However, most of her supporters before the verdict shunned and ignored her after the jury's decision. Many people, both in Fall River and throughout the nation, began to suspect that she had committed the double murder and had gotten away with it. Fall River's high society would not admit her into their social circle, and even her own sister, who proclaimed her innocence for the rest of her life, eventually moved out of the mansion they purchased together and did not speak to her for the last twenty-two years of her life.

One of the thrills of researching history is discovering facts that no one had come across before or finding explanations for heretofore unanswered questions. For this book, I wanted to correct spelling of and give first names to as many individuals as I could. In several cases, references to them in twentieth-century works are lacking and I had to go back to the primary sources. In writing *Yesterday in Old Fall River,* I found, for the first time, the full names of people no other modern Borden historian have listed, or, if they have, mentioned them under the wrong name. Thus, Boston Herald staff artist Blair became George H. and policemen Davis, McAdams, Quigley, Arnold, Brownell, Eldridge and Rooks, among many others, received first name credit for the minor roles they played, as did Taunton, Massachusetts courthouse janitor David M. Piper, landlady Ella Cross, Oak Grove Cemetery official Jonathan E. Morrill and scores of others known in the literature up to this point only as "Mrs. McGuirk" or "the son of C.C. Potter."

Other small yet fascinating facts about the Borden mystery came to my attention. For example, Victoria Lincoln, author of one of the most respected books about the crime, refers to John Vinnicum Morse's friend from South Dartmouth as "Isaac Hastings." He was, in fact, Isaac C. Davis. The only Hastings mentioned in connection with the Borden murders is the city of Hastings, Iowa, where Morse's sister and brother-in-law lived when they gave an interview to the local Hastings newspaper about their relationship with Morse.

Lincoln also popularized the rumor that Lizzie Borden was carried to her grave in 1927 by a group of black pallbearers. Other writers have mentioned that this story was probably untrue and that her pallbearers were a cousin and three men who worked for her at Maplecroft, her final residence after moving out of 92 Second Street with her sister, Emma. Lincoln's story is not entirely false, however. Lizzie was indeed led to the family plot by four white men, but Emma, who soon followed Lizzie to the grave, was carried by African-American pallbearers, apparently because it was an old New England tradition to do so in Lizzie and Emma's day. These trivial facts admittedly add little to a possible solution of the murders, but for Borden aficionados, the devil is in the details and every newly uncovered bit of information is a treasure.

When Frank Spiering wrote his best-seller, *LIZZIE*, his theory had Emma sneaking back into town in a horse and carriage, carrying out the murders and returning to the town of Fairhaven, Massachusetts in time to receive the awful news about Andrew and Abby. Spiering's theory is a clever piece of detective work but, of course, impossible to verify. I came across a statement made by one Delia Summers Manley. She and her sister-in-law Sarah B. Hart, were walking up Second Street to catch a trolley car on Main Street and stopped near the Borden house. There, they had a short conversation with Hart's nephew Ezra P.B. Manley, who was riding in a carriage. Could this be the vehicle Spiering was thinking of when he wrote his account? If so, it solves that part of the mystery and eliminates at least one suspect for modern Borden detectives.

Many writers, most notably Edwin H. Porter, Robert Sullivan, Arnold Brown and David Kent stress the importance of Hyman Lubinsky's testimony at Lizzie's trial. Lubinsky was an ice cream vendor who happened to pass by the Borden home at the time Andrew Borden was murdered and saw a woman outside of the house by the Borden barn. The defense used Lubinsky to impress upon the jury that if it was Lizzie whom Lubinsky saw, she could not have been inside the house killing her father. However, as Leonard Rebello notes in *Lizzie Borden Past and Present*, that woman could have been Ellen Eagan, who suddenly took sick while walking past the Borden residence at the time Lubinsky said he saw a woman walking outside near the Bordens' barn.

It was the discovery of these, and countless other bits of information, that has continued to excite me and move me to publish this volume on what I feel is one of the most fascinating crimes in American history.

A major collection of errors that I have encountered in my research involves the spelling of names used in contemporary accounts of the crime. During the Gilded Age period of United States history, when the crimes took place, the style of newspaper reporting known as "yellow journalism" crowded more than just facts and accurate reporting off of the front page.

It seems that few writers felt it necessary to include correct spelling or, in many cases, even the first names of many of the participants in the crimes. Fall River police officer Wixon, for example, was occasionally given the first name of Frank. At other times, even in the same newspaper, he was called Francis. His middle initial was sometimes reported as "H." and at other times as "X." He has been written up as "Wixon" and as "Wickson." Many of these errors were perpetuated by later writers who depended on the local newspapers for their information. When I came across discrepancies such as these, I used the spelling of the name as it was written in the annual *City Directory* for the cities in which the participants resided.

Misspellings of names are relatively minor problems unless one is trying to discover further facts about the person whose name was originally written in error. In attempting to find out something about New Bedford policeman John Telford, for example, I was puzzled that he was not even mentioned in that city's *Directory* until, in desperation, I read through all of the "T"s and found him as John Talford. In trying to track down the alibi of Thomas Walker, a local drunk and early suspect in the murders, I needed to know something about his boss, tailor Peter Carey. He was either called "Carey," first name excluded, or given the first name of Thomas by the local press. The problem was that there was both a Thomas and a Peter Carey listed in Fall River's *City Directory* and both were tailors! By tracing Walker's statements back to the address of his place of employment, I discovered that the wrong Carey had been listed as Walker's boss.

A lad of about twelve years old named "Kieronack," with no first name supplied, was mentioned in the *New Bedford Evening Standard* as walking past the Borden residence at about the time the murders occurred and observing a man jumping over the Bordens' back fence into the Third Avenue yard of Dr. Jean Baptiste Chagnon. I attempted to find Kieronack's first name in the *Fall River City Directory*, but once again came up empty.

Reading all of the "K"s in the 1893 edition, I finally discovered a family named "Kerouack" listed as relocating to Providence, Rhode Island. The *Directory* did not list the names of minors but did list a Philip and an Oscar Kerouack, both laborers and both living at the same address. Further research led me to assume that the boy was probably the only son of Philip. I further speculated that due to the spelling of his name, Kerouack was most likely of French-Canadian descent and also probably Catholic. I therefore took liberty and put his given name down as Philip, as in Philip, Jr. The odds are in my favor, and it looks better in this work, I believe, than does the heading "Kerouack, ??" Unfortunately, I did find some surnames for which I could discover no given name. Those had to be listed with the notation "??" Hopefully I, or perhaps, you, will some day come across the elusive first names.

As stated above, I found many errors of early newspaper reporters and later writers and have tried to correct them. No doubt, there are many mistakes that I have unknowingly overlooked. Most likely, I have unwittingly committed more than one or two myself. That is why I will not criticize those who made factual errors in their own worthy attempts. Researching this book has shown me how easy it is to confuse or misstate a name or an event. I can only hope that I have cleared up more than I have added to the confusion. No doubt some future writer will discover and correct errors that found their way into print in this attempt to contribute to the explanation of what really happened that August day in Fall River, Massachusetts.

This book could not have been completed without the help of many people and reference works. I first and foremost wish to thank my beautiful wife, Christine, for putting up with over two year's worth of frustration as I tried to get my word processor to express on paper that which was in my head. She also, along with my daughter Leigh, helped find and correct many of the typographical and grammatical errors in the original manuscript.

Professor Jules Ryckebusch of Bristol Community College in Fall River, encouraged me to continue to write and add another volume to the Lizzie Borden story. Maynard F. Bertolet of Merion Station, Pennsylvania, editor of the informative and entertaining *Lizzie Borden Quarterly,* also encouraged me to research the Borden murders and has been kind enough to print some of my findings in his fine publication. Dr. Kent Anderson of Pima College and the University of Arizona in Tucson proofread the manuscript and raised whatever writing skills I happen to possess to a higher level. I also owe a huge debt to my editor at Carolina Academic Press, Glenn Perkins, for improving the quality of my original manuscript.

Of the published works included in my bibliography, the most important in finding background material on many of the personalities involved in the murder or trial was *The Commonwealth of Massachusetts vs. Lizzie A. Borden: The Knowlton Papers, 1892-1893,* published by the Fall River Historical Society. Editors Michael Martins and Dennis A. Binette have provided a treasure chest of information that I have used to explain the lives of many of those mentioned in this work. I truly appreciate the large amount of work and the incredible number of hours it must have taken them just to provide the facts used in that book's glossaries. Another vast source of information about the people of Fall River, Bristol County and southeastern Massachusetts was the Family History Center of the Church of Jesus Christ of Latter Day Saints both in Tucson, Arizona and in Salt Lake City, Utah. The Center has the largest collection of family histories and primary sources in the world. It has made available to me the numerous city directories and histories of Fall River, Taunton, New Bedford and Bristol County that were so important to the completion of this work.

Leonard Rebello's finely researched *Lizzie Borden Past and Present* is also an important fount of information, especially for the birth and death dates of many of the less well-known participants in the Borden saga. He has also traced the history of the many real estate holdings of Borden family members over the years, as well as mentioned names not found in any other secondary source.

This book may be used in several ways. It is a companion to other books and articles on the subject of Lizzie Borden and the Borden murders and trial. One may use it to look up a person when confused about his or her role in the case. I have tried to cross-reference every person mentioned in the body of this work. For example, if the reference to a physician states that he participated in the autopsies of the Bordens, the names of the other doctors involved are also there. Since each physician has his own listing, each passage contains the names of the others involved with him. The same is true for other entries such as pallbearers in the several funerals mentioned in this work and the policemen who were present for the several searches of the Borden residence in the days following the murders.

This text may also be read like any other book, from cover to cover. While writing, I developed a sense of the big picture: who the people were and their relationship to the case. As I wrote about the lesser witnesses at the trial, for example, I realized what the prosecution was attempting to do in calling people like Lucie Collett and John Dinnie to the stand. Prosecutors Knowlton and Adams were trying to show the jury how many people were on the streets or sidewalks around the Borden home and that no one saw a stranger enter or leave during the time the murders occurred. This helped me understand passages in other Borden books that before had left me confused.

I sincerely hope that you experience some of the pleasure reading this book that I had writing it. If it leads to a better understanding of the case by even one person or encourages some future Borden historian to delve further into America's most beguiling murder mystery, then I will consider all of my efforts a smashing success. Who knows? The person who will finally solve the Borden murders once and for all may be reading this volume right now!

Paul Dennis Hoffman
September 2000

Yesterday in Old Fall River

A

Abbott, John Hammill

John Abbott was a Fall River physician. He was given one mention in connection with the Borden case by the *Fall River Herald*. City Marshal Rufus B. Hilliard was quoted as saying that although he was not sure, Abbott may have been present for the first autopsies of Andrew and Abby Borden at 92 Second Street the afternoon of the murders. Abbott was not mentioned in any other account of the crime and had nothing more to do with the case.

Adams, John S.

Adams wrote a crank letter to Rufus B. Hilliard, city marshal of Fall River, concerning the Borden murders. He advised Hilliard to be on the lookout for a man named Dominick Flynn. The letter had no effect on the investigation.

Nothing is known of Adams other than he claimed in the letter to reside in Boston, Massachusetts. He was never heard from again.

Adams, Melvin Ohio (1850-1920)

Melvin O. Adams was retained by Andrew Jennings, Lizzie Borden's personal attorney, as a lawyer for the defense. He cross-examined all 22 prosecution witnesses called by Hosea M. Knowlton's team at the preliminary hearing held in Fall River, August 25-September 1, 1892. Adams also skillfully cross-examined important witnesses at the final trial held in New Bedford, June 5-21, 1893, and brought out several important points.

Lawyer Adams.

He questioned Dr. Seabury Bowen at the inquest and made him admit that Lizzie was under the influence of strong prescription drugs that Bowen himself prescribed. Bowen's admission made her inconsistencies while answering questions at her inquest more understandable. Adams had Bridget Sullivan state that Lizzie had no blood on her dress, skin or hair when the bodies were discovered. In his cross-examination of Professor Edward S. Wood, the Harvard chemist admitted that the killer would most likely have been spattered with Andrew's blood, which Bridget had said Lizzie was not.

Adams also raised serious doubts with the jury as to whether the handleless hatchet was the true murder weapon. Wood stated that there was blood in the notch of the hatchet in question, meaning it had not been washed. Yet there was no blood found on the hatchet. If the handleless hatchet was not the weapon, Adams intimated, then the real weapon was gone from the house. However, Lizzie had never left the premises. Therefore, how could she have committed the crime?

Adams, born in Ashburnham, Massachusetts, graduated from Dartmouth College in 1871 and Boston University Law School in 1875. He had a private practice until he was appointed assistant district attorney. He then served on the staff of Massachusetts Governor John Q.A. Brackett with the rank of Colonel before returning to private practice in 1886. Adams has been described as a handsome man of medium build with a waxed moustache. He was remembered as an elegant dresser with urbane manners and a ready wit, which he used to charm juries.

Adams, Thomas

Dr. Thomas Adams was the minister of the First Congregational Church in Fall River and read the interment service at the funeral of Andrew and Abby Borden at the Borden home on Saturday, August 6, 1892. City Missionary William Walker Jubb also contributed to the service.

Alexander, Mrs.

Mrs. Alexander wrote and signed a crank letter concerning the Borden murders to District Attorney Hosea M. Knowlton. In the letter, posted from Rochester, New York, Mrs. Alexander claimed that she was able to communicate with the dead and could get Andrew and Abby to tell who murdered them. This lead was not followed up by the prosecution.

Alger, Isaac

Alger appeared at the New Bedford courthouse as a prospective witness. He lived in Attleboro, Massachusetts. Although acceptable to the prosecution, Alger was challenged by Lizzie and was not put on the jury. He was listed as being a farmer by profession.

Allen, Charles M. (1852-1920)

Charles M. Allen sold his home on French Street to Lizzie and Emma Borden in 1893 for $11,000. Lizzie later named the house "Maplecroft."

Officer Allen.

Allen was born in Fall River and worked as a bookkeeper an clerk for Allen and Slade Company, the firm founded by Howard B. Allen, his father. Charles Allen had financial interests in several Fall River establishments, including the Fall River Savings Bank and the Naragansett Mills. He died in Fall River on September 24, 1920 and is buried with his wife Alta E. (Gorham) Allen, who died in 1935, in Oak Grove Cemetery.

Allen, Charles N. (1852-1920) *both Charles Allens, had same dates?*

Allen was a prospective juror. While questioned on the stand, he admitted that he had formed opinions concerning the case. He also stated that although he did not feel that he was prejudiced one way or the other, he could not find Lizzie guilty under any circumstances because he did not believe in the death penalty. He did not serve.

Allen, George A. (1838-1901)

Allen, a Fall River policeman, was the first officer to arrive at the murder scene and he testified at the trial as to what he observed. He was actually more of an admitting officer at the station house than a street policeman and was awaiting the arrival of a prisoner at the station when Marshal Hilliard ordered him to 92 Second Street to investigate the crime.

Allen claimed he ran the 400 yards from the station to the Borden home and, finding the front door locked, entered through the side door. He saw Andrew's body in the sitting room and immediately left to return to the station. In the process, he deputized Charles Sawyer, a passerby, to guard the rear door and allow no one to enter except policemen.

Allen soon returned to the murder scene with police officer Michael Mullaly, and at this time learned that the body of Abby Borden had been discovered in the upstairs guest room. Myth has it that when Allen first saw Andrew's body, he ran from the house screaming in a panic. Although the detail adds comic relief to the gruesome event, his reaction has never been confirmed as fact, although at least two authors of books on the crime describe it as true.

Allen was born in Kingston, Rhode Island, fought in the Civil War and moved to Fall River in 1874. He was a machinist in several textile mills before joining the police force in 1889. He was still a policeman when he died at Massachusetts General Hospital in Boston. At Lizzie's trial, witness Dr. Seabury W. Bowen described Allen as short and stocky.

Almy, Frank L. (1833-?)

Almy was related to William M. Almy, Andrew's partner in the funeral business. He was a pallbearer at the funeral and helped carry Abby's casket, along with James C. Eddy, Henry S. Buffinton, J. Henry Wells, Simeon Chace and John Boone. Almy was a prominent Fall River citizen and was an owner of the company that published both the *Fall River News* and the *Fall River Herald*.

He, along with John C. Milne, editor of the *Fall River Daily News*, posted bail in the sum of $500 for John Vinnicum Morse as a guarantee that Morse would show up at the preliminary hearing to give testimony. Later, Almy, Jerome C. Borden, Frank S. Stevens, Joseph A. Borden and Andrew Borden (namesake of the late Andrew Borden), posted a $60,000 bond for Emma Borden when she was named executrix of the Borden estate on August 30, 1892.

Born in Compton, Rhode Island, he moved to Fall River in 1837. He married Charity R. Buffinton in 1886, then Mary K. Cotton after Charity died.

Almy, Genevra M. (Allen) (1826-1903)

Genevra Almy responded to the "sanity survey" conducted by Moulton Batchelder at the request of District Attorney Hosea M. Knowlton. She was a friend of the first Mrs. Andrew J. Borden, Sarah, and of both Lizzie and Emma. Questioned about insanity in the Morse family, Almy denied any knowledge of mental problems suffered by any Morse or Borden. Her Swansea property, called "Landscape Place," bordered one of Andrew's Swansea farms and her family burial plot borders that of the Bordens.

Genevra Allen Almy was born in Tiverton, Rhode Island, to Abram and Rachael (Gardner) Allen. She was the mother of Frank Almy and wife of William M. Almy.

Almy, Henry B.

Henry Almy was called for duty to serve on the Borden jury. It is unclear where he lived in Bristol County, but he was employed by the firm of Almy and Hitch. He claimed that he was morally opposed to capital punishment and was excused from serving.

Almy, William M. (1821-1885)

Almy was a business partner of Andrew Borden. They formed Borden, Almy and Company around 1847 and in 1862 added Theodore D.W. Wood as a partner. Almy and Andrew Borden remained partners for over three decades. William M. Almy died in 1885 and was buried in a plot at Oak Grove Cemetery in Fall River adjacent to the Borden family gravesite.

Ames, Hobart

Hobart Ames of Easton, Massachusetts, was called for jury duty in the Borden trial. He stated when questioned that he was not against capital punishment, but was challenged by the prosecution and therefore did not serve.

Ames, Oliver II

Living in Easton, Massachusetts, Oliver Ames was most likely related to Hobart Ames. He said on the stand that he was prejudiced and did have an opinion as to Lizzie's guilt or innocence. Oliver Ames II was excused and did not sit on the jury.

Apthorp, L.

Apthorp wrote a letter to District Attorney Hosea M. Knowlton dated June 14, 1893. In it, Apthorp related a story of how Lizzie Borden once killed a cat by decapitating it with an axe in July 1890. Apthorp claimed to have heard the story from a friend who was told the tale by Tish Thomas, a manicurist in the Boston beauty shop of Madame Rosalie Butler.

No follow-up to the letter was done by the prosecution. It is possible, according to the editors of the papers of Hosea Morrill Knowlton, *The Commonwealth of Massachusetts vs. Lizzie A. Borden*, that L. Apthorp may be related to the noted music scholar William F. Apthorp, based on the letter's return address.

Archer, Charles F.W.

Archer was a veteran reporter who covered the Borden trial for the *Boston Journal*. He was a graduate of the Massachusetts Institute of

Technology and began his journalism career covering Essex County for the *Boston Advertiser*. He had been on the *Journal* for ten years when the Borden murders occurred.

Arnold, George H.

George H. Arnold was employed as a deputy sheriff in Taunton, Massachusetts, at the time of the Borden trial that took place in New Bedford. Arnold, along with deputy sheriff John W. Nickerson, was on duty at the courthouse. Their orders were to make sure that the only people allowed through the front entrance of the building had legitimate business there. Arnold, Nickerson and officers E.C. Brown and Alfred B. Hodges accompanied the jury to Fall River during the trial to view the murder scene at 92 Second Street at the request of Knowlton. This visit took place on June 6, 1893.

Ashley, Millard F.

Ashley, from Attleboro, Massachusetts, was called for jury duty but was not questioned or picked to be on the jury. Ashley was a carpenter.

Atherton, Herbert L.

Atherton was called to appear for jury duty from his home in Taunton, Massachusetts, but was neither questioned nor put on the jury. Atherton was a machinist.

Auriel, Antonio

Antonio Auriel was arrested as an early suspect in the Borden murders. He was of Portuguese descent, which automatically cast him as a suspect in the eyes of many Fall River residents. He also worked on one of Andrew Borden's Swansea farms. Auriel was arrested at 2:10 P.M. on August 4, 1892, the day of the killings, in a saloon on Columbia Street in Fall River. He was brought to the police station and claimed that Joseph Chaves, a clerk at Talbot and Company, could prove he was not in the area at the time of the murders. Chaves vouched for Auriel, and he was released from custody.

Austin, George B.

Austin was called for jury duty on the Borden case. He travelled from Attleboro but was not questioned and did not serve on the Borden jury. Austin was a jeweler.

B

Babbitt, Gideon H.

Gideon Babbitt of Berkley, Massachusetts, was a member of the grand jury that found there was probable cause for putting Lizzie Borden on trial for the deaths of her father and stepmother.

Bailey, George P.

George P. Bailey reported for jury duty at the New Bedford courthouse on June 5, 1893. He admitted that he was biased in the case and had already formed an opinion. Bailey was excused from serving on the Borden jury. He was from Mansfield, Massachusetts.

Baker, Ansel G.

Ansel Baker answered the call for jury duty in the Borden murder case. He resided in New Bedford, Massachusetts and worked as a foreman for the Morse Twist Drill and Machine Company. He declared that he had no interest in the case, although he had already formed an opinion which he would not change. Baker was described by a reporter for the *New York Times* as "elderly," with a gray beard and "pleasant features." He was excused and did not serve on the Borden jury.

Baker, Charles Lewis (1862-?)

Charles L. Baker witnessed and signed the last will and testament of Lizzie Borden as a witness, as did Carl A. Terry and Ellen R. Nottingham on January 30, 1927. Baker was a lawyer in the firm of Baker, Seagrave and Terry.

Baker, John L.

John L. Baker of Seekonk, Massachusetts was a member of the grand jury that indicted Lizzie Borden on December 2, 1892.

Baldwin, Charles F.

Thomas A. Matherson reported to the Fall River police that he overheard Baldwin state that he knew who had murdered the Bordens. Officers interviewed Baldwin, a carpenter, on August 8, 1892, but he denied ever claiming he had information about the crimes (see Thomas A. Matherson).

Barker, Frederick T.

Barker was a Fall River policeman who stood guard at the landing inside the Central Police Station when Lizzie Borden arrived from her Second Street home for her inquest on August 9, 1892.

Barlow, Thomas C. (c.1877-?)

Thomas C. Barlow is remembered today as the "Me" of "Me and Brownie." He was a witness at the Borden trial and described his adventures with friend Everett Brown in the Borden barn the day of the murders.

Barlow claimed that he and Brown were in the barn's loft *before* police officers Michael Medley and Philip Harrington checked the loft for Lizzie's footprints. Medley and Harrington reported seeing no footprints in the loft; thus Lizzie lied, Fall River authorities believed, and could have been in the house killing Andrew. If Barlow and Brown were telling the truth, however, they would have left footprints in the barn before the two officers inspected the loft.

"Me and Brownie" — Thomas Barlow and Everett Brown.

The testimony of "Me and Brownie" seemed to detract from the statements made by the two officers in court. The defense, who called the boys as witnesses, hoped it would aid their case. When cross-examined by the prosecution, however, Barlow admitted that it took the two friends 15 minutes to go three blocks to the Borden residence because they were playing and roughhousing on the way to the murder scene. Barlow also admitted in cross-examination that he was not entirely sure when he and Brown arrived at 92 Second Street, which opened up the possibility that they were in the barn after the two officers inspected the loft. This admission lessened Barlow's importance to the defense.

Barlow was considered something of a juvenile delinquent because he worked in a local billiard hall stacking pool balls. Barlow was remembered for saying at the trial, "Me and Brownie went in the side gate, went to the barn and up to the hayloft. It was cooler in the barn than outside... The police officers put us out of the yard."

Barnes, Charles E.

At Lizzie's trial, Barnes, an ex-minister from Boston, was an assistant to Norfolk County court reporter Frank H. Burt. He along with

William H. Haskell and William B. Wright, assisted Burt in his duty of being in charge of the court stenographers.

Barrows, Eugene M.

Barrows was a prospective juror who lived in New Bedford. Although he stated that he was unbiased in the case and had an open mind as to Lizzie Borden's guilt or innocence, he was challenged by Lizzie and did not serve on the jury. Barrows was in the paint business with George Kirby and Co.

Bartlett, Bourne S.

Bartlett, from New Bedford, appeared for jury duty, but was not questioned and did not serve.

Batchelder, Moulton (1836-1929)

Batchelder was a state police detective at the time of the Borden murders, and in that capacity was called upon to investigate the case by District Attorney Hosea M. Knowlton. He was instructed to conduct a "sanity survey" to see if acquaintances of the Morse and Borden families noted any signs of insanity that might be used as leads to solve the murders.

Batchelder interviewed Captain James C. Stafford, Anne Howland, Abraham G. Hart, Southard H. Miller, Rescome Case, John S. Brayton, Genevra Allen Almy, David Sewell Brigham and George A. Pattey. He gave written reports of the interviews to Knowlton. The district attorney was basically unimpressed with the results of the interviews and felt Batchelder gave him no information that could be used against Lizzie at trial.

Batchelder was born in Plainfield, Vermont, and moved to Lawrence, Massachusetts, in 1856. After fighting in the Civil War, Batchelder joined the police force in Lawrence, became an assistant city marshal in 1873 and city marshal, the equivalent of chief of police, in 1878. He resigned from that position in 1881 to become a detective on the Massachusetts State Police force and in that position had arrested six murderers, prepared the cases for trial and got six convictions. He died in Lawrence, Massachusetts at the age of ninety-three.

Bates, Frank M.

Frank M. Bates arrived for jury duty on June 5, 1893 from Fairhaven, Massachusetts. He was not questioned and did not serve on the jury picked to decide the guilt or innocence of Lizzie Borden. Bates was a carpenter.

Baylies, Theodore B.

Theodore B. Baylies attended the Borden trial in June 1893 as a reporter for the *New Bedford Morning Mercury*.

Beach, Henry Harris Aubrey (1843-1910)

Beach was a noted professor with medical expertise. He was recommended by Dr. George Gay as a medical expert to Massachusetts Attorney General Albert Enoch Pillsbury in the Borden murder case. Although asked to participate in the investigation, Beach was not active in the case.

Beach was born in Middletown, Connecticut, to Elijah and Lucy S. (Riley) Beach. As a youth, his family moved to Cambridge, Massachusetts, where he attended public school. After serving in the United States Army during the Civil War, he entered Harvard Medical School and received his degree of Doctor of Medicine in 1868. He set up his medical practice in Boston as a surgeon and also held the position of demonstrator of anatomy at Harvard Medical School between 1879 and 1882. He then resigned to teach clinical surgery at Massachusetts General Hospital in Boston. Beach was a renowned surgeon, teacher and lecturer into the twentieth century.

Alderman Beattie, official who saw the murderer.

Beattie, John

Beattie was an alderman on the Fall River City Council at the time of the Borden murders. He publicly remarked that he believed Lizzie killed her father and stepmother. His theory was that Lizzie was calculating enough to wear a loose wrapper to protect her clothes from blood splatters and gloves to cover her hands, then burned the wrapper and gloves in the kitchen stove before the police were alerted. Beattie's remarks were published in the *Fall River News* on August 8, 1892. Because he was an alderman, his opinion held more weight, at least for a while, than that of the average citizen.

Bell, Eliza J.

Bell was named in the sensational story written by reporter Henry J. Trickey in the *Boston Globe*'s October 10, 1892 edition. Private detective Edwin D. McHenry told Trickey that Bell was prepared to swear at Lizzie's trial that shortly before he was murdered, Andrew had told Sarah Whitehead, the younger sister of Abby Borden, that he has prepared a will and that Sarah would be well-off financially for the rest of her life. This could have been used by the prosecution as a motive for the murders.

Soon after the *Globe* published the story, which was reported all over the United States within a matter of days, it was proven to be a complete hoax. It is probable that Eliza J. Bell was a ficticious character and a product of detective Edwin D. McHenry's imagination.

Bence, Eli (1865-1915)

Bence was a clerk in a drug store owned by D.R. Smith near the intersection of Columbia and S. Main Streets. He testified at both Lizzie's inquest and at the preliminary hearing. Bence was also prepared to testify at the final trial in June 1893, but the court ruled all of his testimony inadmissible.

Bence was prepared at the final trial to state that on Wednesday, August 3, 1892, the day before Abby and Andrew Borden were brutally murdered, Lizzie entered Smith's drug store and attempted to purchase ten cents worth of prussic acid, a strongly toxic substance. The prosecution planned to use Bence's testimony to prove that Lizzie planned to kill her parents, thus proving premeditation.

The prosecution discovered Bence's story after Officer Philip Harrington interviewed Bence on Friday, August 5 at the drug store. Also present during the alleged incident were clerk Frederick B. Hart and customer Frank H. Kilroy. The *Fall River Globe* broke the story on Friday, August 5, and assured its readers that Bence claimed to know Lizzie by sight.

Both Bence and Kilroy were questioned at the inquest. At the final trial, George Dexter Robinson, leading attorney for Lizzie's defense team, protested the inclusion of any evidence concerning prussic acid since this toxin was not involved in the actual murders. The court agreed with Robinson's argument and testimony by all witnesses concerning the acid was thrown out. This was a major defeat for the prosecution, which soon after the ruling concluded its case.

Bence was born in Braintree, Massachusetts, and clerked in many Fall River drug stores before working for Smith between 1890 and 1895. He later owned his own drug store in Pittsfield, Massachusetts.

He was described at the time of the trial as having dark gray hair, heavy-lidded eyes and a thin moustache that covered part of his upper lip. In dress, Bence was partial to a long dust coat over a shirt with a white starched collar. He held his body rigid, yet had a calm, professional air about him. He died in Pittsfield, Massachusetts.

Bennett, William A.

William A. Bennett was a pharmacist who owned his own drug store on N. Main Street in Fall River. For a time, Bennett employed William R. Martin, a potential witness, as a clerk, but Bennett was not called upon to testify by either the prosecution or the defense (see William R. Martin).

Bennett, William A.

Bennett was named in the *New Bedford Evening Standard*, June 6, 1893 edition, as being called for jury duty from his home in North Attleboro. According to the *Evening Standard*, Bennett claimed that he could not, as a member of the jury, vote Lizzie guilty even if he was convinced by the evidence, and was therefore excused. Because of the similarity to the name William A. Bennett, pharmacist (see above), it is possible the *Evening Standard* was mistaken, although "Bennett" and "William" were (and still are) common names and the towns in which each of the Bennetts resided was different. This William A. Bennett worked for the Bennett and French Co.

Bentley, George

George Bentley was a baker who resided at 185 N. Main Street in Fall River. He told policemen Philip Harrington and Patrick Doherty on August 13, 1892 that he saw a suspicious-looking "Italian" who left a strange trunk at the railroad station in Fall River. According to Bentley, the trunk contained an old carpet stained with what could have been blood. Bentley's information was considered unimportant by the police and they did not follow up on his statement.

Billings, Warren T.

Billings was in charge of reporters covering the Borden trial in New Bedford for the *Boston Herald* in June 1893. Along with *Boston Herald* reporter George H. Brennan and *Herald* artist George H. Blair, he personally covered the trial. Billings sent *Fall River Globe* reporter Thomas Hickey, who also wrote for the *Boston Herald*, to interview Taunton jail matron Hannah Reagan about a reported argument in Lizzie's jail cell between the accused murderess and her sister Emma Borden (also see Hannah Reagan).

Birch, John

John Birch reportedly owned some land on S. Main Street, south of the McManus store. In her inquest testimony, Lizzie mentioned the fact that Andrew had recently purchased this tract from Birch. This land would be an asset of Andrew's and part of his fortune, and, therefore, part of his estate.

Blackwood, Algernon (1869-1951)

Blackwood, a reporter for the *New York Sun*, was present at the Borden trial in New Bedford in June 1893. Theodore B. Baylies' memoirs, *Episodes Before Thirty* (1924), mentioned Blackwood's observation of the trial.

Algernon Blackwood was born in Kent, England, on March 3, 1869. He was a student at Edinburgh University before emigrating to North America, where he worked in Canada and the United States as a farmer and hosteler before becoming a reporter for the *New York Evening Sun* and the *New York Times*. He later wrote novels which included elements of the supernatural, according to Borden researcher Leonard Rebello. He died in London on December 10, 1951.

Blaine, Martin

Blaine was the executive treasurer of the Globe Yarn Mill Company of Fall River, of which Andrew Jackson Borden was the most important director. According to Blaine, Andrew Borden was in the offices of the yarn mill and ran into Blaine shortly before Borden left to return home for the last time on the morning of August 4, 1892.

Blaine attempted to make small talk about the hot weather and asked Andrew if he were planning a trip to one of Andrew's Swansea farms to escape the heat. Andrew surprised Blaine by answering, "I'm having…a lot of trouble at home. I can't talk about Swansea until it's settled." Soon after saying this, Andrew left the building by the side entrance and walked towards the center of town.

No footnote or other proof exists proving the conversation took place. This story was related in Frank Spiering's *LIZZIE* as proof that Andrew could have enemies, especially among his own family members.

Blair, George H.

Blair was a staff artist for the *Boston Herald*. As such, he covered the Borden trial along with reporters Warren T. Billings and George H. Brennan. Blair was also a popular cartoon artist for the *Boston Sunday Herald*.

Blaisdell, Josiah Coleman (1820-1900)

Judge Josiah Coleman Blaisdell presided over the inquest of Lizzie Andrew Borden on August 9-11, 1892 and issued the warrant for her arrest on August 12 for the murders of her father Andrew Jackson Borden and stepmother Abby Durfee Gray Borden. Lizzie was arraigned before Judge Blaisdell that same day and pleaded "not guilty" to the charges.

Blaisdell also presided at the preliminary hearing, which was held in Fall River on August 25-September 1, 1892 to determine if there was probable cause to charge Lizzie with the crimes. After Blaisdell announced his belief that there was probable cause, the case was handed over to the grand jury. Blaisdell took no part in the grand jury proceedings and at the final trial held in New Bedford, June 5-June 21, 1892, Blaisdell was replaced by a three-judge panel consisting of Judges Albert C. Mason, Justin Dewey III and Caleb Blodgett.

Blaisdell was born in Campton, New Hampshire and moved to Fall River in 1843 where he entered the shoe business.He studied law in the offices of James Ford, Esq. and was practicing law in Fall River by 1853. He rose to prominence over the years as a state representative and state senator and served as mayor of Fall River for one term, 1858-1859.

He was appointed an assistant justice for the Second District court of Bristol County in 1874 and in that capacity presided over the inquest and preliminary hearing of Lizzie Borden. His son married Minnie Borden, a distant relative of Lizzie. When asked by Lizzie's lawyer, Andrew Jennings, at the preliminary hearing to drop the charges against his client, Blaisdell sadly replied, "Suppose for a single moment that a *man* had been found in the vicinity of Mrs. Borden—was the first to find the body—and the only account he could give was the unreasonable one that he was out in the barn looking for sinkers–then he was out in the yard–then he was out for something else–would there be any question in the minds of men what should be done with such *a man?*"

Bliss, Zeba F. (?-1901)

Bliss was from Taunton and called to appear in New Bedford for jury duty. He was not questioned, probably because the twelve jurors had already been chosen, and sent home.

Blodgett, Caleb (1832-1901)

Associate Justice Caleb Blodgett was on the panel of three judges who presided over the trial of Lizzie Borden. The other two were Chief Justice Albert C. Mason and Associate Justice Justin Dewey III. At the trial, Blodgett sat on the bench to the right of Chief Justice Mason. Justice Blodgett was the senior of the three judges and except for the Borden trial had a rather mundane career. Blodgett's specialty as an attorney was bankruptcy law. He was appointed to the bench in 1882 by Massachusetts Governor John Davis Long (the predecessor of George Dexter Robinson who, as governor, appointed Justin Dewey III to the bench and became the leader of Lizzie Borden's defense team in 1893).

Judge Caleb Blodgett.

Blodgett was born in Dorchester, New Hampshire, and graduated from Dartmouth in 1856. He was a high school teacher in Leominster before he read law at the offices of Bacon and Aldrich of Worcester, Massachusetts. He was admitted to the bar in 1860 and eventually moved to Boston in partnership with Halsey J. Boardman. The partnership was dissolved in 1882 and Blodgett was appointed a judge of the superior court that same year, in which capacity he served until he retired in 1900. Blodgett had a full white beard, was partially bald and had a full jaw. He was characterized by one observer as having the "caricatured appearance of a New Hampshire farmer."

Bodman, Henry A.

Bodman was named foreman of the grand jury that met from November 7–December 2, 1892 to hear the evidence against a number of people, including Lizzie Borden. No other biographical information about Henry A. Bodman is known except that he worked for H.A. Bodman and Sons.

Jury on Trial of Lizzie Borden.

Boone, John H.

Boone was a prominent Fall River merchant tailor, property owner and business associate of Andrew J. Borden. He was one of the pall-bearers at Abby Borden's funeral on Saturday, August 6, 1892. The other men who helped lay Abby to rest were Henry S. Buffinton, James C. Eddy, J. Henry Wells, Simeon B. Chace and Frank C. Almy.

Booth, Francis A.

An accountant from New Bedford, Booth was questioned by both the prosecution and defense as a potential juror. He was challenged by Lizzie and dismissed.

Borden, Abby Durfee Gray (1828-1892)

Abby Durfee Gray Borden was one of the two murder victims whose bodies were found on August 4, 1892 at 92 Second Street in Fall River, Massachusetts. The other victim was Abby's husband, Andrew Jackson Borden. Abby was killed between 9:30 A.M. and 10:30 A.M. Her body was discovered by Adelaide Churchill and Bridget Sullivan at 11:30 A.M. in the second floor guest room which she was cleaning at

Abby D. (Gray) Borden.

the time of her death. Her corpse was found between the bed and the bureau near the north wall. She had been attacked with a hatchet and had a total of 19 wounds in the back of her head and another at the neck where it joins the shoulders.

Abby Borden became the stepmother of Emma and Lizzie Borden when she married widower Andrew on June 6, 1865. The Durfee family had as respected a name in Fall River, as had the Bordens, but Abby's parents, Oliver and Sarah (Sawyer) Gray were considered less than successful. Oliver was a tin peddler who sold goods from a pushcart around Fall River and his family lived on Fourth Street in a house located in a poorer section of town, much like the family of Andrew Borden.

Before marrying Andrew, Abby lived with her father and his second wife Jane, their daughter (and Abby's half-sister) Sarah (Gray) Whitehead and her husband George, and Sarah's two children George and Abby Borden Whitehead. The latter was named after her aunt, Mrs. Andrew J. Borden. Sarah (Gray) Whitehead was 36 years younger than Abby and their close connections were more akin to a mother-daughter relationship than it was to being children of the same father.

After Abby married, her relationship with Sarah most likely deepened since the new Mrs. Borden's presence was resented by thirteen year-old Emma and two year-old Lizzie. Abby was reported to have seen Sarah almost daily and frequently brought cakes and pies over to the Fourth Street house.

Andrew and Abby met at the Central Congregational Church in Fall River. Widower Andrew was probably looking for a substitute mother for his two young daughters and perhaps Abby saw Andrew as her last chance to avoid spinsterhood. No one knows exactly when or why the girls began to dislike Abby so, though some Borden chroniclers believe that Lizzie learned to resent her stepmother from Emma.

Abby's relationship with her two stepdaughters was cool at best during the whole of her marriage to Andrew and worsened when Andrew showed a rare generosity to Abby's sister Sarah Whitehead in 1887. Andrew and Abby owned part of Abby's Fourth Street home, which came into their possession after Abby's father Oliver died (see Sarah Bertha (Gray) Whitehead). They eventually gave their share to Sarah Whitehead.

Lizzie and Emma were angry that Andrew showed partiality to the family of Abby without a similar gift to them. Even after Andrew's attempt to mollify the girls by giving them real estate and stock, they still were not satisfied. Three years later, on the way home from a European vacation that Andrew paid for, Lizzie remarked to her cousin and travelling companion Anna Borden that she was reluctant to return to her "unhappy home," in Anna's words, and voiced resentment against Abby.

Abby at the time of her death weighed between 200-220 pounds. To some she was stocky, possessed no sense of humor, and displayed almost no outward signs of love or affection. Others, however, saw her as timid and generous with a kindly disposition, easy to please and eager to please others. She was generous with her own family, yet found it impossible to satisfy Emma and Lizzie. She did, however, have characteristics that were acceptable to Andrew: she was loyal, undemanding, and a conscientious housekeeper.

Some Borden historians believe Lizzie feared that if Andrew died before his wife, Abby would inherit the Borden estate and the Whiteheads would get all of Andrew's wealth, leaving Emma and Lizzie destitute. As an argument for Lizzie's guilt, they point out that Abby had to die before Andrew so that the sole heirs of the estate would be the Borden sisters. Autopsy reports show that Abby died approximately ninety minutes before her husband.

Borden, Abraham Bowen (1798-1882)

Abraham Borden was the father of Andrew Jackson Borden. Although he was a member of an illustrious family whose ancestors traced their American origins back to colonial days, Abraham was a fish peddler and the first member of his family to not possess wealth. He and his family lived at 12 Ferry Street, in an area of Fall River that some called a slum. Andrew, Abraham's only son, inherited water rights in Fall River and the Ferry Street house upon his father's death. Some writers of the Borden mystery feel that Andrew believed his mission in life was to regain the fortune and power of the Borden name that Abraham had lost.

Abraham Borden married twice. His first wife, Phebe Davenport bore all of Abraham's children including Andrew, the first born, and Laura Ann, also known as Laurana, who married Hiram Harrington in 1854. Phebe Borden died the year before that marriage. Abraham married Phebe Davenport Wilmarth, his second wife, the year after his first wife died. Phebe Wilmarth Borden was called Bebe or Beebe. She and Abraham had no children together.

Borden, Alice Esther (1855-1857)

Alice Esther was the second child of Andrew and Sarah Borden. She lived until the age of two and died of hydrocephalus, a brain malady, three years before Lizzie was born.

Borden, Andrew

Andrew Borden, who was named after his relative, the murdered Andrew Jackson Borden, was treasurer of the Merchant Mills company in Fall River. He was a pallbearer at the Borden funeral on Saturday,

August 6, 1892 and helped Richard C. Borden, Abraham G. Hart, George W. Dean, Jerome C. Borden and James M. Osborne carry Andrew's casket.

A few months before the murders, both Andrews desired to purchase the same Main Street house on "the hill," the exclusive area of Fall River. The asking price was $15,000. Andrew Jackson Borden supposedly wanted to move there to please his daughters, who wanted to live in the most respected neighborhood in town. When he discovered that his namesake also wanted the property, Andrew proposed that the younger man purchase a large piece of land up on the hill at a good price, then Andrew would buy half of it and the two Bordens could live on the hill as neighbors. The land was never bought, however, perhaps because the murders occurred before the closing.

Andrew Borden also contributed to the $60,000 bond that Emma needed to post after being named administrator of the Borden estate on August 30, 1892. The others who helped raise the money for the bond were Jerome C. Borden, Joseph A. Borden, Frank L. Almy and Frank S. Stevens.

Borden, Andrew Jackson (1822-1892)

Andrew Jackson Borden was murdered by numerous blows from a hatchet on August 4, 1892 as he lay sleeping on a sofa in his sitting room. His wife Abby Durfee Gray Borden was murdered approximately ninety minutes earlier as she cleaned the guest bedroom on the building's second floor. Andrew's head and the whole of his face were covered in blood and gore. One blow cleaved through his nose and upper lip and his left eye was cut in two. Many of the wounds had penetrated his brain.

There were eleven cuts total, any one of which could have killed him. The first blow probably did. He died at approximately 11:00 A.M. His youngest daughter Lizzie discovered the body sometime between then and 11:15 A.M., at which time she yelled up to the Borden maid, Bridget Sullivan, who was napping in her own attic bedroom.

Andrew Borden, seventy years old at the time of his death, was 6'2" tall with a gaunt face and small eyes that have been described as black

Andrew Jackson Borden, c.1890.

and dull. Both his voice and skin were "thin and dry" according to one of his biographers, and he sported a lipless mouth that photographs show turned down at the edges. His personality apparently matched his physical characteristics. He was remembered as dour, miserly and so brusque as to be unfriendly. He was singularly lacking in personal warmth. He seemed the stereotypical hard New England Yankee.

Although his family history was replete with rich, successful businessmen, Andrew was born poor to the family of Abraham and Phebe (Davenport) Borden. His father was a fish peddler, and the family house at 12 Ferry Street was run-down and in one of the poorer parts of Fall River.

Yet Andrew became a successful businessmen like many of his ancestors. He began a profitable furniture and undertaking establishment with William M. Almy as his partner in 1853. Stories abound as to how he cheated clients while in the funeral business. One tale tells how he used his business skill to talk the bereaved into purchasing the most expensive funeral whether they could afford it or not. He then "lent" the relatives of the deceased the money for the funeral with the grievers' property as collateral. If they could not pay, Andrew ended up owning the property for a small payment. Another story that circulated after his death was that he bought cheap, short coffins and cut off the legs of the deceased to fit them. Neither of these stories has ever been verified.

At the time of his death, Andrew owned many valuable real estate lots all over Fall River. He was also was a directing officer in the Union Savings Bank, First National Bank, Durfee Safe Deposit and Trust Company, Globe Yarn Mill Company, Troy Cotton and Woolen Manufacturing Company and the Merchants Manufacturing Company.

For all of his wealth, however, Andrew was a known miser. He sold eggs around Fall River from a basket he carried with him on his business journeys around town. He lived in a cheap house in the wrong section of the city on Second Street and refused to install a telephone, gas lines or hot water facilities. He used wood rather than coal for fuel and had no running water inside the house except in the sink room off the kitchen and in the basement.

His only large expenditure, a personal monument to his success, was the construction of the A.J. Borden building in downtown Fall River. It was completed in 1890 as an office and commercial building, and Andrew rented much of the space to other businesses. It was built of gray granite and contained twelve stores and forty offices.

Andrew married Sarah Anthony Morse, a young farm girl, in 1871. Together, they had three children: Emma Lenora, the oldest daughter, Lizzie Andrew, the youngest and one in between, Alice Esther, who died in 1858 at age 2. Two years after Sarah died in 1863, Andrew married Abby Durfee Gray.

The relationship between Andrew and Lizzie was said to have been close. Lizzie was supposed to have given Andrew her high school ring as a token of her love for him. Lizzie said that he wore it all the time, although at her trial, neither of the undertakers involved with the funeral, James E. Winward and James Renwick, remembered having seen the ring on his finger.

Andrew Jackson Borden was remembered by many contemporaries and later biographers, but not with fondness. One of the latter recalls him as being a dour-faced man who maintained his dignity with "a rent book in one hand and a basket of eggs in the other." A second said of him, "thrift may be a virtue, but Andrew Borden made it a vice."

Borden, Anna Howland (1858-1940)

Anna H. Borden was a cousin of Emma and Lizzie Borden. In 1890 Anna was Lizzie's travelling companion when they took the "Grand Tour" of Europe, as many young upper-class American women did during the "Gilded Age" period. They sailed that summer and in Europe saw plays featuring famous actors, visited world famous museums and bought many souvenirs. On the return voyage, Lizzie and Anna shared a cabin where Anna later claimed Lizzie spoke of her hatred for Abby and her reluctance to return home to 92 Second Street. Lizzie further told Anna that she found Fall River dull and boring and yearned for the excitement of the world.

At Lizzie's trial, the prosecution submitted into evidence a letter from Anna describing Lizzie's thoughts that summer. The defense objected to putting the letter into evidence on the grounds that the wording of the letter was too vague. The court ruled in favor of the defense and Anna's letter was not presented as evidence to the jury.

Borden, Emma Lenora (1851-1927)

Emma was the older sister of Lizzie and the daughter/step-daughter of Andrew and Abby Borden. She testified at Lizzie's inquest and was a star witness for the defense at the final trial in June 1893.

Emma was born on March 15, 1851 to Andrew and Sarah Anthony (Morse) Borden. She was twelve years old when her mother died and made a deathbed promise to Sarah that she would always watch out for little Lizzie, then almost three. Emma showed nothing but the strongest support for her sister during the trial and believed in Lizzie's innocence until the day of her death.

Emma and Lizzie lived together on "the hill" in Fall River at Maplecroft, the French Street mansion they purchased after the trial was over. Emma resided there until a falling out with Lizzie caused her to move

Emma Lenora Borden (as an adult).

in 1905. She resided for a while at the home of the sister of the late Reverend Mr. William Walker Jubb in Fall River. She then moved to Providence, Rhode Island, and finally to New Market, New Hampshire, where she lived under an assumed name until her death ten days after that of Lizzie. She was buried in the family plot at Oak Grove Cemetery, Fall River where also lie Andrew, Abby, Lizzie, mother Sarah and the child Alice.

Emma remains a fascinating mystery woman to many who are captivated by the Borden murder story. Physically, Emma was small in stature and appeared almost frail. She reportedly had sharp features, a narrow face and reminded many contemporaries of the quiet, shy middle-aged old maid she had in fact become.

Some historians of the murders feel Emma was dominated by the personality of younger yet stronger Lizzie. One reporter at the trial described her as a "prim little woman, very frail, with a careworn face... that had a scared expression." The nationally known columnist Joe Howard of the *New York World* called Emma, "a little old-fashioned New England maiden, dressed with exceeding neatness in plain black, with the impression of a Borden in every feature." Yet one modern-day writer on the mystery believes that Emma was the real killer and planned it so that Abby would die before Andrew, thus insuring that she and Lizzie, not Abby's relations, would inherit Andrew's estate.

On the day of the murders, Emma was on vacation in Fairhaven, Massachusetts, fifteen miles from Fall River and the murder scene. She was vacationing with friends and relatives at the home of Helen Brownell, a friend and dressmaker. Emma had been there for two weeks before the murders. A telegram sent by Dr. Seabury W. Bowen informing her about the killings sent the elder sister hurrying back to Fall River, which she reached during early evening on the day of the crime.

The Sunday after the murders, Emma decided to clean up blood spatters near the site of Andrew's murder in the sitting room. Two weeks later, she received a strange letter dated August 17, 1892 from one Samuel Robinsky, who purported to be a Jewish peddler living in Waltham, Massachusetts. He wrote that he saw the real murderer sitting at the side of a road in New Bedford and would soon visit Emma and give a more exact description. He never appeared and all efforts to locate him failed. Robinsky was never heard from again.

Emma was the main defense witness at the trial, and her testimony and cross-examination took up most of the afternoon proceedings of June 16, 1893. She told of Lizzie giving her father a ring as a token of love and admitted that both she and Lizzie were angry when Andrew gave the Fourth Street property to Abby's half-sister Sarah Gray Whitehead. She also stated that relations between Lizzie and Abby were cordial until she was reminded that she had said at the inquest that relations were strained.

Emma explained while on the stand that she suggested Lizzie burn the dress which both the Fall River police and the prosecution interpreted as an attempt to destroy evidence of wrongdoing. Emma said that the dress had been ruined by paint stains in May of that year and Emma needed the nail in the closet for one of her dresses. She also denied prosecution witness Alice Russell's statement that Emma did nothing to stop Lizzie from destroying the dress.

Another major dispute at the trial was whether an argument took place between Lizzie and Emma while Lizzie was in custody at the jail in Fall River awaiting trial. Supposedly, Lizzie accused Emma of giving her away and Emma denied that she did so.

Emma said on the stand that no such discussion ever took place, even though the matron of the jail, Hannah Reagan, testified that she overheard the quarrel (see Hannah Reagan). Emma must have been seen by the jury as a truthful and sympathetic witness because most observers felt her testimony contributed heavily to the verdict of "not guilty."

After the trial, Emma wore black mourning clothes for the rest of her life. She became a recluse while living at Maplecroft. She did, however, frequently attend services at the Central Congregational Church, walking the seven blocks from French Street. She always sat alone in the Borden family pew.

Emma had few friends. Her closest acquaintance besides Lizzie was Alice Lydia Buck, the daughter of the Reverend Edwin Augustus Buck, a supporter of the Borden sisters during Lizzie's trial. When Emma found life with Lizzie intolerable because of the parties that Lizzie threw for her show business friends, she fled to the Buck home before moving to Fairhaven. She then moved to Minden House, a resident hotel in Providence, Rhode Island, and on to her final home in New Hampshire. After Emma left French Street, she never saw or spoke to her sister again, for reasons known only to her.

On the night before Lizzie died, Emma had a vision of her sister's death. The day after Lizzie died, June 2, 1927, Emma fell down a flight of stairs in her New Hampshire home and broke her hip. She died eight days later on June 10. Victoria Lincoln, in her book *A Private Disgrace*, wrote that Lizzie was carried to her grave by "colored men." Many have disputed this, and they are correct. All four of her pallbearers were white. Emma, however, was indeed taken to Oak Grove by African-Americans on June 13, 1927 following an old social custom. At the time of her death, Emma's estate was valued at half a million dollars.

Borden, Jerome Cook (1845-1930)

Jerome Cook Borden was a first cousin to murdered businessman Andrew Jackson Borden. He was a pallbearer at the latter's funeral along with Richard B. Borden, Andrew Borden, Abraham G. Hart, George W. Dean and James M. Osborne on Saturday, August 6, 1892. He contributed to the settlement of Andrew's estate that same month, and appeared as a witness at both the preliminary hearing and the final trial. His testimony concerned his memories of a visit he made to the Borden house on the day after the murders and on the existence of Andrew's will.

Jerome Borden contributed money to help secure the $60,000 bond required of Emma under Massachusetts law when she became executrix of Andrew's estate on August 30, 1892. He cooperated with Frank L. Almy, Joseph A. Borden, Andrew Borden and Frank S. Stevens to put up the bond money.

Borden took the stand at Lizzie's trial on June 16, 1893. He testified that on Friday, August 5, he entered 92 Second Street without anyone observing him, even though at the time he walked into the house it was supposed to have been under police watch and two officers were on guard by the front door.

Since the murders, rumors circulated that Andrew Borden had left a will giving everything he owned to his wife Abby. If true, this could have provided a motive for Lizzie to kill her father and destroy the will. Andrew Borden was supposed to have discussed the will with several people, including his cousin Jerome and associates Abraham G. Hart and Charles Cook. At the trial, Borden testified that Andrew never mentioned a will to him. Cook and Hart also denied discussing that topic with Andrew. This testimony helped Lizzie, for with no will, there was no reason for her to kill her father in order to keep his estate.

Jerome C. Borden was born in Fall River to Cook and Mary A. (Bessey) Borden. He began his career as a bank clerk and later entered the Cook Borden and Co. lumber business started by his father. Borden married Emma E. Tetlow in 1870 and was an officer in both the Union Savings Bank and the Troy Co-operative Bank as well as a director in several local firms at the time of his death.

Borden, Joseph A.

Joseph was a relation of Andrew Jackson Borden. As such, he helped relatives Andrew Borden, Richard B. Borden, Jerome C. Borden, and family friends Frank L. Almy and Frank S. Stevens secure the $60,000 bond Emma Borden needed to act as administrator of her late father's estate.

Borden, Laura Ann

See Harrington, Laurana.

Borden, Lizzie Andrew (1860-1927)

Lizzie Borden was the prime suspect in the deaths of her father and stepmother, which occurred in the Borden home in Fall River, Massachusetts, on August 4, 1892. She was put on trial in New Bedford, Massachusetts, in June 1893. The jury brought back a verdict of "not guilty" on June 20.

Lizzie Borden, c.1889.

For someone charged with two horrific murders, Lizzie was not physically imposing. She was 5'4" and weighed about 135 pounds. Even at that, she told reporters at the trial that she had gained weight while in jail and had to have some of her dresses let out. She had small ears, hands and feet, according to writer Edwin Radin. Victoria Lincoln, another writer who actually saw Lizzie in person in the 1920s, differs with Radin. Lincon described Lizzie as having hands that were large and "elegantly white," broad shoulders and a thick waist, a thick lower jaw and a rough and pale complexion which would turn red when Lizzie became angry or nervous.

Lizzie was born on July 19, 1860 to Andrew and Sarah (Morse) Borden. Sarah died when Lizzie was two years old, and her older sister Emma assumed the role of mother and protector of Lizzie even after Andrew married Abby Durfee Gray on June 6, 1865. She attended high school up to her junior year and gave Andrew her high school ring as a token of her love for him.

She took the Grand Tour of Europe in 1890 with her cousin Anna and was active in Fall River upper-class organizations such as the Central Congregational Church, the Christian Endeavor Society and the Woman's Christian Temperance Union. She was an upstanding member of her church's missionary committee and taught Sunday school. In addition, she was a member of the board of the Hospital of the Good Samaritan. These efforts earned her the strong vocal support of two well-respected city ministers, W. Walter Jubb and Edwin A. Buck.

From the time the news of the double murders circulated around Fall River, many people believed that only a family member had the motive and opportunity to kill the Bordens. Lizzie's uncle, John Vinnicum Morse, was able to account for every second in the time frame of the murders; he was nowhere near the house. Sister Emma was fifteen miles away in Fairhaven, Massachusetts, visiting friends. The only viable suspect besides the live-in maid, who would have gained nothing by the deaths of her employers, was Lizzie.

An inquest was held at the Fall River police station on August 9-11, 1892, and on August 12 Lizzie was arrested and charged with the murder of Andrew Jackson Borden. The testimony given by Lizzie at the inquest was the only formal statement she ever made about the deaths of Andrew and Abby Borden, and those statements were not allowed into evidence at her trial (see John William Coughlin).

The preliminary hearing took place in Fall River from August 25-September 1, 1892. Then, the grand jury heard the evidence between November 7 and November 21, 1892. Lizzie was indicted by the grand jury on three charges: the murder of Andrew Jackson Borden, the murder of Abby Borden and the double murder of both Andrew and Abby Borden. She was arraigned in superior court on May 5, 1893, and the trial at which she was acquitted lasted from June 5-June 20, 1893.

After her acquittal, Lizzie continued to live in the Second Street house with Emma until 1893 when the sisters bought a large home on "the hill," an exclusive area in the city, from Charles M. Allen for $11,000. Lizzie named the house Maplecroft. Ignored after the trial by the Fall River society that supported her so strongly during her ordeal, Lizzie traveled extensively along the east coast. She became interested in the stage and supported theater people by attending plays as far away as Boston and Washington, D.C. Her relationship with actress Nance O'Neil was the scandal of Fall River and possibly resulted in Emma moving out of Maplecroft in 1905.

After Emma left, Lizzie began calling herself "Lizbeth" and spent most of her last twenty years as a recluse in her home on French Street in the company of her staff and pet Boston bull terriers Donald Stuart, Royal Wilson and Laddie Miller. She had expensive furniture, a large library and was driven around town first in a carriage, later in an automobile, by her chauffeur Ernest Terry.

By the time Lizzie's health started to fail in the 1920s, most of the important players in the Borden melodrama were long dead. In 1926 she entered Truesdale Hospital in Providence, Rhode Island, for a gall bladder operation under the pseudonym Mary Smith Borden. She was reported to have been a difficult patient and refused to eat the hospital fare. Although she recovered from the operation and returned to Maplecroft, her health was never the same and she died from complications of the operation on June 1, 1927. The *Fall River Globe* listed the cause of death as pneumonia.

Lizzie had a small funeral with no one in attendance and Congregational Church choir member Vida Pearson Turner singing Lizzie's favorite song, "My Ain Countree," to an empty room. The pallbearers at her funeral where she was laid to rest with her father, mother, stepmother, and infant sister Alice Esther, were Fred Coggeshall, Ernest Terry, Norman Hall and Edson Robinson. Her sister would follow Lizzie to the family plot in Oak Grove Cemetery in Fall River only ten days later.

Borden, Mary Ann

Mary Ann Borden was present at the funeral services of Andrew and Abby Borden. The *Fall River Herald* stated that Andrew had been the guardian of Mary Ann Borden's estate. Although probably a relative of Andrew, and therefore of Lizzie and Emma Borden, no other account or information about her was written in contemporary newspaper accounts.

Borden, Mary Smith

When Lizzie entered Truesdale Hospital in Providence, Rhode Island, for a gall bladder operation in 1926, she checked in under the name Mary Smith Borden to avoid any publicity. The hospital workers knew who she was but kept her secret.

Borden, Richard Butler (1834-1906)

Richard Borden was Andrew Jackson Borden's cousin and the treasurer of Troy Mills in Fall River. He was a pallbearer at Andrew's funeral with Abraham G. Hart, George W. Dean, Jerome C. Borden, Andrew Borden and James M. Osborne. He was born in Fall River on February 21.

Borden, Sarah Anthony (Morse) (1823-1863)

Sarah Anthony Borden was the first wife of Andrew Jackson Borden and the mother of Emma Lenora, Alice Esther and Lizzie Andrew. She was also the sister of John Vinnicum Morse, which is why he is known in the Borden saga as "Uncle John."

Sarah Anthony Borden was born on September 19, 1823 in Somerset, Masachusetts to Anthony and Rhody (Morrison) Morse and married Andrew on Christmas Day 1845. Sarah died in Fall River on March 26, 1863 of uterine congestion and spinal disease. She left two young children, Emma, aged 12 and Lizzie, four months short of her third birthday. Alice, the middle child had preceded her mother in death seven years earlier. Sarah was a farm girl with no dowry. Although she was poor, Andrew apparently fell passionately in love with her, a rare emotion for the Andrew Borden known to history.

One writer on the Borden mystery, Arnold R. Brown, states that Abby was an improvement as a mother over the late Sarah. He also hypothesizes that the marriage soon soured and Andrew had an affair with Phebe Hathaway Borden. The result was, according to Brown, an illegitimate son named William Borden who was born in 1856, the same year Alice Esther was born to Sarah and Andrew. Brown believes that it was William who killed the Bordens on August 4, 1892.

Borden, Simeon, Jr. (1860-1924)

Simeon Borden, Jr. worked for Bristol County, Massachusetts. His official position was clerk of courts. As such, he was the trial clerk at Lizzie Borden's trial for the murder of her father and stepmother.

Simeon Borden was born in Fall River to Simeon and Irene (Hathaway) Borden and received his early education in the Fall River public school system. He graduated from Brown University in 1882 and began his legal career as a clerk in his father's law firm. He was appointed assistant clerk of courts in 1888 and admitted to the Massachusetts bar in 1894.

Borden was elected clerk of courts for Bristol County, a position his father once held, by a large majority. Simeon Borden had extensive business interests and was a director of several Fall River corporations and charitable organizations until his death. He and Lizzie had a great-great-great-great grandfather in common, making them distant relatives.

Boulds, Thomas (1845-1896)

Boulds was a witness for the prosecution at Lizzie's trial on June 14, 1893. He testified about strangers he might have observed around the Borden home on the day of the murders. Various books and newspapers have spelled his last name Bowles or Bolds. This author has chosen the spelling used by the Fall River Historical Society.

Thomas Boulds, a native of England, was living in Fall River by 1889. He remained a resident of that city until his death. At the time of the murders, Boulds was working as a laborer and gardener for Mrs. Adelaide Churchill, the Bordens' next door neighbor. He lived directly north of the Bordens in what was known locally as the Buffinton house at 90 Second Street with the widow Mrs. Churchill and her son Charles.

Boulds was present at Louis L. Hall's stables at 129 Second Street, a few houses south of Lizzie's home when the bodies of the Bordens were discovered. Mrs. Churchill rushed to the stables to ask Boulds to fetch a doctor. Boulds was with a group of men at the time, including news dealer John Cunningham.

When Mrs. Churchill told Boulds to telephone for a doctor because there had been an incident at the Borden residence, Cunningham called three newspapers, including the *Fall River Daily Globe* and then the police from Augustus P. Gorman's paint store. Boulds left the stables and arrived at Dr. Seabury Bowen's house, across the street from his own, just as Bowen had returned from a call in Tiverton, Rhode Island, between 11:10 A.M. and 11:20 A.M.

At the trial, Boulds testified that he observed Bridget Sullivan, the Borden family maid, cleaning windows on the north and west sides of the Borden home, but she was gone when he returned at 11:20 A.M. He said he saw no intruders or strange people around 92 Second Street during the time the murders took place.

Bowen, Phebe Vincent (Miller) Bowen (1848-1907)

Phebe Vincent Bowen was the wife of Dr. Seabury Warren Bowen, the Borden family physician. She was a witness at both the preliminary hearing in session, August 25-September 1, 1892 and the final trial, held June 5-20, 1893. Mrs. Bowen's testimony concerned Lizzie's actions and physical appearance on the morning the bodies of her father and stepmother were discovered.

Bowen testified that she saw Lizzie on August 4 shortly after the murders were discovered. She remembered Lizzie looking pale and faint, but had no blood on her skin, hair or clothes. The jury could infer from this that Lizzie had had very little time to clean herself after the murders and so, with no blood on her person, could not have murdered Andrew and Abby.

Phebe Bowen, however, also stated that when she went to the Borden home to comfort Lizzie, she noticed Lizzie had her hands in her lap most of the time, and that her hands were clean, not dirty as one might expect from a person who had recently returned from a hot and dusty barn.

When Mrs. Bowen heard about the murders, she took the time to change from her house dress before venturing across the street, since during the 1890s, no self-respecting woman would leave her home in such informal attire. This should be noted since at her inquest, Lizzie stated that when Abby received a note that said someone was ill and needed her, Lizzie asked Abby if she planned to change her clothes before leaving, and Abby said she did not. Those who believe Lizzie was the true culprit point to this statement as proof that there was no note, and Lizzie was lying to hide the fact that Abby was dead in the guest room and Lizzie had killed her.

Phebe was the daughter of Southard Harrison and Esther G. (Peckham) Miller (See Southard Harrison Miller). She married Seabury Bowen in 1871. Phebe and her husband lived directly across the street from the Bordens at 91 Second Street on property shared with her father. Phebe was active in the local Baptist Church and belonged to many civic organizations.

Bowen, Seabury Warren (1840-1918)

Dr. Seabury Bowen was a family friend of the Bordens and also their physician. He and his wife Phebe lived directly across the street from the Bordens at 91 Second Street in a house they shared with the family of Southard Harrison Miller, Phebe's father. The doctor also conducted the first of two autopsies on the Bordens. Bowen, assisted by Dr. William Andrew Dolan, performed the examination of the bodies on the Bordens' dining room table the day of the murders.

Bowen testified at the inquest and as a witness for the prosecution at the preliminary hearing and the final trial. He was also the physician of the Emery family that John Vinnicum Morse had visited while the murders were taking place.

When Abby fell sick on Wednesday, August 3, the day before the murders, she was certain that she had been poisoned. She ran across the street to Dr. Bowen's house for an examination. Bowen told Abby that her illness was probably the result of spoiled food. That was the last time Bowen saw Mrs. Borden alive.

That Wednesday was also the last time Bowen saw Andrew Jackson Borden alive. When Bowen went to the Borden house later in the day to check on Abby, her husband in a burst of anger told the doctor to leave the house, and that he would not pay for Dr. Bowen's visit.

On the day of the murders, the first outsider to enter the Borden house after the bodies were discovered was Mrs. Alelaide Churchill. Dr. Bowen was the second. He went to the telegraph office on Pleasant Street between Second and Main to relay the news of the murders to Emma, who was in Fairhaven, Massachusetts with friends. Bowen left the Borden house to send the message but not before the arrival on the scene of the first Fall River policeman, George A. Allen.

Bowen testified at Lizzie's trial on June 8, 1893 that on the day of the murders, he had just returned from "personal calls" in Tiverton, Rhode Island. He went to the Borden house when he heard of the killings, spoke to Lizzie, saw Andrew's body and then took his pulse. When he pronounced Andrew dead, he asked Lizzie about Abby. Lizzie answered that Abby had left the house after receiving a note.

Bowen then left to telegraph Emma and when he returned to the house was told of Abby's death upstairs in the guest room. It was then that he realized Lizzie had on a different dress from the one he saw her wearing when he first entered the house. She was wearing a pink wrapper, whereas she had previously had on a calico dress of a drab color. Lizzie also told Bowen that at the time of the murders she had been in the barn looking for "irons."

Bowen also said that he prescribed the drugs bromo-caffeine and sulphate of morphine to relieve Lizzie's mental distress. This information provided a possible reason why Lizzie's inquest testimony was contradictory and confused. In cross-examination by defense lawyer Melvin O. Adams, Bowen said that Lizzie was taking prescription pills up until the time of her inquest and arrest. When Bowen was on the stand, the validity of Lizzie's inquest statements as evidence had not yet been successfully challenged by the defense. By June 15, however, the court ruled that nothing from the inquest would be admitted into evidence.

Seabury Bowen was born in Attleboro, Massachusetts. He received his B.A. from Brown University in 1864 and graduated from Bellevue Hospital Medical College in 1867. Bowen began practicing medicine in Fall River that same year and held the post of city physician on the staff of Fall River Hospital. He married Phebe Vincent Miller in 1871.

Bowen continued practicing medicine in Fall River after the trial and died in that city while in retirement. The evening Lizzie was acquitted, Dr. Bowen and his wife attended a dinner party given in honor of Miss Borden and in celebration of the jury's verdict.

Bowles, Thomas

See Boulds, Thomas.

Braley, William E. (?-1928)

William E. Braley was a sketch artist for the *Fall River Daily Herald*, which published many of his drawings of the Borden trial. He had recently completed his studies at New Bedford's Swain School of Design when he was hired by the *Daily Herald*.

Braley graduated from the Lowell School of Design in 1897 and was later appointed Fine Arts Supervisor for the Fall River public school system, a post he held for over a quarter of a century. He died in Fall River and is buried in Oak Grove Cemetery.

Brayton, John Summerfield, Sr. (1826-1904)

John S. Brayton was one of the respondents of the "sanity survey" conducted by Moulton Batchelder at the request of District Attorney Hosea M. Knowlton. The survey was taken to learn of any insanity in the Borden or Morse families. The written report stated that Brayton said that he "never heard of any one of them (members of the Morse family) as being Insane (sic) or having any streak of Insanity (sic)."

Brayton was a Fall River businessman and lawyer. He was born in Swansea, Massachusetts to Israel and Kezia (Anthony) Brayton. Brayton went to Brown University and studied in the law offices of Thomas D. Eliot, Esq. in New Bedford, Massachusetts. He then attended Harvard Law School. Brayton was admitted to the bar in 1853 and practiced for 15 years. During that time he held numerous public offices, including that of representative in the Massachusetts House of Representatives and clerk of courts for Bristol County for seven years.

He was an original incorporator of Union Hospital in Fall River and had business interests in textile manufacturing and railroads. Brayton also helped organize the First National Bank in Fall River and the B.M.C. Durfee Safe Deposit and Trust Company. He was president of both of these businesses when he died.

Brayton, William

Andrew Jackson Borden used some of the profits he realized from his undertaking business to buy property. The story told in Fall River involving him and William Brayton was used as an example of Andrew's business sense and ruthlessness.

According to the story, when one Horace Brayton died, he was buried by Borden, Almy and Co. Brayton's survivors fought among themselves as to dividing up the late Horace Brayton's estate, especially several valuable real estate plots. Andrew offered to purchase the parcels at a price under their current value.

Fearing one relative would get everything, all of the survivors except William Brayton were willing to sell to Andrew. Brayton threatened court action against Andrew, but finally went along with the rest of his family and sold out to Borden. For years after, the story goes, William went around Fall River denouncing Andrew and speaking of revenge. By then, Andrew had resold the property at a handsome profit.

This story could have been pure fabrication. Proof of its veracity has never been discovered. It fits into the same category as Andrew buying cheap coffins and charging full price and the gruesome tale of cutting the legs off tall corpses so that they would fit into shorter, cheaper burial boxes.

Brennan, George H.

Brennan was a reporter for the *Boston Herald* who with reporter Warren T. Billings and staff artist George H. Blair covered Lizzie's trial in 1893. Borden scholar David Kent gives Brennan's first name as George, while fellow author Leonard Rebello lists him as Charles H. Brennan.

Briggs, Charles E.

Briggs was one of the over one hundred people who were called for jury duty and did not serve. Briggs was a jeweler from Attleboro, Massachusetts.

Brigham, David Sewall (1823-1893)

David Sewell Brigham of 150 Second Street responded to Moulton Batchelder's "sanity survey," given to numerous people at the request of District Attorney Hosea M. Knowlton. Brigham is listed in Knowlton's papers as being an ex-City Marshal of Fall River. Later, Brigham's name briefly surfaced as a possible suspect in the Borden murder case (see John Crompton Newton).

Batchelder recorded the following statement from Brigham "I use (sic) to know the Morses never heard of them as being Insane, but this girl Lizzie Borden is known by a number of people here to be a woman of a bad disposition if they tell what they know."

Brigham, Mary E. (c.1860-1942)

Mary E. Brigham was a friend of Lizzie Borden who testified for the defense. She was the wife of George Brigham and the mother of Florence Brigham of the Fall River Historical Society and a Fall River institution to this day.

When Mary Brigham descended into a deep depression in 1891 after losing a young son, Lizzie stayed by her side and helped Mary recover. When Lizzie was accused of murder the next year, Mary returned Lizzie's demonstration of sympathy and friendship.

According to a report in the *Fall River Globe,* when druggist Eli Bence testified at the inquest that he, fellow employee Frederick B. Hart and customer Frank H. Kilroy saw Lizzie in D.R. Smith's drug store the day before the murders attempting to buy prussic acid, Lizzie turned to Mary Brigham and whispered, "I was never in that store in my life." Later, when a reporter asked Brigham if Lizzie had said that, Mary answered in the affirmative and added that Lizzie stated she did not leave her house at all that morning, even though three witnesses (Bence, Kilroy and Hart) stated otherwise.

After testifying at the inquest, Lizzie was accompanied to her house from the Fall River Police Station, where the inquest was held, by Mrs. Brigham and City Marshal Rufus B. Hilliard. When Lizzie was arrested on August 12, 1892, the day after the inquest, Brigham, along with Lizzie's sister Emma and her attorney Andrew Jennings, accompanied the accused to the jail. At the final trial, Mary Brigham took the stand and stated that jail matron Hannah Reagan's story of an argument between Lizzie and Emma in Lizzie's cell was a lie and that Reagan herself had told Mrs. Brigham that the tale was untrue.

Brightman, Hiram

Weston L. Cook suggested to members of the Fall River police department that Brightman knew about the Borden murders. Brightman, who lived on Wilson Road "at the head of Boston Rd." said that there was a stranger loitering in the area with "burned cork or soot" on his face and hands. That sighting had been on Sunday, July 31, however, and no one had seen him since. Because the murders had not occurred until August 4, the police considered Brightman's claim another dead end and there was no search for this sooty individual (see Weston L. Cook).

Brightman, Peleg P.

Brightman was an early suspect in the Borden killings. He worked as a paperhanger and occasionally did jobs for Andrew. A neighbor saw Brightman digging in his own back yard and thought Brightman was burying a hatchet. The police investigated and found that whatever Birghtman was doing, he was not covering up a weapon. Brightman's hatchet was found on his kitchen shelf. He was not questioned further by the authorities and was never arrested.

Brightman also worked in South Somerset near two pieces of property owned by Andrew Borden. A rumor circulated that a bloody hatchet had been found on a nearby farm wrapped in newspaper and hidden in a laborer's house. Marshal Hilliard sent Officer Philip H. Harrington to the farm and interviewed Brightman. The laborer said he knew nothing of a bloody hatchet and allowed the policeman and some reporters to search the house. Nothing of interest was discovered. These stories were taken from two different sources, and could have been two different versions of the same incident. A very similar story about a bloody hatchet was reported about a Portuguese farmer named Joseph Silvia. The two stories have so much in common that probably either 1893 Borden author Edwin Porter or the *New Bedford Evening Standard* confused the names (see Joseph Silvia).

Broadhead, W.O.

W.O. Broadhead, according to Borden writer Leonard Rebello, was one of the most experienced reporters present at the Borden trial. He covered this media event for the *New York Evening Sun*.

Brocklehurst, John

Sergeant John Brocklehurst was a Fall River police officer. He was in charge of a group of twelve policemen who kept crowds of curious onlookers from the Borden family at Oak Grove Cemetery during the funeral of Andrew and Abby Borden on Saturday, August 8, 1892.

Brown, E. Carlisle (1842-?)

Brown was a Taunton, Massachusetts deputy sheriff who, along with deputy sheriffs Alfred B. Hodges, George H. Arnold and John W. Nickerson, accompanied the jurors at Lizzie Borden's trial from New Bedford to 92 Second Street in Fall River to view the murder scene on June 6, 1893.

Brown, Everett P. (c.1877-?)

Everett P. Brown was the "Brownie" in the "Me and Brownie" testimony of Thomas C. Barlow. Brown and Barlow were playing in the barn loft of 92 Second Street the day of the murders. Both boys, about 16 at the time, claimed to be in the loft *before* Officer William H. Medley said he had inspected the barn and discovered no footprints in the loft. Brown and Barlow went to the murder scene from Brown's house at 117 Third Street.

Brown and Barlow's testimony was supposed to cast doubt on statements given by Officer Medley. If Medley was correct, Lizzie was never in the loft as she had claimed. Perhaps she had lied to cover up the fact that she was, at that very time, murdering her father. If, on the other hand, Brown and Barlow were accurate, Medley was simply careless, and Lizzie could have been in the loft as she stated at the inquest.

Brown said at the trial that on the day of the murders he and his companion attempted to enter the Borden house but Charles Sawyer, the volunteer guard on duty, would not allow them in. They then crept into the barn. "Brownie" said they were in the loft for about five minutes and, when they finally came down, were ejected from the yard by some policemen.

Brown's testimony was good news for the defense, but was weakened in cross-examination by the prosecution. The witness admitted he was not sure of the time, so they could have been up in the loft after Medley had made his inspection. He also stated that he was not sure whether he saw Medley in the barn at all that day. "I might have seen Officer Medley," he said on the stand "or I might not. I wasn't taking notice of who I saw there." Cross-examination greatly weakened the testimony of both Barlow and Brown.

Later in life, Brown fought in the Spanish-American War as a soldier. One may find his likeness as an adult on a composite photograph in remembrance of Fall River citizens who fought in the War of 1898 on a conference room wall in the Fall River Historical Society.

Brown, Jerimiah N.

Jerimiah Brown, from Swansea, was called to New Bedford for jury duty. He was not questioned and did not serve.

Brown, Thomas Joseph Lee (1864-1954)

The name Thomas Lee Brown appeared on a list of possible witnesses written in the handwriting of District Attorney Hosea M. Knowlton. The subject matter of his testimony was listed "As to escape." This probably refers to the prosecution planning an argument to defense claims that the real killer somehow escaped from the Borden home undetected. Although Brown was near the Borden property at the time of the murder, he was not called upon to testify at the trial. He and Fred Lavalle were working in the yard of the Fall River Ice Company and reported seeing nothing of a suspicious nature the morning of the murders (see Fred Lavalle).

Brown was born in Fall River and began a business career as a bookkeeper. He was employed for several years by the Arctic Ice and Cold Storage Co. in Fall River and in 1905 became a partner in Lee and Brown, which specialized in express agents and teaming. When the partnership dissolved in 1918, he continued in the business under his own name. He married three times and died in Fall River.

Brownell, Gilbert K.

Brownell was from New Bedford. He was questioned as a prospective juror and said that he had served on a jury during the court's last term. Based on that, he was allowed to return home to his boot and shoe business.

Brownell, Helen M. (1838-1919)

Helen Brownell was the friend Emma visited at 19 Green Street in Fairhaven, Massachusetts, during the time Andrew and Abby Borden were murdered. Emma had been there for almost two weeks when she was notified by telegram that her father and stepmother were dead. Brownell's mother was seventy-eight year-old Rebecca (Delano) Brownell, the widow of Allen Brownell of Fairhaven and was living with her daughter Helen during the summer of 1892 in a house owned by Moses Delano (see Moses Delano).

In late July of that year, Emma and Lizzie both argued with Andrew over his actions concerning his interest in a house on Ferry Street in Fall River (see Sarah Bertha Whitehead). Both sisters left the house angry on the day of the argument. Lizzie planned to see friends in Marion, Massachusetts, and Emma decided to stay with the Brownells. The two sisters travelled together as far as New Bedford where Lizzie turned back. Emma continued on to Fairhaven.

Helen Brownell was approximately thirteen years older than Emma and possibly a distant relative. When Fall River policemen later interviewed them, both Brownells strongly stated that Emma was with them at the time of the murders.

Brownell, Milton A.

Brownell was a New Bedford policeman. On the first day of Lizzie's trial, June 5, 1893, he was one of three officers who controlled crowds of onlookers hoping to be admitted into the courtroom to view the trial. He informed the people that no one would be allowed entrance because of the large number of prospective jurors waiting to be questioned by lawyers for both the prosecution and the defense. The other two policemen on duty that day were John C. Rooks and Daniel J. Humphrey.

Bryant, Charles H.

Bryant was a mason by profession and helped policemen Dennis Desmond, Francis L. Edson, Patrick Connors and William H. Medley search the Borden residence on August 8, 1892, two days after the murders. Bryant removed portions of fireplaces and a chimney at the Borden house as part of the search for the murder weapon.

Buck, Alice Lydia

Alice Lydia Buck was one of five daughters of the Rev. Edwin Augustus Buck, City Missionary of Fall River and an ardent supporter of Emma and Lizzie Borden during the latter's trial. After Lizzie and Emma moved to Maplecroft, the Borden's new home, Emma became unhappy with the behavior of her younger sister. She most likely disapproved of Lizzie's associations with show business folk and wild parties that supposedly were held in the home. Emma also demanded that Lizzie fire their coachman, Joseph Tetrault, something that Lizzie did not want to do. Emma apparently was voicing her concerns about her sister's lifestyle to the Rev. Buck before his death in 1903.

In 1905, when Emma moved out of Maplecroft, she lived at Alice Buck's home at 114 Prospect Street. Alice had become one of Emma's closest friends since the end of Lizzie's trial.

After a few months in the home of Alice Buck, Emma moved first to Fairhaven, Massachusetts, then in 1908 to Providence, Rhode Island

and from there to her final home in Newmarket, New Hampshire in 1923.

Little is known about Alice Buck after Emma left. She lived in her father's house for the rest of her life and never married.

Buck, Edwin Augustus (1824-1903)

The Reverend Edwin A. Buck was City Missionary and a strong supporter of Lizzie Borden. He was with Lizzie almost every day from the time the murders took place until her acquittal on June 20, 1893. He was at every public appearance where Lizzie was present and most effective in presenting Lizzie to the public in a sympathetic way. Also, in her last public interview, given to *Boston Sunday Post* reporter Edwin J. Maguire in 1913, Emma Borden said that it was on the advice of E.A. Buck that she left Maplecroft and Lizzie forever in 1905.

After the bodies of Andrew and Abby were discovered on the morning of the murders, Lizzie went up to her bedroom to change from her blue dress into a pink wrapper. She allowed only a few people to enter her room to comfort her. One of them, along with family doctor Seabury Bowen and family friend Alice Russell, was the Reverend Mr. Buck. The city missionary was even present when members of the Fall River police force questioned her several times that day.

Andrew and Abby's funerals were held on Saturday, August 6 at 92 Second Street, the Bordens' home. Rev. Thomas Adams of the Central Congregational Church, where Andrew held a pew but rarely attended, and Buck jointly conducted the services. The following Friday, August 12, when Emma Borden and Lizzie's uncle John Vinnicum Morse arrived at the Second District court at 9:00 A.M., Buck was already conversing with Lizzie before she was about to be arraigned.

Buck also accompanied Lizzie on the trip from Fall River to the jail in Taunton that Friday after she was formally accused of the double murders. After they arrived at the jail, Buck spoke some encouraging words to the accused and returned to Fall River.

Rev. E.A. Buck also played a part in the controversy as to whether or not Lizzie and Emma had an argument while the latter visited her sister in her cell (see Hannah Reagan). After an article about the possibly incriminating discussion was published in the *Fall River Globe*, Andrew Jennings, Lizzie's attorney, drew up a statement saying the story of the argument was false.

Mr. Buck read the statement to Reagan and requested that she sign it. Reagan first wanted permission from her boss, Marshal Rufus B. Hilliard. Buck showed the statement to Hilliard who said that if Reagan signed the paper, it would be without his consent. Reagan did not sign the document. On the witness stand, Reagan denied that the reports in the press about the argument were untrue. She stated that Buck never spoke to her about them and that she never wanted to sign the statement at any time.

The jury at Lizzie's trial reached a verdict of "not guilty" on June 20, 1893. After Lizzie was set free, neither Rev. Buck nor her other pastoral supporter, Rev. William Walter Jubb, had much contact with her for the rest of their lives. They seemed to have forgotten Lizzie after the trial ended. Buck was married to the former Elmira Walker.

Buffinton, Benjamin

Buffinton was mentioned in one article in the *New Bedford Evening Standard* on August 11, 1892. He was a deputy sheriff and former tax assessor in Fall River. The story stated that Buffinton was at the Borden home on the afternoon of the murders, interviewed both Lizzie and Bridget Sullivan and examined the premises. He reportedly asked both ladies about the houses surrounding the Second Street residence and what they observed that morning. Nothing further is mentioned about Buffinton or the information he may have acquired.

Buffinton, Elisha W.

Elisha Buffinton of Fall River was a foreman for a local company. He was a member of the grand jury that indicted Lizzie Borden for the murders of her father and stepmother. Buffinton was elected clerk of the grand jury.

Buffinton, Henry S.

Henry S. Buffinton was one of the pallbearers for Abby at the double funeral on Saturday, August 6, 1892. The other pallbearers who helped carry Abby's casket were James C. Eddy, John H. Boone, J. Henry Wells, Simeon B. Chase and Frank L. Almy. Buffinton was a business associate of Andrew, a financier and a property owner.

Burke, Frank H.

See Burt, Frank H.

Burnham, Michael

The Reverend Michael Burnham was Andrew's pastor at the Central Congregational Church before he left Fall River for a church in Springfield, Massachusetts, in 1882. He was present at Lizzie Borden's preliminary hearing as an observer. In 1894 Burnham left Springfield to lead the Pilgrim Congregational Church in St. Louis, Missouri.

Burrell, John Thomas (1857-1904)

John T. Burrell was a cashier at the Union Savings Bank, of which Andrew Jackson Borden was a major stockholder. Burrell testified at both the preliminary hearing and the final trial.

Burrell, along with Abraham G. Hart, Everett M. Cook, Jonathan Clegg, Joseph Shortsleeves and James Mather, testified as to the movements of Andrew Borden between 9:30 A.M. and 10:45 A.M. on the morning of the murders before he returned home for the last time. Cashier Burrell described a meeting between Borden and Hart. According to Burrell, Andrew Borden entered the Union Savings Bank sometime between 9:15 A.M. and 9:45 A.M. and left after five or ten minutes.

John Burrell was born in Fall River and began his banking career as a clerk and later as a teller at the National Union Bank. He then was a bookkeeper for a furniture dealer, but returned to banking in 1882. He began his employment at the Union Savings Bank in 1888 and remained there as a cashier until his death at the age of forty-seven.

Burroughs, Frank

Frank Burroughs was a Fall River native who later became a lawyer in New York City. He was mentioned in a featured news article published in the *Boston Globe* on October 10, 1892 that was soon proven to be a hoax (see Henry G. Trickey).

According to the article, Burroughs was willing to testify that in January of 1892, Lizzie talked with him in Fall River about property rights. Lizzie then saw him again five weeks before the murders of Andrew and Abby Borden in New Haven, Connecticut, where Burroughs was preparing a court case for the New York, New Haven and Hartford Railroad. Lizzie again asked him about wills and inheritance of property, specifically who receives the property if the wife dies before the husband. Lizzie supposedly saw him again one week before the killings, again in Connecticut. Burroughs soon heard about the murders and became suspicious.

This story is probably false in its entirety, published as part of the "Trickey-McHenry Affair." For some, it offered a reason why Abby died first: Lizzie had to kill her before Andrew died, so as the last surviving spouse, his property would go to his family (Emma and Lizzie) rather than to the Whiteheads, the relatives of Abby.

In 1971, in his history of the *Boston Globe*, Louis M. Lyons told the story of the Trickey-McHenry hoax but wrote that a "real lawyer" was quoted as saying Lizzie asked him about property rights. Burroughs was never asked to testify.

Burt, Ansel O.

Ansel Burt, from Taunton, Massachusetts, was called for jury duty, although he was not questioned on the stand or picked. Burt worked as an assessor.

Burt, Frank Hunt (1861-1946)

Frank Hunt Burt was the official court reporter of the Norfolk County (Massachusetts) courts. At the trial of Lizzie Borden, Burt was in charge of the official court stenographers. He was assisted by William B. Wright, William H. Haskell and C.E. Barnes. The official typists, of whom Hunt was in charge, were A.M. Dollard, F.M. Cushing, F.D. Ross and Mrs. William H. Haskell. The duty of the typists was to transcribe the dictated stenographic notes taken at the trial by Annie White. All of those named above, with the exception of Annie White, were from Boston.

Burt was born in Northampton, Masachusetts to Henry M. and Francis A. (Hunt) Burt. Four years after graduating from high school in Springfield, Burt moved to Newton, Massachusetts and entered the publishing business as an employee of his father. He became a stenographer upon leaving publishing in 1886 and remained in the stenographic business for the next 60 years.

As a stenographer, he was assigned to the Borden trial. He also re-entered publishing by taking over the Mt. Washington, New Hampshire newspaper *Among the Clouds*, a summer daily, upon the death of his father. Burt belonged to several important stenographic organizations including the National Shorthand Reporters Association and the New England Society of Shorthand Reporters. He died in Arlington, Massachusetts at the home of his son at the age of eighty-five.

Burt, Phebe

Phebe Burt was present at the funerals of Andrew and Abby Borden. She was listed in the Fall River City Directory of 1893 as the widow of James D. Burt and lived just a few houses north of the Bordens at 84 Second Street.

Butler, Harry

Harry Butler was present at the trial of Lizzie Borden as a reporter for the *New Bedford Evening Standard*.

Butler, William F.

Butler, from New Bedford, was called for jury duty but was not chosen. He bought and sold oak lumber and was a builder of boats.

Butman, Thomas

Butman was a deputy sheriff in Taunton. He officially called the roll of the twelve jurors at the end of the Borden trial. The jurors had discussed the evidence after the controversial instructions of Judge Justin Dewey on June 20, 1893. All members of the jury answered "present" when Butman called their names. The jurors had deliberated for only one hour. The verdict of the twelve jurors, "not guilty," was announced by foreman Charles I. Richards at 4:35 P.M.

C

Cain, Lawrence

Lawrence Cain was a Boston Police captain headquartered at Station One. He and Police Inspector J. Ryder, also of Station One, helped Fall River authorities search for Samuel Robinsky, who described himself as an itinerant peddler in a letter he sent to Emma Borden. Robinsky wrote that he could lead authorities to the real killer of Andrew and Abby Borden. Nothing further was heard from Robinsky, and the Fall River police asked Boston officials to see if he was living in any town near there. Robinsky was never located (see Samuel Robinsky, Emma Borden George L. Mayberry and J. Ryder).

Caldwell, John R.

John R. Caldwell was a journalist employed by the *New York Herald*. He was on assignment in Massachusetts covering the Borden trial in June 7, 1893. His vivid descriptions of Lizzie Borden's arraignment in Fall River created nationwide interest in the case, according to the *New Bedford Evening Standard*.

Caldwell also testified at the trial as to what he overheard Mrs. Hannah Reagan say about an argument between Lizzie Borden and her sister Emma in Lizzie's Fall River jail room. Caldwell happened to be in the Fall River police station guard room with reporter Mrs. J.H. Percy and overheard City Marshal Rufus B. Hilliard tell Reagan in the corridor that if she signed a statement saying the argument never took place, it would be against Hilliard's orders. While speaking to Mrs. Reagan, Hilliard spotted Caldwell and ordered him to leave the area, which he did after "remonstrating with the marshal," as Caldwell described the incident on the stand (see Hannah Reagan).

Callanan, Thomas F.

Callanan was a Taunton policeman who was on duty with Charles Taber on June 7, 1893. Their responsibility was to keep the growing crowd of people outside the courtroom from entering the building. According to the *New Bedford Evening Standard*, the crowd was quiet that morning.

Cannon, Thomas E.

Thomas E. Cannon was a member of the grand jury that heard the evidence against Lizzie Borden and decided that she was "probably guilty" of the charges against her. He was a resident of Freetown, Massachusetts.

Carberry, John W.

John W. Carberry covered the Borden trial as a reporter for the *Boston Globe*. Bert Poole and L.F. Grant, *Boston Globe* staff artists, accompanied him. Carberry had replaced the late Henry Trickey who had been involved in a hoax played upon that newspaper.

Carey, Peter

Carey owned a tailor shop on Main Street in Fall River. He vouched for the presence at the shop of suspect Thomas Walker on the day of the Borden murders. Walker was an alcoholic who frequently missed work because of his drinking, but he did happen to show up the day of the murders. The police then dismissed Walker as a suspect.

Carpenter, Joseph Wilmarth, Jr. (1855-1899)

Carpenter was an early suspect in the killing of Andrew and Abby Borden. He was cleared when his claim that he was far away from Fall River on the day of the murders proved true.

Carpenter had been a bookkeeper for the undertaking firm of Borden and Almy. He was caught embezzling money from the firm in an amount of $6,700 over a period of years, a lot of money in the late 1800s. Carpenter was arrested but the charges were quietly dropped.

After Andrew's death, a rumor circulated that Carpenter threatened to tell of dishonest practices such as how the firm cheated clients by substituting cheap coffins after bereaved relatives had paid for expensive ones (see Andrew Jackson Borden). Since Carpenter later paid the firm back at least some of the missing funds, it is more likely that he and the company reached an out-of-court agreement to have the charges dismissed.

A New York publication, *Once A Week*, offered a $500 reward for the missing note that Lizzie said Abby received on the day of the murder. Among other responses, the New York paper was told that Carpenter, who had left Fall River before fully repaying Almy and Borden, was seen in the city shortly after the killings. Peter Driscoll, a Fall River barber, also said he saw the ex-bookkeeper in town at about that time.

In August 1892, Carpenter was living in Albany, New York, and was on a sales trip far from Fall River. This was verified by Mrs. Victoria Foreman, Carpenter's landlady. When Mrs. Foreman told her story to Fall River police officer Philip Harrington, Carpenter was no longer a suspect.

Carpenter was born in Fall River and worked there until fired by Borden and Almy. He and his wife Ann then relocated to Holyoke, Massachusetts, until Ann moved back to Fall River alone in 1882 to live with relatives. Carpenter, meanwhile, moved to Buffalo, New York and then to Albany as a traveling salesman for an ink manufacturing company. He died in Worcester, Massachusetts, at the home of his sister.

Carr, William (1821-1893)

William Carr answered questions about the sanity of the Bordens and the Morses. This was part of the "sanity survey" that Moulton Batchelder undertook at the request of District Attorney Hosea M. Knowlton. Carr, who had lived in Fall River for 40 years at the time of the murders, said that he knew the Bordens better than he did the Morses. He called the Bordens peculiar, but had no knowledge of insanity in either family.

Carr was born in Warren, Rhode Island to William and Temperance (Smith) Carr. He married Elizabeth Valentine Durfee of Fall River in 1848. Carr served as a director of the Borden Mining Company and the Metacomet National Bank. He also worked as an agent for the Fall River and Providence Steamboat Company. He was active in Fall River community affairs until his death.

Carrier, Isaac G.

Isaac Carrier was a prison official at the Taunton jail at the time Lizzie Borden was a prisoner there. He kindly told Lizzie that she did not have to wear the required prisoner uniform while she was awaiting trial.

Carter, Henry M.

Carter, a Fall River resident, lived at 88 Snell Street. Police officers Philip Harrington and Patrick Doherty checked out a lead that Carter-was involved in an argument with Andrew J. Borden concerning his rent and a $66.00 water bill. The officers were satisfied with what Carter told them and he was not considered a suspect after his interview of August 6, two days after the Bordens were murdered.

Carter, Robert H.

Carter, of New Bedford, Massachusetts was called to the courthouse for jury duty and might have been chosen to hear the Borden trial. Under questioning, however, he admitted that he had already formed an opinion that he probably would not change and was excused. Carter was a druggist.

Case, Rescome (1817-1901)

Case responded to the "sanity survey" given by Moulton Batchelder at the request of Hosea M. Knowlton, head of the team that was assigned to prosecute Lizzie Borden for the murders of her father and stepmother. He was quoted as saying, "I assure you I have my opinion of Lizzie Borden and I hope they will get more evidence.... We never heard that any one of them is or ever was Insane (sic) but <u>I think some of them are worse then</u> (sic) <u>Insane</u>." (underlines appear in Batchelder's notes). He was also interviewed by Fall River policemen Philip Doherty and Philip Harrington on August 21, 1892 and told them that Lizzie and Abby did not get along well with each other.

Case was born to Pardon and Ellipha (Macomber) Case in Westport, Massachusetts. He was a carpenter by trade and at the start of his career was apprenticed to James S. Ford and Southard Harrison Miller. He later did carpentry work for those two men as well as for other manufacturers. Case married twice and was active in the Congregational Church. He had lived at 199 Second Street for fifty-seven years by August 1892, the month of the Borden killings.

Chace, Abigail

Abigail Chace and her parents were mentioned in the sensational news story known as the "Trickey-McHenry Affair" (see Henry G. Trickey). According to reporter Trickey's story in the *Boston Globe* on October 10, 1892, she and her parents lived at 198 Fourth Street and were guests at the Borden house the evening prior to the murders. Abigail reportedly heard Andrew yelling at Lizzie because Lizzie had become pregnant. Andrew demanded to know the name of the man involved or Lizzie would have to move from the house.

After reading the story, Andrew Jennings, Lizzie's lawyer called the whole article untrue and claimed that Abigail and her parents never existed. In this claim, Jennings was correct.

Chace, Frederick

Frederick Chace was the supposed father of Abigail (see Abigail Chace). "I will know the name of the man who got you in trouble!" the story quoted Andrew as screaming.

A reporter for the *New Bedford Evening Standard* reported that day in his paper, that Borden lawyer Andrew J. Jennings said, "I have endeavored to find out about Mr. and Mrs. Fred Chace at the number indicated, 198 Fourth Street. There is not only no such number, but not any within 50 (house numbers) of it."

Chace, Joseph P.

Joseph P. Chace of Somerset, Massachusetts, served on the grand that indicted Lizzie Borden on December 2, 1893 on three charges of homicide.

Chace, Mary C. (Mrs. Nathan D.)

Mrs. Chace resided two houses down from the Borden home on Second Street. She lived on the top floor of the building where Vernon Wade's grocery store was located. Mrs. Chace told police officer P.T. Barker (according to the stenographic notes of Annie M. White) that she saw a man picking pears in the back yard of the Borden residence on the day of the murders. (Her name is occasionally spelled Mary Chase, as in Ms. White's stenographic record.)

Those who hoped that she might have seen the murderer were disappointed. The pear snatcher turned out to be Patrick McDonald, a mason's helper employed at John Crowe's stoneyard, which was just to the rear of the Borden house. McDonald sheepishly admitted that he was stealing a few pears from the Borden yard, but that he did nothing more illegal than that.

Chace, Simeon B.

Simon B. Chace, a property owner and financier, was a pallbearer for Abby Borden at the double funeral for her and Andrew on Saturday, August 6, 1892. The other pallbearers for Abby were Henry S. Buffinton, James C. Eddy, John H. Boone, J. Henry Wells and Frank L. Almy.

Chagnon, J.B.

See Chagnon, Wenceslas Jean Baptiste.

Chagnon, Marianne (Gigault) Phaneuf (?-1895)

Marianne Chagnon was the wife of Dr. Jean Baptiste Chagnon. She lived with her husband and daughter in their home on Third Street adjacent to the Borden's back yard. Chagnon testified at both the preliminary hearing and final trial about strange noises she heard from the direction of 92 Second Street on the evening before the murders.

On the stand at Lizzie's trial in New Bedford, Marianne was called by the defense to testify. She stated, as did her mother who took the stand just before her, that she heard sounds on Wednesday evening, August 3. She admitted that she was confused as to exactly where the sounds originated and said that dogs occasionally got into her rubbish barrel, which was located at the rear of her house near the back of the Borden residence. During cross-examination, Mrs. Chagnon admitted that the sounds could have come from somewhere else. Both Marianne and her stepdaughter Marthe said the sounds occurred between 11:00 P.M. and 11:30 P.M. and lasted for approximately five minutes.

Marianne Chagnon was born in Canada. She was the widow of Desire Phaneuf, a merchant from St. Damase, Quebec, Canada when she married Jean Baptiste Chagnon in Biddeford, Maine in 1885. Mrs. Chagnon died in 1895 from injuries she received when she jumped from a convent window in St. Hyacinthe, Quebec, Canada.

Chagnon, M. Marthe (1873-?)

Marthe, or Martha, as she was called, was a witness at Lizzie Borden's preliminary hearing and at the final trial. She testified, as did her step-mother, that she heard strange noises the night before the Bordens were killed. The defense hoped to use this testimony as proof strangers could have been near the Borden house around the time of the killings, although the sounds were heard about twelve hours before the Bordens died (see Marianne Phaneuf Chagnon).

Marthe was the first witness called by the defense at Lizzie's trial. She stated that she had heard a pounding noise, as if someone was hammering on wood. She said the sounds lasted for five minutes and she did not investigate the source of the racket.

In the cross-examination conducted by Hosea M. Knowlton, Miss Chagnon admitted that she could not be sure the sounds emanated from the Borden home. The district attorney reminded her that at the preliminary hearing, she had said the sounds came from an icehouse, which was in a different direction from the Borden home.

M. Marthe Chagnon was born in Canada to Dr. Wenceslas Jean Baptiste Chagnon and his first wife Victorine (Desnoyer) Chagnon. She married a dentist from North Adams, Massachusetts in 1897 and was widowed when he died in 1907 at the age of thirty-three. She then worked as a nurse in a Rhode Island hospital and later moved to Montreal, Canada, where her two sisters resided. The last known official record mentioning her is dated 1936. She was described by writer Frank Spiering as being "delicately pretty" and speaking with a slight accent.

Chagnon, Wenceslas Jean Baptiste (1837-1912)

Dr. Chagnon owned the house northeast of the Borden residence on Third Street. It was there that his wife and daughter heard strange banging noises the night before the Bordens were murdered. At the trial, Fall River deputy sheriff Frank H. Wixon said that the murderer of the Bordens could have jumped the fence that separated the Borden property from that of the Chagnons because the fence was not very high.

Dr. Chagnon was born in Rouville, Canada. He received his medical degree in 1860 from the University of New York. After further study in Paris, France, Chagnon practiced medicine in Canada for 18 years and saw action in the Franco-Prussian War. He immigrated to the United States in 1879 and settled in Fall River.

Chagnon was married three times and fathered 20 children. He and his first wife Victorine were married in 1861 and had thirteen children, including Marthe. He married Marianne in 1885 and Isabelle Ballou of Fall River in 1897. Together, he and Isabelle had seven more children. Chagnon and his wife Marianne lived at 91 Third Street, behind the Bordens, at the time of the murders.

Charrete, Francios

Listed as Francios Charret in the stenographer's notes, Charrete, a laborer, worked for Romuald St. Amant. He told police officer Joseph M. Heap that he saw a man acting out of desperation begging St. Amant for a ride to New Bedford from Fall River. He also saw St. Amant refuse the stranger's request and return to the stranger money that he offered St. Amant for the lift (see Joseph M. Heap, Joseph Michaud, Jean H. St. Laurant, Romuald St. Amant, Exentive St. Amant and Alexander Côté).

Chase, Albert E.

Albert E. Chase was a Fall River policeman. The *Fall River Herald* briefly mentioned Chase as standing guard at the front door of 92 Second Street after the Bordens' bodies were discovered. Chase stood guard during the daylight hours and Officers John McCarthy and Michael Reagan shared the night duty. Although no date appears in the article, it seems to have been written about the time Lizzie was arraigned for the homicides and pleaded "not guilty." This occurred on

August 12, 1892. Chase also investigated the "confession" of Charles H. Peckham (see Charles H. Peckham).

Chase, Mark P. (1843-1921)

Mark Chase testified at the preliminary hearing and at the final trial. His testimony concerned his observations on the morning of August 4, 1892 on Second Street at the time of the murders. Chase was one of several witnesses produced by Lizzie's defense attorneys to show that strangers were in the vicinity of the Borden home and therefore could have killed the victims. The other witnesses besides Chase who gave testimony to that effect were Marthe and Marianne Chagnon, Mary A. Durfee, Delia S. Manley, Sarah B. Hart, Dr. Benjamin Handy, Joseph Lemay and Hyman Lubinsky.

Chase worked at the New York and Boston Dispatch Company, which was located near the Borden residence. On the morning of the crimes, Chase was sitting in a large chair in the shade of an old elm tree. He testified that at about 9:30 A.M., he saw a black carriage in front of 92 Second Street. He noticed it because he was in the horse business and the animal attached to the carriage was, Chase noted, a beautiful specimen. Chase had never seen that horse before and wondered who its owner was. He arose and left his chair to go indoors at around 11:00 A.M. and when he returned to his chair, the horse and carriage were gone.

Chase was born in Somerset, Masachusetts. After serving in the Civil War as a wagoner for Company H of the 3rd Massachusetts Volunteers, he relocated to Fall River around 1870, where he was a freightmaster for the Old Colony Railroad at the steamboat wharf. He left Fall River for Westport, Massachusetts, in 1887 and returned in 1892, where he worked as a hostler at the New York and Boston Dispatch Company. After his wife Sarah died in 1901, he remained in Fall River for nine more years, then moved to Togus, Maine. At the time of his death, he was living in Sterling, Connecticut.

Chase, Mary

See Chace, Mary.

Chausse, Joseph

A New Bedford native, Chausse was called for jury duty in the Borden trial. On the stand, he admitted that he was prejudiced and was excused. Chausse was listed in the *New Bedford City Directory* as a grocer.

Chaves, Joseph

Chaves provided the alibi for Antonio Auriel, a Portuguese laborer who was an early suspect in the Borden case. Chaves worked as a clerk for Talbot and Co. He placed Auriel far from Second Street at the time of the murders and shortly thereafter, Auriel was released.

Cheetham, Annie

Annie Cheetham was most likely the niece of Adelaide Churchill. Cheetham, who was unmarried, lived with Churchill in the Buffinton House next door to the Bordens at 90 Second Street. She claimed that at the time of the murder of Andrew Borden, she was seated in her kitchen window writing a letter. The window looked south, directly at the Borden house. Cheetham said she saw no one on the Borden property. She was never called upon to testify and probably made these statements while being interviewed by City Marshal Rufus B. Hilliard on the day the murders occurred.

Cheever, David Williams (1831-1915)

After the Bordens' funeral service at the Oak Grove Cemetery on Saturday, August 6, 1892, a second autopsy was performed on the bodies. As part of the autopsies, the heads of both Andrew and Abby were

Dr. David W. Cheever, government's medical expert.

removed and all flesh, cartilage and brain matter scraped from the severed heads. The skulls were then sent to Harvard University.

Dr. David Cheever was a Harvard medical expert who studied the skulls and testified at the trial in June 1893 concerning the hatchet wounds to both Andrew and Abby. Both he and Dr. Frank Winthrop Draper, also of Harvard, testified at Lizzie's trial for the prosecution as to the head wounds of the victims.

Cheever said that, in his opinion, Abby predeceased Andrew by between one and two hours. He also stated that he believed the blade of the murder weapon was no more than 3 1/2" long. He observed that the blade of the "handleless" hatchet fit the wounds "accurately" and that the first wound on Abby's skull showed that she faced her killer. Cheever also said it was possible for a woman of average strength standing astride Mrs. Borden's prone form to strike with enough force to kill her.

In cross-examination, Cheever said the blood spatter pattern for Abby would depend on which blow cut the main artery and killed the victim. If Abby were already dead when the artery was cut, there would have been almost no spray of blood. The killer could have gotten blood on his or her shoes, but the spray pattern was mostly guesswork.

The result of Cheever's testimony was that the prosecution claimed Cheever supported the state's contentions that Abby died before Andrew, the spray pattern of blood was almost entirely guesswork and that Lizzie could have killed her and remained relatively free of blood. Also, Cheever supported the prosecution's ideas that the crime was particularly brutal and hideous, the handleless hatchet was most likely the murder weapon and a woman could have commited the deed.

David Williams Cheever was born in Portsmouth, New Hampshire. He received a B.A. from Harvard in 1852, travelled in Europe for eighteen months and then attended Boylston Medical School. He continued his studies at Harvard Medical School and received a degree of Doctor of Medicine in 1858. He was appointed demonstrator of anatomy at Harvard in 1861 and named Assistant Professor of Anatomy in 1866.

Cheever enjoyed a brilliant career as a doctor and an educator and was the youngest senior surgeon at Boston City Hospital. He became a Professor of Surgery at Harvard in 1882, a post he held until named Professor Emeritus in 1893. He also kept up a private practice during this time and received an honorary Doctor of Laws degree from Harvard in 1894. Cheever wrote several books and articles and frequently contributed to professional medical journals.

Church, Charles H. (1830-1914)

On District Attorney Hosea M. Knowlton's handwritten list of witnesses was the name of Charles H. Church. His testimony was to be about prussic acid, the chemical poison Lizzie Borden was accused of trying to purchase the day before the murders of her father and stepmother. Another witness who was supposed to testify about prussic acid, clerk William R. Martin, was employed by Church, a druggist at the time of the murders. Eventually all testimony concerning prussic acid was excluded due to the vociferous objections of Borden lawyer George D. Robinson.

Church was born in New Bedford, Massachusetts. He was educated in New Bedford as a youth and then was an apprentice to his own father as a sailmaker. After showing no talent at that trade, Church was employed by druggist Charles A. Cook. He worked for Cook for one year, then moved to Boston and found work as an apothecary. Church moved to Brooklyn, New York and then back to New Bedford in 1852. He purchased Warren B. Potter's drug business and enlarged it in 1855. He remained a druggist all his life and founded the New Bedford Druggist Association.

Churchill, Adelaide (Buffinton) (1850-1926)

Adelaide Churchill was a neighbor of Lizzie Borden. She lived in what was called locally the "Buffinton House" where her late father, a hugely popular mayor, resided in the mid-1800s. Living with her was her son Charles, her niece, her sister and her handyman, Thomas Boulds. The house was located at 90 Second Street, directly to the north of the Borden home. Churchill was one of the first people on the murder scene after Lizzie discovered her father's body. Twenty min-

Mrs. Adelaide B. Churchill, c.1880.

utes later, Mrs. Churchill discovered Abby's body in the second floor guestroom. Adelaide Churchill testified at Lizzie's inquest, preliminary hearing and final trial.

Mrs. Churchill had just returned home from M.T. Hudner's Market on Main Street on the morning of the murder. When she looked out of her kitchen window, she saw Bridget Sullivan running across the street to Dr. Seabury Bowen's house and Lizzie standing by the side door in apparent distress. She called to Lizzie who told her Andrew had just been murdered. Churchill immediately rushed out of her house to Lizzie's aid.

Upon entering the house, she saw Andrew's body and asked Lizzie questions, including where she was when Andrew died. Lizzie answered that she had been in the barn. Mrs. Churchill then asked her about Abby's whereabouts. Lizzie told her of the note her stepmother had received. When Bridget rushed into the house and said Dr. Bowen was not at home Churchill left the house, found Tom Boulds at a nearby livery stable and told him to telephone for help. It was this conversation that news dealer John Cunningham overheard. The reporter then telephoned the police as well as the *Fall River Globe, News* and *Herald* from Augustus P. Gorman's nearby paint shop. The call to the police station was logged in at 11:15 A.M.

After returning to Lizzie's house, Churchill and Bridget went upstairs to look for Abby and saw her body from the landing. Mrs. Churchill went into the room and viewed the body. She then returned to the first floor and exclaimed, "There is another one!" At the trial, Churchill said that even after the second body was discovered, "I never saw Lizzie in tears that morning at any time."

By then Lizzie's friend Alice Russell was also present in the house. Both Russell and Churchill attended to Lizzie in the kitchen, mainly by fanning her. Lizzie stood up from the chair she was sitting on and, passing her father's body on the sitting room couch, went upstairs to her room to change into a pink wrapper from the blue dress she was wearing.

At the trial, when cross-examined by defense lawyer George Robinson, Alelaide Churchill admitted she saw no blood on Lizzie or her dress as she and Alice Russell tended to her in the kitchen. Since her dress was a light blue calico, a bloodstain would have been easy to spot. Robinson's point was that since there was no blood on Lizzie's dress, she could not have committed the crimes. It is interesting to note that Churchill's memory of the dress Lizzie wore that morning in the kitchen does not match the dress that Lizzie gave to the police. It does, however, seem to be an accurate description of the dress she burned on Sunday morning, August 7.

Robinson also got Churchill to say that she heard the claim from Bridget rather than from Lizzie that Abby had received a note about a sick friend. In re-direct questioning by prosecutor William Moody, however, Churchill said that Lizzie told her first, then Bridget spoke of it. This convinced Churchill that there really was a note, since she had heard of it from two different sources. Whether this was true or not, it could have confused the jury as to the existence of the note, as writer Robert Sullivan observes.

Adelaide Churchill was remembered as looking younger than her forty-eight years, plump and with a gentle, kindly face. She was born in Fall River to Edward P. and Comfort (Taber) Buffinton. She married Charles H. Churchill, who worked for the Fall River water department. Adelaide Churchill was widowed in 1879. She was active in the Congregational Church and took an interest in civic events until her death.

Clark, Henry A.

Henry Clark had a tailor shop at 38 S. Main Street in Fall River. Police officers Philip Harrington and Patrick Doherty questioned him on September 21, 1892 about whether or not Andrew Borden had mentioned the existence of a will before he was murdered. Clark told the two policemen that Andrew had never mentioned a will to him.

Clark, Nathan (1825-?)

Nathan Clark was called for jury duty in the Borden trial. He lived in Taunton, was hard of hearing and was sixty-eight years old. He was excused from jury duty due to his age.

Clarkson, Alfred (1846-1917)

Clarkson claimed to have entered the barn loft before the policeman who testified at the trial that he saw no footprints at all in the loft's dust. If the jury believed Clarkson, they might also have believed the police incompetent and that Lizzie was telling the truth when she said she was not in the house at the time of the murders. Alfred Clarkson testified at the preliminary hearing and at the final trial.

Clarkson said that he had been up in the barn loft before Officer William H. Medley went there to check Lizzie's story of where she was when Andrew was killed. Medley said he saw no footprints in the loft, and Lizzie, therefore, was lying about her location when her father died. If Clarkson was correct and inspeced the loft before the policeman went up, Medley should have seen Clarkson's prints. This would make Medley an extremely unreliable witness and be of great help to Lizzie Borden's defense team.

Prosecutor William H. Moody's cross-examination weakened Clarkson's testimony. Clarkson admitted that Medley could have been in the barn when he walked in and they simply did not see each other. At the inquest, Clarkson said he was in the barn at 11:38 A.M. Under pressure from Moody at the trial, however, Clarkson admitted that was only an estimate.

Also, two other witnesses, Charles Sawyer and John J. Manning said they saw Clarkson on the grounds at 11:40 A.M., not in the barn. Therefore, it was possible Clarkson was on the premises but not in the barn when Medley made his trip to the loft. If so, then Medley could have been correct when stating he saw no prints, and Clarkson could have gone up to the loft after Medley had left the barn. The prosecution made its point that Clarkson had contradicted his inquest testimony and that it was still possible Lizzie was never in the barn.

Alfred Clarkson was born in England and came to the United States in 1853. His name is first found in Fall River records for 1872. He was a steam engineer and by the time of his death had earned a reputation as an inventor in that profession.

Clegg, Jonathan (1842-1923)

Jonathan Clegg testified at the Borden trial about the movements of Andrew Jackson Borden in downtown Fall River the morning that he was murdered. Clegg, along with John T. Burrell, Everett M. Cook, Joseph Shortsleeves and James Mather were questioned as to Andrew Borden's movements between 9:30 A.M. and 10:45 A.M. on August 4, 1892.

Clegg was a hatmaker who had agreed to rent space in the Borden Building at 39 S. Main Street. He said that he met Andrew Borden near City Hall at 10:20 A.M. to describe changes Clegg wanted in the space he was soon to use. Their discussion ended at 10:29 A.M. Andrew continued his journey up Main Street, went into the store Clegg planned to rent, and talked with Shortsleeves and Mather, two carpenters whom Andrew had hired to renovate the store. Borden left the area at about 10:20 A.M. Clegg never saw Andrew Borden again.

Clegg was born in England and emigrated to the United States around 1876. He held several jobs before founding a haberdashery shop on N. Main Street in 1884. After he quit the clothing business, he became an insurance agent. He was in this business for more than a decade. Clegg died in Fall River.

Cleveland, Edmund J.

The Reverend Mr. Cleveland officiated at Lizzie Borden's funeral at Oak Cemetery on June 4, 1927. He was pastor of the Church of the Assumption in Fall River.

Clifton, Jireh W.

Clifton was from New Bedford. He was called to jury duty but was not questioned and did not get picked. Clifton was in the stove business.

Cobb, Alson W.

Cobb was a deputy sheriff from Mansfield, Massachusetts, who, with deputy sheriffs Russell Lincoln of Raynham and A.C. Kirby of Taunton, was assigned to guard the west door of the courthouse where the trial was held and keep unauthorized people from entering the building.

Cobb, George A. (1842-?)

A prospective juror from New Bedford, George A. Cobb was excused from jury duty because he said he had formed an opinion about the case and was prejudiced. He was excused. Cobb was in the tin and hardware business.

Cobb, James H.

James Cobb, from Acushnet, Massachusetts, was present for jury duty. He was not asked any questions and did not serve on the jury.

Coggeshall, Abner

Coggeshall, who worked for the street department in Fall River, was said to have heard screams coming from 92 Second Street at the time the Bordens were murdered. He told policemen Philip Harrington and Patrick Doherty on August 13, 1892 that he never made that statement and was not near Second Street at that time. Coggeshall's boss, Assistant of Streets Frank Thurston confirmed this. This was another of many dead-end leads that the local authorities traced during the weeks after the murders.

Coggeshall, Alexander H. (1840-1930)

Alexander H. Coggeshall owned stables at 143 Second Street, close to the Borden residence. He was questioned by the Fall River police on September 25, 1892 and later summoned as a witness to appear at the trial of Lizzie Borden in New Bedford, Massachusetts, in June 1893. Although he was present, he was not put on the stand by either the prosecution or the defense. Presumably, he would have been questioned as to what he observed on Second Street the day of the murders.

Coggeshall was born in Westport, Massachusetts. He married Sarah E. Tripp, also of Westport. Fall River records first mentioned him as living in that city in 1870 and listed his occupation as wood dealer. He went into partnership with Herbert L. Law in 1872 forming Law and Coggeshall Stables. After two years, he went into business for himself. Coggeshall died in Fall River after he retired from the livery business.

Coggeshall, Fred W.

Legend has it that Lizzie Borden was carried to her grave by five black pallbearers. That story, found in Victoria Lincoln's book *A Private Disgrace* (1967), is inaccurate. On the Saturday after her death, Lizzie's body was brought from Maplecroft to Oak Grove Cemetery by four white pallbearers. Fred Coggeshall, her coachman, was one of them. Ernest Terry, Norman Hall and Edson Robinson were the other three.

Coggeshall, Thomas

Thomas Coggeshall, a well-known local drunk, was the victim of a practical joke about three weeks after the Borden murders. On August 30, 1892, someone covered the drunken Coggeshall's hand, arm, face and chest with a substance resembling blood and threw him out of a Fall River bar into the street where he paraded around as Andrew Borden. An outraged crowd of about 500 people gathered around him until the police arrested him for disturbing the peace.

Cole, Francis (Frank) Granger (1844-1915)

Frank Cole was one of the twelve jurors who found Lizzie Borden "not guilty" of murder. He was described in the papers of Hosea M. Knowlton as being a Republican who had no interest in religion and neither wife nor children at the time of the trial. He had never before served on a jury. The *New Bedford Evening Standard* described him as middle-aged and good looking with black "searching eyes," sharp features and a demeanor of "firmness."

Cole was born in Rehoboth, Massachusetts to George and Nancy (Rounds) Cole. He fought in the Civil War and was a jeweler in Attleboro, Massachusetts where he was also active in civic affairs and the Baptist Church. He later married Josephine B. Peck of Rehoboth.

At the session of the trial when prospective jurors were questioned, Cole said he had formed an opinion but was not prejudiced. Although others gave similar statements on the stand, many were rejected, while Cole was acceptable to both the prosecution and the defense. Many years after the trial, Cole told his great-niece Alice E. Dyer that he could not believe a woman was capable of such a violent and bloody crime. He would say nothing more about his decision for acquittal.

Collett, Lucie (1874-1900)

Lucie, or Lucy as her name is written in some of the literature on the Borden case, was sitting on the Chagnons' porch on Third Street on August 4, 1892. She was called as a witness at the preliminary hearing and for the prosecution at the final trial as to what she saw that morning.

The family of Dr. W. Jean Baptiste Chagnon was attending a wedding anniversary that Thursday and needed someone to answer the telephone. Originally, Dr. Pierre A.A. Collett's son was supposed to watch the house but he did not show up. Jean Napoleon Normand, Dr. Collett's clerk, then asked the physician's daughter Lucie to go to the Chagnon residence.

Upon arrival at 10:50 A.M., Lucie discovered that the front door was locked, so she sat on the front porch until after 11:00 A.M. Some

Miss Lucy Collet.

observers later reported seeing a man jump over the Borden fence, which bordered the Chagnon property to the east on Third Street, but Lucie, who was there, saw no one.

Lucie's testimony for the prosecution was weakened somewhat when she admitted she was unsure as to the exact time she was at the Chagnon residence. Her observations were not considered to be of great importance.

Lucie Collett was born in Quebec, Canada to Pierre A.A. and Gerogianna (Verrault) Collett. After her parents came to Fall River, Lucie lived there for the rest of her life. She married her father's clerk, Jean Normand, in 1896.

Colvin, S.S. (1869-?)

Colvin reported about the Borden trial for the *Providence Journal*. He attended Brown University and began his career with the *Providence Telegram*.

Cone, Dwight Eleazer (1854-1927)

Cone was an autopsy clerk who, five days after the funeral of Andrew and Abby Borden, entered the vault at Oak Grove Cemetery where the bodies were placed before burial. With him were Drs. William A. Dolan, Frank W. Draper and John H. Leary. Without the knowledge of the Borden family, the physicians removed the heads of both victims and sent them to Harvard University for examination. The actual skulls were later introduced at Lizzie Borden's trial as evidence.

Cone was born in Brookfield, New York and early in life was a teacher. His goal was to save enough money to put himself through medical school. He attended Albany Medical College in Albany, New York and finished his studies at the University of the City of New York in 1875. He practiced medicine in New York state and Rhode Island before moving to Fall River in 1882. Cone was a founder of Fall River Hospital in 1886. Cone was a Mason and active in several medical associations. He died unexpectedly in 1927 while attending a clambake in Swansea, Massachusetts.

Connelly, Annie (1884-?)

Janice Duckworth reported that eight year-old Annie and her friend, ten year-old Mamie Smith, heard cries from the Borden house the day of the murders. Two police officers, Philip Harrington and Patrick Doherty interviewed Connelly on August 8 in her home at 41 John Street. Both Connelly and Mamie Smith denied ever saying they heard cries or saw anything concerning the murders (see Janice Duckworth, Sarah Scholnick and Mamie Smith).

Connor, Annie C. (1861-1936)

Annie Connor lived in Wadleigh Falls, New Hampshire and was middle-aged and unmarried when she first met one of the Bordens. Along with her sister Mary, Annie Connor purchased a house in Newmarket, New Hampshire on November 9, 1915 for $2,500 even though they were not known to have that much wealth in their possession. The Connor sisters moved into the Newmarket house in 1916 with a strange woman. That woman was Emma Borden.

Annie was remembered by George Bennett, a neighbor of the Connors in Wadleigh Falls who later visited them in Newmarket. Annie had a friendly disposition and always dressed in fine clothes. Bennett said Emma never came downstairs from her bedroom while he was visiting. Other neighbors of the Connors in Newmarket also remember spotting Emma from a distance. Soon after Emma died, Annie and Mary Connor sold the Newmarket house.

Connor, Mary K. (c.1860-1921)

Mary, like her sister Annie, was middle-aged and unmarried in 1915 when they bought a house in Newmarket, New Hampshire from George Leavitt. They also lived on a 65-acre farm in Wadleigh Falls, about two miles from the newly purchased house, where they had resided all of their lives. They moved into the new house with a woman who turned out to be Emma Borden. Emma most likely provided the money for the $2,500 selling price. In physical appearance, Connor was simply described as being older and paler than her sister Annie.

Connors, Patrick (1853-1926)

Connors was on the Fall River police force and participated in the search of the Borden residence on Monday, August 8, 1892. He was accompanied by Captain Dennis Desmond, William H. Medley and Martin Quigley, all policemen, and by attorney Andrew Jennings and Pinkerton detective O.M. Hanscom. Connors was present as a witness at the Borden trial but was not called upon to testify.

Patrick Connors was born in County Cork, Ireland. He came to the United States with his family in 1840 and was living in Fall River by 1868. He was a laborer for years before he received an appointment to the police department in 1879. Connors was assigned day duty in 1886 and became a captain in 1893. He remained a police officer for over forty years and retired in 1923 with several commendations of excellence for his investigatory skills. Connors remained active in Catholic charity work and died after a lengthy illness in Union Hospital, Fall River.

Cook, Charles C. (1854-1934)

Charles C. Cook (called Charles T. Cook in Edwin H. Porter's *The Fall River Tragedy* (1893)) managed some business property Andrew Borden owned on the corner of Anawan and S. Main Streets in Fall River. He was also an insurance agent. Cook testified at the preliminary hearing as to whether or not Andrew had made a will before his death.

An article in the August 18, 1892 edition of the *Fall River Globe* claimed that Andrew Borden told Cook he was thinking of drawing up a will because he was getting along in years. Although Cook denied the truth of the story in the same article, he attended the preliminary hearing in Fall River and denied Andrew ever mentioned making a will to him.

At that hearing, Cook said that he usually saw Andrew Borden but did not notice him on the morning of the murders. Cook last saw Borden on July 31, 1892, and Andrew never mentioned a will. Cook further stated that three weeks before he last saw the deceased, Borden told him that he had no will.

After Lizzie was acquitted, she entrusted her business affairs to Cook. As a token of appreciation for years of faithful service, Lizzie left Cook $10,000 and some land she owned across the street from Maplecroft, her home on French Street in her will.

Cook, Charles H. (1836-1911)

Charles Cook's name was on a list of witnesses handwritten by District Attorney Hosea M. Knowlton. The leader of the prosecution team at Lizzie's trial wanted to trace Andrew Borden's movements in downtown Fall River on the morning he was murdered. Cook testified at the preliminary hearing. He was summoned to attend the trial as a witness but was not called to the stand.

On the morning of the killings Cook, H.P. Durling, William Hacking and George C. Douglas were sitting on the front porch of Mrs. Adelaide Churchill's home, known as the "Buffinton House." On that fateful Thursday morning they saw no one enter or leave the Borden residence, which was located directly south of Churchill's house. Cook also went into the barn after the bodies were discovered and later that day gave a statement to the Fall River police (see John Donnelly).

Charles H. Cook was born in Rhode Island to Dennis and Louisa P. (Francis) Cook. He spent his youth in Fall River and fought in the Civil War for a nine month term, 1862-1863. He held several different types of jobs in Fall River after returning from the war, including that of coachman. He died in Taunton, Massachusetts.

Cook, Everett M. (1855-1931)

Everett M. Cook, along with John T. Burrell, Abraham G. Hart, Jonathan Clegg, Joseph Shortsleeves and James Mather, was called to testify at the trial as to the movements of Andrew Jackson Borden on the morning of August 4, 1892, the day Borden and his wife were murdered.

Cook was a cashier at the First National Bank. Andrew was one of the bank's directors and entered the bank at 9:45 A.M. The cashier just happened to look up at the clock as Borden walked in. After seeing Cook, Borden left to meet with two carpenters who were doing renovations for him inside the Borden Building.

Cook was born in Fall River to William and Esther Cook. He became an employee of the First National Bank after graduation from high school and remained there as a cashier until he retired. Cook was a well-known banker and a member of several business clubs. Cook married Mattie L. Brightman and died in the city of his birth.

Cook, Samuel H.

Samuel Cook of New Bedford was called to serve on the grand jury that indicted Lizzie Borden for the murders of her father and stepmother. He was listed in the *New Bedford City Directory* of 1892 as being in the marine and fire insurance business. He was excused and did not serve on the grand jury.

Cook, Weston L.

"West" Cook was listed in the *Fall River City Directory* of 1892 as a farmer. According to the stenographic notes of Annie M. White, he also worked at the "Durfee ice houses." Cook suggested that the police interview Hiram Brightman of Wilson Road. Neither interview brought the authorities any closer to the killer of Andrew and Abby Borden (see Hiram Brightman).

Cook, William S.

Cook was a reporter for the *New Bedford Evening Journal*, and as such attended the Borden trial in New Bedford in June 1893.

Cooper, Bearsley S.

Bearsley S. Cooper was an early suspect in the killings of Andrew and Abby Borden. The Fall River police believed for a while that Cooper was Dr. Benjamin Handy's "wild-eyed man" (see Benjamin Handy). He was a horse trader by profession. Cooper was able to prove that he was in New Bedford at the time the murders took place, selling a horse to a respected resident of that city. Cooper was never arrested and after his alibi was confirmed had nothing more to do with the Borden murder case.

Correira, Manuel José (1871-?)

Bertha Manchester was hacked to death in her Fall River farmhouse with a hatchet on May 31, 1893, five days before the Borden jury was chosen. Her killer was Manuel José Corrriera (see Bertha Manchester). All of Fall River heard about the murder and its parallels to the Borden killings were obvious to everyone in Bristol County. At the time Manchester was killed, Lizzie was in the Taunton jail. If a crazed murderer was still on the loose, it certainly was not Lizzie Borden.

The timing of this crime was perfect for Lizzie's defense team. When Correira was captured on June 4, 1893, the Borden jury had already been chosen and was not aware of Correira's arrest.

Bertha was the youngest daughter of Stephen "Old Steve" Manchester. He was known to be so unsavory and nasty that two wives had deserted him. At the time of her death, Bertha was twenty-two years old and a large, sturdy farmer's daughter who managed the land as well as could any man (see Stephen Manchester).

Manchester's body was found in her kitchen and the circumstances of her death were similar in some ways to the Borden murders. It

José Correiro, held for the murder of Bertha Manchester.

turned out that Correira had been hired as a farmhand by Stephen Manchester, and subsequently fired. The next day, Correira returned to get his final pay, but "Old Steve" was not there. Bertha was, but she spoke no Portuguese and Correira knew no English.

Correira, probably frustrated and believing he was not going to get paid, killed Bertha, who put up a mighty struggle. Correira was arrested, stood trial and was sentenced to life in jail. He served 26 years in Charlestown Prison until pardoned by Massachusetts Governor Eugene Foss, after which time Correira returned to his native Azores Islands.

Correira could not have killed the Bordens since he did not arrive in the United States until April 1893. The members of the Borden jury, however, were not aware of that.

Costello, Matthew

A native of Somerset, Costello was questioned as a possible juror at the Borden trial. On the stand, Costello said that he had formed an opinion and was morally against capital punishment. Realizing that he would vote "not guilty" no matter how strong the evidence, Costello was excused from serving on the jury.

Côté, Alexander

Alexander Côté was a plumber who lived at 32 Jencks Street in Fall River. Côté recalled seeing a strange man at Arcand's stable who asked him for a ride to New Bedford at about 3:00 P.M. on August 4, the day the Bordens were hacked to death. Côté refused the man's request (see Joseph H. Heap, Francios Charette, Joseph Michaud, Jean St. Laurent, Romuald St. Amant, and Exentive St. Amant).

Coughlin, John William (1861-1920)

Coughlin was a physician and the mayor of Fall River at the time of the murders. He played a large, if unwitting, role in preventing Lizzie's

Dr. John W. Coughlin, mayor of Fall River.

inquest statements from being presented to the jury. Coughlin testified at the final trial in June 1893 about a visit he and City Marshal Rufus B. Hilliard paid to the Borden house on Saturday evening, August 6, 1892.

Coughlin and Hilliard visited 92 Second Street at 7:45 P.M. on the night of the Bordens's funeral to warn Lizzie, Emma and John Vinnicum Morse to remain at home because of concern that the crowd milling outside the Borden home would turn violent. During the conversation Lizzie insisted that she be told if she were a suspect. Coughlin reluctantly said, "Well, Miss Borden, I regret to answer, but I must answer—yes, you are suspected." No warrants, however, were issued against Lizzie until the following Monday.

Mayor Coughlin's confession that Lizzie was a suspect was a grave error, for it opened the door to defense claims that her inquest testimony be excluded from the trial on the grounds that her answers were involuntary and therefore violated her Fifth Amendments rights. That was the argument defense lawyer George Dexter Robinson used, and the court agreed with his reasoning; all inquest testimony was excluded.

John William Coughlin was born in Fall River. After a local public school education, he worked as a steam and gas fitter until employed in the office of Dr. W. Jean Baptiste Chagnon, who inspired Coughlin to become a doctor (see Wenceslas Jean Baptiste Chagnon). He studied with Dr. Charles C. Terry and later attended the College of Physicians and Surgeons in Baltimore, Maryland where he received a medical degree in 1885. Coughlin opened a practice in Fall River and was elected mayor of his native city four consecutive times beginning in 1890. He remained politically active for the rest of his life and served on the Frothingham Commision during the First World War.

Cowles, Edward (1837-1919)

Cowles was an alienist, which was nineteenth century terminology for psychiatrist. Dr. Cowles was asked in a September 22, 1892 letter written by Massachusetts Attorney General Albert Enoch Pillsbury to help the Commonwealth decide if Lizzie was insane. Cowles turned down the offer, answering, "...my inferences have been against a theory of insanity in the person charged with the crime."

Edward Cowles was born in Ryegate, Vermont, and received a B.A. from Dartmouth in 1859 and an M.A. from Dartmouth Medical School in 1861. A Doctor of Medicine degree from the same college followed in 1863 as did a medical degree from the College of Physicians and Surgeons at Columbia University.

Cowles was an assistant surgeon at the Retreat for the Insane in Hartford, Connecticut. He served in the army during the Civil War and was discharged in 1872. He then became head resident at Boston City Hospital in Boston, Massachusetts. In 1879, he resigned to succeed Dr. George F. Jelly as superintendant at McLean Hospital for the Insane in Somerville, Massachusetts (see George F. Jelly).

Cowles later helped plan a new hospital in Waverly, Massachusetts, when the Somerville facility relocated. He remained there until he retired in 1913. In addition to treating patients, Cowles was also a professor of mental diseases at Dartmouth, 1885-1914, then was named professor emeritus. He also taught at Harvard and Clark Colleges. Cowles received an honorary Doctor of Laws degree from Dartmouth and authored many journal articles on mental disorders.

Coyle, Patrick

Patrick Coyle of Taunton, Massachusetts, served on the grand jury that decided Lizzie Borden must stand trial for the murders that occurred in Fall River on August 4, 1892.

Cranston, Orville W.

Orville Cranston of New Bedford was questioned as a prospective juror in the Borden trial. He admitted to being prejudiced and was excused.

Crapo, Margaret L. (Wallace) (1829-1896)

Margaret L. Crapo was listed on Hosea M. Knowlton's handwritten list of witnesses under the heading "As to not seeing prisoner escape." Mrs. Crapo was summoned as a witness at the trial but was not asked to take the stand.

Margaret L. Wallace was born in Saugerties, New York, and married John D. Crapo, a dealer in alcoholic beverages, who died in 1877. Her address was listed as 39 Third Street, Fall River in 1892. She died in that city.

Cross, Ella

Ella Cross ran a boarding house at 17 John Street in Fall River. One of her boarders was Henry Mahr, an early suspect in the Borden murders. Mrs. Cross produced letters and telegrams proving that Mahr was in London, England at the time of the crimes (see Henry Mahr).

Crossman, Oliver H.

Crossman, of Taunton, was asked as a prospective juror whether or not he could render a fair verdict. Crossman said that he was prejudiced and was excused.

Crowe, John

John Crowe owned the property on Third Street to the east of the Borden pear orchard, just south of the Chagnon property. On the Crowe's land was a stoneyard where laborers Joseph Desrosiers, John Dennie and Patrick McGowan were working when Fall River policeman Frank H. Wixon jumped a six-foot fence on the Borden property to see if a person could escape from the Borden house by that route. Wixon's actions startled the laborers.

On June 14, 1893 an Associated Press report stated that a boy, the son of C.C. Potter, discovered a hatchet on the roof of Crowe's barn while looking for a ball (see Arthur Potter). No one knows what later happened to the hatchet. Some Borden historians have speculated that this hatchet, not the one without a handle that was presented at the trial, was the true murder weapon.

Cummings, James T.

Cummings was a lawyer who represented Bridget Sullivan at the preliminary hearing when Sullivan appeared as a witness. He was possibly a relative of Dr. Michael Kelly, who lived with his family and maid directly south of the Borden residence at 96 Second Street.

Cundall, Benjamin (1824-?)

Benjamin Cundall, from Somerset, was called as a prospective juror at the Borden trial. He said he had no opinion in the case, did not feel that he was biased but had extremely poor eyesight. He was acceptable to Lizzie Borden, but challenged by the prosecution and did not serve on the jury.

Cunneen, James E. (1832-1914)

Cunneen, a prominent local businessman, was on Hosea M. Knowlton's handwritten list of possible witnesses. He was listed under the heading, "As to not seeing prisoner escape." He happened to be near the Borden house at the time of the murders and testified at the preliminary hearing and before the grand jury. Summoned as a witness at the trial, he appeared but was not called to give testimony.

Cunneen was born in New York state and moved to Fall River with his family in 1839. He began working when seven years old and later fought in the Civil War. He was in real estate and insurance and served as an alderman from 1870-72. Cunneen invested heavily in Fall River mills and was superintendent of the Seaconnet Mill. He was married twice, first to Mary A. Organ, then to Mary J. Kelleher.

Cunningham, John J. (1864-1912)

John J. Cunningham was a freelance reporter. He is the caller who notified the police to report a "stabbing" in the Borden home at 92 Second Street using the telephone at the paint store of Augustus P. Gorman. He was questioned at the preliminary hearing and at the Borden trial as to what he observed on the morning of the murders.

When Mrs. Adelaide Churchill rushed to Hall's Stables at 129 Second Street to tell her handyman Tom Boulds to report a murder to the police, Cunningham overheard the exchange. He then went into Augustus P. Gorman's paint store and made four phone calls: one to the *Fall River Globe*, one to the *News*, a third to the *Herald* and finally to the Fall River police station, where City Marshal Rufus B. Hilliard answered the telephone at 11:15 A.M. on Thursday, August 4, 1892. After receiving Cunningham's call Hilliard ordered Officer George A. Allen to proceed to the Borden residence.

After making the calls, Cunningham saw Bridget Sullivan and Alice Russell rushing towards the Borden house. He met Officer Allen and went there himself to see what was happening. When Cunningham and Allen arrived at the Borden's home, two newspaper reporters, John J. Manning of the *Globe* and Walter P. Stevens of the *News* were already on the scene.

Manning and Stevens quickly searched the grounds for clues. They went to the south side of the property between the Borden and Kelly homes and spotted no footprints of an escaped murderer there. They then went into the back yard and tried to open the cellar door, which was locked from the inside. Neither went into the house. Cunningham also saw Allen appoint a passerby, painter Charles S. Sawyer, as a guard at the Bordens' side door.

Cunningham was born in England. After moving to the United States, he became a partner in Cunningham Brothers, which specialized in selling newspapers and periodicals. Cunningham once had the largest newspaper route in Fall River. As a news dealer he had verbal agreements with all three of the local newspapers to report any late-breaking stories. In 1891, Cunningham was made a "callman" for the Fall River Fire Department, a position he held until his death.

Currien, George W.

From Attleboro, Currien was called to jury duty for the Borden trial. He stated when questioned that he had formed no opinion about the murders and considered himself unbiased. He was challenged by Lizzie Borden, however, and was sent home.

Cushing, Florence W.

Cushing, from Boston, was an official type writer along with William B. Wright, Mrs. William H. Haskell and A.M. Dollard. Their job was to type the stenographic notes that Annie White made during the trial as the notes were dictated to them after each day's testimony had ended.

D

Daily, William

William Daily was at one time suspect in the Borden murders. He was from Roxbury, Massachusetts, a town near Boston. Daily was arrested at approximately 2:00 P.M. on the day of the killings. He told the police he had arrived in Fall River on Wednesday evening, the day before the Bordens were murdered. Daily had bloodstains on his clothes, which he said were two days old. The police believed Daily's story and he was released from custody.

Daly, Maurice

Daly was a carpenter in Fall River. While the inquest of Lizzie Borden and others proceeded at the Fall River police station, Daly, Officer Philip H. Harrington and Marshal Rufus B. Hilliard went to the Borden house and remained there for half an hour. Daly removed sections of wood from where the bodies were discovered. The wood came from areas near doors and windows and were stained with the victims' blood. The *New Bedford Evening Standard* referred to Daly as "Morris Daley."

Dammon, Silas D.

Silas D. Dammon of New Bedford admitted that he was biased concerning the murder case. He was then excused from sitting on the Borden jury. Dammon made his living as a ship carpenter.

Davidson, Arabel

Arabel Davidson was the half-sister of John Vinnicum Morse, Lizzie Borden's uncle by Andrew Borden's first marriage. Her name appeared in the newspaper of her hometown, Hastings, Iowa where Morse had once lived. When Morse lived in Hastings, he owned a farm that shared a common border with the farm of the Davidsons. They had known Morse since 1857.

Several years before the murders, Morse had resided with the Davidson family. Because of a disagreement, relations between them and John V. Morse were strained. In the article, Arabel Davidson said that Morse never forgot a grudge and was unforgiving to those whom he felt had crossed him. The interview, written as a result of Pinkerton Detective Superintendent O.M. Hanscom's trip to Hastings to investigate Morse, as well as growing national interest in the Borden murders, was filed as a wire story and picked up by other papers on August 14, 1892.

Davis, Elihu M.

Chosen for possible jury duty, Davis was questioned by prosecution and defense attorneys. He said that he was not biased but had formed an opinion. Davis also claimed that he was hard of hearing. He was excused. Davis worked as a machinist.

Davis, Fred E.

Fred E. Davis was a Fall River policeman. When prisoner and accused murderess Lizzie Borden arrived in Fall River from the Taunton jail on August 22, 1892 for her preliminary hearing, Davis and Officer Thomas McAdams escorted her from the entrance of the Central Police Station to the room of jail matron Hannah Reagan where Lizzie stayed until she was returned to Taunton.

Davis, George W.

George W. Davis was a farmer from Dartmouth called for jury duty in the Borden murder trial. He was described in the *New Bedford Evening Standard* as of the "manly looking type." He said that although he had formed an opinion, he believed he could still render a fair decision. He admitted, however, that he felt capital punishment was wrong and was excused.

Davis, Isaac C.

Davis, who was born in Westport, Massachusetts, was a butcher by trade. By 1892 he was blind and living in South Dartmouth. John Vinnicum Morse, the uncle of Lizzie and Emma Borden, lived with Davis and his family. Morse had worked for Davis before heading west to seek his fortune in 1855.

Morse advised the Davis family on business matters and was a close friend of Davis's son William. Davis consistently proclaimed Morse's innocence in the Borden murders when the latter was the chief suspect. When a reporter for the *Fall River Daily Herald* interviewed Morse and asked him why he was in town on the day of the murder, Morse answered that he was buying an ox for Davis.

Davis, William A. (1852-?)

Like his father Isaac, William A. Davis was in the meat business. He was in the ice business as well. Davis owned the house on S. Mill Rd. in South Dartmouth where his father lived, and where John Vinnicum Morse had resided since his return from Iowa. Davis also had a wife Sophia, who he married on Christmas Day 1872, and three children. Davis accompanied Morse when he went to Fall River on June 3, 1893 to meet with Andrew Jennings, one of Lizzie's lawyers.

Davol, Ezra

Davol, of Taunton, presented a document to the court while the jurors were being chosen for the Borden trial and was allowed to leave. Davol was a printer.

Dean, Albert

Albert Dean, from Berkley, Massachusetts, arrived in New Bedford for jury duty, but was neither questioned nor picked.

Dean, George W.

George Dean was a retired industrialist at the time of the murders. He was a friend of Andrew Jackson Borden and acted as one of the pallbearers at his funeral on Saturday, August 6, 1892. The other pallbearers for Andrew included Richard B. Borden, Abraham G. Hart, Jerome C. Borden, James M. Osborne and Andrew Borden, the deceased's relative and namesake.

Dean, Harry C.

Dean arrived in New Bedford for jury duty on June 5, 1893 but was not questioned and did not sit on the jury. Dean was a resident of Taunton, Massachusetts.

Dean, William Francis (1839-1904)

William Francis Dean was chosen to sit on the jury that eventually acquitted Lizzie Borden of the murder of her father and stepmother. He was described as a Republican with a wife and child. He had sat in a jury box before. The *New Bedford Evening Standard* noted that although he was in middle age, he still had a lot of hair, looked around with a "searching eye" and called him "an interested spectator of all that is transpiring."

Dedrick, Albert C. (1864-?)

Dr. Albert C. Dedrick assisted at the first autopsy of the Bordens performed on the dining room table at 92 Second Street the afternoon of the murders. Dedrick assisted Dr. William A. Dolan, the Fall River Medical Examiner, along with physicians John William Coughlin, John H. Leary, Thomas Gunning, Emmanuel C. Dutra, J.Q.A. Tourtellot and Anson C. Peckham. Dedrick also testified at the trial in New Bedford.

Dedrick took the stand at the Borden trial on June 12, 1893. Dedrick's testimony concerned the wounds on Andrew's face and Abby's head. He stated to the jury that Abby had preceded Andrew in death.

Albert C. Dedrick was born in Cranston, Rhode Island on October 10, 1864. His father was a doctor and an assistant surgeon during the Civil War. Dedrick graduated from New York's Bellvue Hospital Medical College in 1888 and moved to Fall River that June where he began his medical practice. He was a member of several social and medical organizations. He married May Leslie Law of Fall River in 1894.

Delano, Moses (1815-?)

Delano owned the house at 19 Green Street in Fairhaven, Massachusetts where Emma was vacationing when her father and stepmother were killed. She and Lizzie were to travel together to visit Helen Brownell, but Lizzie turned back to Fall River when they reached New Bedford.

de Lipman, Max

See Lipman, Max de.

Derossier, Joseph

See Desrosiers, Joseph.

Desmond, Dennis, Jr. (1854-1926)

Dennis Desmond, Jr. was a Fall River policeman. He was called to investigate a robbery at the Borden residence in 1891. After the Bordens were killed, he participated in searches of the house on Friday, the day after the murders, and Monday, August 8. Desmond testified at Lizzie's trial as a witness for the prosecution.

On August 8, 1892, Desmond, Assistant City Marshall John Fleet, State Detective George Seaver, Medical Examiner William A. Dolan and City Marshal Rufus B. Hilliard, made a search of the Borden home. It is possible that Officer Philip Harrington participated in that search as well. On the stand at the trial, Desmond insisted that the search was thorough, in spite of Fleet's earlier assertion on the witness stand that it was casual.

Mr. Desmond shows how he rolled the hatchet up.

Officer William Medley took the witness stand before Desmond, but on the same day, June 10, 1893. Medley claimed that he had discovered the handleless hatchet in the Borden cellar and had shown it to Desmond, who told Medley to wrap it in brown paper he found in a nearby water closet. Medley said at the trial that after wrapping the hatchet, he took it to the station house.

On the stand, Desmond agreed with most of Medley's statements except that Desmond said he, Desmond, had wrapped the hatchet in newspaper he had found in the water closet. Lizzie's attorney George Dexter Robinson asked him on the stand to demonstrate how he had wrapped the evidence, which Desmond proceeded to do.

Dennis Desmond, Jr. was born in Fall River to Dennis and Mary Desmond. He began his career with the Fall River Police Department in 1888 as a patrolman and was promoted to captain in 1893. He later served as Assistant City Marshal and became captain of the Central Division in 1903. His wife Adeline died in 1923 and Desmond retired the next year. He held a unique record—that of having commanded every police department division in Fall River by the time he retired. After leaving the force, Desmond relocated to Somerset, Massachusetts and lived there for the remainder of his life.

Desrosiers, Joseph (1870-?)

Joseph Desrosiers was a stonecutter who worked in the stoneyard of John Crowe. He testified at both the preliminary hearing and the trial as to his observations on the morning of the Borden killings. The *New Bedford Evening Standard* described the witness as a handsome Frenchman with a "fastidious moustache."

Joseph Desrosiers lived at the King Philip on Main Street, according to his testimony at the Borden trial, although he is not listed in the *Fall River City Directory* at that or any other address. He, along with John Dinnie and Patrick McGowan, was working in the stoneyard on Third Street directly behind the Borden property when Andrew and Abby Borden were murdered.

Desrosiers spoke English poorly, and his testimony at the trial was in French. Police officer Adelard Perron acted as his translator before the jury. Desrosiers said that at the time the murders occurred, he saw no strangers in the Bordens' backyard or on the Borden or Crowe properties. He testified that he had worked all day on August 4, 1892, from 7:00 A.M. until 5:00 P.M.

Devine, John J. (1852-1930)

Devine was a Fall River policeman who, on the day of the murders, participated in the search of the Borden house and that evening probably saved John Vinnicum Morse from being torn apart by a mob.

Devine was one of seven officers who were involved in the first search of the Borden house that began at about 11:45 A.M., August 4, 1892. The others involved in the inspection were Officers Frances X. Wixon and Michael Mullaly who, along with Devine, arrived at the house at 11:37 A.M. Deputy Marshal John Fleet, Inspector William H. Medley, Officer Charles Wilson and Sergeant Philip H. Harrington came upon the scene minutes later. Devine assisted in the search of the Borden cellar and examined a number of axes and hatchets found there.

Later that night, as John Vinnicum Morse was returning from a trip to the post office, a mob who suspected him to be the killer chased the terrified Morse up the street. He was saved by Officer Devine and a squad of police who had been tracking his whereabouts all that day (some writers have said it was Officer John Minnehan who performed this life-saving deed).

Devine was born in England. He became a Fall River policeman in 1877 and retired from the force in 1922 with the rank of lieutenant. He was active in many professional organizations and died in Fall River.

Dewey, Justin III (1836-1900)

Justin Dewey was one of the three justices who jointly presided over the Lizzie Borden trial. Chief Justice Albert C. Mason named Associate Justices Caleb Blodgett and Justin Dewey as two of the three judges re-

Judge Dewey.

quired by law to sit on capital cases. He named himself as the third judge. Of the three, Dewey had the least experience on the bench.

A major controversy later arose over the naming of Dewey to the trial. Dewey had been appointed to the bench by former Governor George Dexter Robinson, who in 1892 was the leader of Lizzie Borden's defense team. It was Dewey and the other justices who, speaking for the court, ruled that the reading of Lizzie's incriminating inquest statements and all mention of prussic acid were to be excluded.

Finally, it was Dewey who gave the instructions to the jury before they began deliberation. Contemporary Judge Charles G. Davis felt Dewey's remarks were not only a plea for acquittal, but actually more effective than Robinson's summation of the case. At the time, however, the press took little notice of the connection between Dewey and ex-Governor Robinson. In spite of the controversy that surrounded the final verdict and the decisions of the panel of justices, Dewey told the *Boston Globe* on June 21, 1893, "I am perfectly satisfied with the verdict...I was satisfied when I made my charge to the jury that the verdict would be not guilty."

Dewey was considered handsome with his white beard, aquiline nose and his deep-set and intense eyes. He was the father of three daughters, all in their twenties. Some felt that perhaps he saw them in Lizzie Borden. Although Lizzie was almost 33 when acquitted, perhaps the Justice could not believe that a young lady could commit such atrocious crimes.

Justin Dewey III was born in Alford, Massachusetts and graduated from Williams College in 1858. He studied law in the Great Barrington, Massachusetts law office of Increase Sumner. He was elected to the Massachusetts House of Representatives in 1862 and again in 1877. He went to the state Senate in 1879. Dewey received his appointment in 1886 as a justice of the Massachusetts Superior Court by Governor George Dexter Robinson.

Dexter, Henry Alton

Dexter was a state officer mentioned in the preliminary hearing testimony of Assistant City Marshal John Fleet. Dexter, Fleet and two other Fall River policemen consulted with each other while searching the Borden home on the afternoon of the murder. Dexter's only mention, however, is in Edwin H. Porter's *The Fall River Tragedy* (1893). He was not noted in any other account of either the search of 92 Second Street or of the murders in general.

Dias, Charles H.

Dias was a salesman from New Bedford. He appeared for jury duty at the Borden trial but was neither questioned nor chosen.

Dimond, ??

A "Miss Dimon" living on Fourth Street in Fall River is briefly mentioned in the stenographic notes of Annie M. White. There is no Dimon mentioned in the *City Directory* of 1892, but there is the name Dimond. White probably misspelled the name; she had done this before. Dimond was interviewed by private detective Edwin D. McHenry, later to become a factor in the notorious "Trickey-McHenry" Affair" that almost ruined the *Boston Globe* newspaper (see Edwin D.

McHenry and Henry G. Trickey). McHenry later made an official statement about the interview that was recorded on paper by Annie White.

According to McHenry, Dimond and her sister, Mrs. Potter, "milliners on Fourth Street," told him that they knew Lizzie Borden was exercising in a gymnasium and occasionally boasted of her strength. McHenry's account said that the gymnasium was in the "Troy block" of Fall River. Nothing official action resulted from McHenry's information.

Dinnie, John (1858-?)

Dinnie, a worker at the Crowe stoneyard, testified at the preliminary hearing and at the final trial. He said at the trial that he worked at the stoneyard, which bordered the rear of the Borden property, from 6:45 A.M. until noon and saw no strangers on or near the Borden backyard. He also said he saw no one enter Third Street from the direction of the Borden house.

Born in Scotland, Dinnie arrived in the United States in 1882 and had lived in Fall River since 1884. He was employed by Crowe as a stonemason. By 1905, he referred to himself as a contractor. He lived in Fall River until 1908 when he moved to Chicago, Illinois.

Dixon, John W.

John W. Dixon, from the city of Taunton, admitted on the stand when questioned for the Borden jury that he was biased. He was quickly excused. Dixon worked as a pattern fitter.

Doherty, Patrick H. (1859-1915)

Patrick H. Doherty was a Fall River policeman. He was one of the first police officers to arrive at 92 Second Street after the murders were reported. He saw the bodies, questioned Lizzie in her bedroom and later that evening interviewed drug clerk Eli Bence at D.R. Smith's drug store. Doherty testified at the preliminary hearing and the final trial.

Doherty as a witness at the trial made it seem that he had been the first person on the murder scene. He was not. While travelling on foot to 92 Second Street, he ran into Deputy Sheriff Francis X. Wixon near Adelaide Churchill's house, which at 90 Second Street was next door to the Borden home. When they arrived at about 11:37 A.M., John J. Manning, a reporter for the Associated Press was already there waiting on the steps (see John J. Manning and John J. Cunningham). Officer George A. Allen has also preceded Doherty. The courtroom burst into laughter when Manning related this story on the witness stand. It demonstrated to all the supposed incompetence and slow reaction of the police force.

At the trial, Doherty described how he and Dr. Bowen inspected the bodies of the deceased. Andrew's blood was fresh and liquid while Abby's was "hard." He saw blood spots on the pillow shams and on the bed was a bunched section of severed hair from Abby's head on the bed in the guest room where she was attacked.

Doherty then made his way into the kitchen and saw Lizzie and Mrs. Churchill. He asked Lizzie where she was when Andrew was murdered. Lizzie answered that she was in the barn. He asked if any Portugsese worked for the family, and Lizzie said no. Lizzie told Officer Doherty that William Eddy and Alfred C. Johnson managed Andrew's Swansea farms but they would not hurt him. Officer Doherty later saw Lizzie in her bedroom and asked to be admitted. Lizzie requested that he wait a moment, then opened the door. Doherty entered and looked around the room.

Later, when Doherty saw Lizzie downstairs again, he noticed that she was wearing a light blue dress. This was not the dress later shown to him at the trial (the dress that Lizzie gave the police as being the one she wore on the murder morning).

Bridget Sullivan said on the stand that Doherty at some point went down to the cellar with Officer William H. Medley, Assistant City Marshal John Fleet and Dr. Seabury Bowen. They took away three hatchets from a box where Andrew kept wood for the furnace. One of them was the famous "handleless hatchet" which was introduced by the prosecution at the trial as the murder weapon. Doherty also went into the barn and remembered it as being "very warm...breathing was bad...stifling hot there."

At around 7:00 P.M. that evening, he and Officer Philip H. Harrington went to Smith's drug store and spoke to Eli Bence, who told the policemen Lizzie had come into the store the day before to buy ten cents worth of prussic acid. She was denied the acid because she lacked a doctor's prescription. Doherty remained on duty the night of the murders until 9:00 P.M.

By the time Bridget Sullivan was called to testify at the inquest later that week, she had moved out of the Borden residence and lived with her cousin Patrick Harrington at 95 Division Street. Doherty picked her up there to go to the inquest which was held at the Fall River Police Station.

Doherty was born in Peoria, Illinois. He traveled with his family as a youngster and eventually found a job with the Fall River Iron Works. He later served as a deck hand on the Fall River Line steamer Bristol and was accepted in the police department in 1885. He married Nora Coughlin two years later and was promoted to the rank of captain in 1892. He retired in 1915 and died a short time later.

Dolan, William Andrew (1858-1922)

Dr. William Dolan was the Fall River Medical Examiner. He performed two autopsies on the Bordens and sent body parts and three hatchets found in the Borden cellar to Boston for analysis. Dolan testified at both the preliminary hearing and the final trial. The doctor also performed the autopsy on Bertha Manchester, who was slain with an ax in June 1893 (see José Corriera and Bertha Manchester).

At 11:45 A.M. on Thursday, August 4, Dolan was returning from a house call when he spotted a large crowd milling around 92 Second Street. He entered the house and talked to Lizzie in her bedroom. At this time, only Andrew's body had been discovered. Lizzie told Dolan that Mrs. Borden had left the house because of a note she had received, which Lizzie said Abby probably burned on her way out.

Dolan performed the first autopsy on the murdered couple on the Bordens' dining room table at 3:00 P.M. He was assisted by Drs. Seabury Bowen, Albert C. Dedrick, John William Coughlin, John Leary, Thomas Gunning, Emmanuel C. Dutra, J.Q.A. Tourtellot and Anson C. Peckham. The autopsy team, led by Dolan, removed both of the Bordens' stomachs and tied the ends to preserve the contents. He sent the stomachs along with a total of three axes and hatchets found by the police in the cellar by messenger to Dr. Edward S. Wood, professor of chemistry at Harvard for testing and analysis.

The following day, August 5, Dolan and policemen John Fleet, George F. Seaver and Dennis Desmond searched the Borden home. They inspected the house and yard, emptied closets and examined every article of clothing for signs of blood. As Dolan later said, "We examined everything down to the slightest bump on the wallpaper." They found nothing.

Five days after the August funerals of Andrew and Abby Borden in Oak Grove Cemetery, Dolan and Dr. Frank W. Draper, assisted by Dr. John H. Leary and autopsy clerk Dr. Dwight E. Cone, performed a second autopsy in a holding vault at the cemetery. Dolan removed the Bordens' heads and later removed all flesh and tissue, revealing the bare skulls which clearly showed the damage done by the murder weapon. Plaster casts and photographs were made of the skulls. When the skulls, photos and plaster casts with the wounds outlined in blue were displayed at the trial on June 14, one of the jurors, Louis B. Hodges, fainted.

Dolan was born in Shirley, Massachusetts, and moved to Fall River while still a young boy. He graduated from St. Joseph's College in Yonkers, New York, in 1879 and studied medicine at the University of Pennsylvania. He graduated from there in 1882, returned to Fall River in 1883 and set up a practice.

Dolan was appointed medical examiner for the Third District of Bristol County in 1892, the year of the Borden killings, and in that capacity was the medical officer in charge of the case. He was active in many professional organizations and was still practicing medicine in Fall River when he died.

Dollard, A.M.

Dollard, along with Mrs. William H. Haskell, F.W. Cushing and F.D. Ross, all of Boston, were the official type writers. Their job was to type Annie White's stenographic notes from the trial as they were dictated to them (see Florence W. Cushing and Florence D. Ross).

Donaghy, Thomas, Jr.

Thomas Donaghy was a shoe clerk from New Bedford, Massachusetts. He appeared for jury duty on the Borden trial but was not chosen to be one of the twelve men who acquitted Lizzie Borden of the murders of her father and stepmother.

Dondis, Jacob

Dondis bought Emma Borden's one-half share in the A.J. Borden Building in 1923 for about $340,000. Lizzie owned the other half.

Donnelly, John

Donnelly was a "hack driver," the equivalent of the taxi cab driver of modern times. He went up into the loft of the Borden barn and searched the area before police officer William H. Medley inspected the loft. Medley, however, reported no footprints were present in the barn's dust.

This incident was revealed by mason Charles H. Bryant when he gave an interview to a reporter from the *New Bedford Evening Standard* on August 13, 1892. Donnelly himself confirmed the story as a sworn witness at the preliminary hearing on August 31.

Donnelly said while up in the barn, he noticed an impression in a pile of hay on the north side of the loft, but he could not tell if the imprint was of a human or an animal form. Donnelly stated that Charlie Cook from the telephone company was with him at the time. Cook was never called to testify.

Donnelly told no one of seeing the hay pile before appearing at the preliminary hearing because, he said, "As I could not disturb the hay at all, I thought (I'd) let them see it themselves." This testimony helped Lizzie's defense. It showed someone was in the barn before Medley and that the policeman missed the footprints. If true, Medley also could have missed Lizzie's prints.

Doolan, Mary

Mary Doolan was referred to in the Borden case simply as "Mrs. Kelly's girl." She lived in the Kelly home at 96 Second Street, the house directly south of the Bordens, from 1893 to 1896. She was listed in District Attorney Hosea M. Knowlton's list of witnesses. Probably born in Ireland, Doolan was summoned to appear at the trial in New Bedford but was never called to take the stand.

Douglas, George L. (1864-1923)

George L. Douglas testified at the preliminary hearing and before the grand jury but did not appear at the final trial held in New Bedford in 1893. He was sitting on the steps of Mrs. Adelaide Churchill's home, directly north of the Borden residence, with Oliver H. Perry Durling, Charles Cook and William Hacking at the time of the murders on August 4, 1892. None of those at the Churchill house saw anyone enter or leave 92 Second Street.

Douglas was born in Fall River and employed as a hostler at Douglas Brothers, a livery, boarding and horse exchange stable on Morgan Street. He relocated from Fall River to New Bedford in 1897 and worked as a motorman there. He returned to Fall River for a short period, then went back to New Bedford where he earned his living once more as a motorman. He died in Taunton, Massachusetts.

Douglas, Mrs. S.A.

Mrs. Douglas wrote a crank letter to City Marshal Rufus B. Hilliard shortly after the Borden murders became national news. She offered to travel to Fall River and obtain a confession from the killer for the fee of eight or ten dollars per day. Her letter was mailed from River Point, Rhode Island. There is no evidence that Hilliard replied to Mrs. Douglas' letter.

Douglass, Oscar R.

Oscar Douglass of Swansea was present at the jury selection for the Borden trial. After being questioned, he was challenged by the prosecution and sent home.

Downs, Edward P. (1877-1950)

Downs was summoned as a witness at the Borden trial in New Bedford but was not called to testify. It is not clear what the nature of his testimony would have been. He was a youth at the time of the Borden murders.

Downs was born in Fall River to John A. and Catherine (Hannon) Downs. He was employed as a wood dealer and became a clerk in 1904. For many years he was employed by Louis P. Drape, Inc., fish dealer. He married Johanna Gleeson and lived in Fall River all of his life.

Dowty, William E.

A *Fall River Daily Herald* reporter wrote that Officer William E. Dowty and someone else, possibly Marshall Rufus B, Hilliard, travelled to Swansea to question a Portuguese laborer. This is similar to the circumstances under which Joseph Silvia was questioned by officers Philip Harrington and William H. Medley. Dowty's name does not appear again in the Borden story. Although there was a William E. Dowty on the police force in 1892, it is possible a reporter or someone else investigating the murders confused Dowty with someone else.

Draper, Frank Winthrop (1843-1909)

Draper was a professor at Harvard Medical School. He assisted Dr. William A. Dolan in the second autopsy performed on the Bordens on August 11, 1892, five days after the funeral. Also present were Dr. John Leary and autopsy clerk Dr. Dwight E. Cone. It was at this autopsy that the heads of both victims were removed and sent to Harvard for further study (see William A. Dolan and Dwight E. Cone). Draper testified at the trial as to his findings based on this autopsy. He described the wounds and the possible murder weapon. When the actual skulls were accidently displayed at the trial on June 14, 1893, Lizzie Borden fainted.

As a witness for the prosecution, Draper testified that he and Dolan made plaster casts of the skulls, examined the intestines and measured and inspected all of the wounds on both bodies. He claimed that Andrew died approximately one hour after Abby. This was important since it would have a legal bearing on which side of the family would inherit Andrew's estate.

At the trial, Draper was given the actual skulls of the victims and, when given the handleless hatchet to fit into the wounds, said that it could have been the murder weapon and could have been wielded by a woman of ordinary strength. This, of course, would include Lizzie Borden. He speculated on the positions of the deceased at the instant of death and admitted there was no way to determine the direction of the spattered blood.

Lizzie's defense lawyer, Melvin O. Adams committed a blunder when he gave Draper a new hatchet and asked him if it fit into the wounds. Adams' point was to be that virtually any hatchet could duplicate the wounds, not just the one found in Lizzie's cellar. Adams must have been the most surprised person in the courtroom that day when Draper said the new hatchet did not fit the skull wounds.

Draper was born in Wayland, Massachusetts. He received his B.A. from Brown University in 1862. After seeing action in the Civil War, Draper attended Harvard Medical School. After graduating in 1869, he interned at Boston City Hospital, established a practice in Boston and was a visiting physician at Children's Hospital and City Hospital there. Draper served as Medical Examiner for Suffolk County from 1877-

1889. He taught medicine at Harvard, wrote for many medical journals and was recognized as a leading expert in the field of medical jurisprudence. He died in Brookline, Massachusetts.

Driscoll, Daniel F.

Driscoll was a New Bedford grocer who appeared for jury duty at the Borden trial. He admitted while being questioned that he was biased, and was asked to step down.

Driscoll, Peter M. (1853-1899)

Peter M. Driscoll was a barber in Fall River. He claimed to have seen disgraced Borden and Almy bookkeeper Joseph W. Carperter, Jr. in his barber shop at the Wilber House on Sunday, August 1, three days before the murders of Andrew and Abby Borden were committed (see Joseph W. Carpenter, Jr.). Driscoll insisted that he had shaved Carpenter that day even after Fall River police told him that he was mistaken.

Driscoll was born in Boston. He was employed as a barber in Fall River and became a partner in the firm of Driscoll and Sheffield, Fashionable Hairdressers in 1880. The firm dissolved two years later and Driscoll continued to cut hair under his own name until 1896. He was married to Harriet A. Read of Westport, Massachusetts until her death in 1882, then married Harriet D. Vadenais of Fall River, who died in 1898. Driscoll himself died of what was diagnosed as acute melancholia in 1899.

Driscoll, Timothy W. (1863-?)

Timothy Driscoll lived in Easton, Massachusetts. On the stand as a potential juror in the Borden trial, Driscoll claimed he had no interest in the case and could remain unprejudiced. He was challenged by Lizzie and did not serve on the jury.

Duckworth, Janice

Janice Duckworth lived at 43 John Street in Fall River. She spoke to Sarah Scholick, who told her that two young girls, Mamie Smith and Annie Connelly heard screams coming from 92 Second Street at the time the Bordens were murdered. Scholick also told Duckworth that the two young girls saw a man leaving the Borden property cleaning his hands with a handkerchief.

Doherty spoke to all four "witnesses" on August 8, 1892. No solid leads resulted from any of these interviews (see Sarah Scholick, Annie Connelly and Mamie Smith).

Dunn, John W.

John W. Dunn purchased the house where Andrew and Abby Borden were murdered, 92 Second Street, Fall River from Lizzie and Emma Borden in 1918 for "One dollar and other valuable considerations," according to the Registry of Deeds, Briston County, Fall River, Massachusetts.

Durfee, Mrs. John R.

Mrs. John R. Durfee was present at the funerals of Andrew and Abby Borden on Saturday, August 6, 1892. Her husband was a bookkeeper at the Durfee Mills, in which Andrew had a business interest.

Durfee, Mary A. (1856-1924)

Defense witness Mary A. Durfee testified at the trial that she saw a man in an angry argument with Andrew Borden approximately eight months before he and Abby were killed. She did not recognize the man or know the subject of the argument.

Mrs. Durfee stated on the witness stand that in November 1891, while her late sister was still alive, she saw a stranger talking loudly with Andrew on the front steps of 92 Second Street. Durfee was on her way to get some medicine for her sister, who died before Thanksgiving 1892. She remembered that the strange man exclaimed, "You have cheated me and I'll fix you for it." Judge Albert C. Mason, speaking for the court, ruled that the incident occurred too long before the crime and did not allow Durfee to describe the exchange before the jury.

Mary A. Durfee was born in Newport, Rhode Island, to George and Elizabeth Bentley. She married Joseph Franklin Durfee of Fall River, a clerk for a local provisions dealer in 1876. She lived at 124 Second Street and died in Fall River.

Durling, Oliver H. Perry (c.1873-?)

Durling was sitting on the front steps of the Buffinton House at 90 Second Street, next door to, and south of the Borden residence. With him were Charles Cook, William Hacking and George L. Douglas. They testified at the preliminary hearing and again before the grand jury that they were there during the time the murders occurred on August 4, 1892 and saw no one enter or leave the Borden house. He was not summoned to testify at the final trial in June 1893.

Durling was born in New Jersey to James W. and Charlotte Douglas. He graduated from Fall River's Bradford Matthew Chaloner Durfee High School in 1892 and held the rank of major in that school's cadet force. He was employed as a clerk in Fall River before moving to Providence, Rhode Island, in 1900. He and his wife Martha's last known address was in Pittsburgh, Pennsylvania, in 1915.

Dutra, Emmanuel C.

Dr. Emmanuel C. Dutra assisted Drs. William A. Dolan, Seabury W. Bowen, Albert C. Dedrick, John W. Coughlin, John H. Leary, Thomas Gunning, J.Q.A. Tourtellot and Anson C. Peckham during the first autopsy of the Bordens, which took place on the Bordens' dining room table at 3:00 P.M. on the day of the murders.

Dwight, Thomas (1843-1911)

Thomas Dwight was a well-respected anatomist who acted as a consultant for the defense. He examined the skulls of Andrew and Abby Borden and served as a medical expert for Lizzie Borden's attorneys.

Dwight was born in Boston and spent his early years with his family in France. He graduated from Harvard in 1866 and received a Doctor of Medicine degree from Harvard Medical School the following year. Dwight went abroad for further study and then opened medical practices in Nahant and Boston, Massachusetts. He became an instructor of comparative anatomy at Harvard and lectured at Bowdoin College. He also became an instructor of histology and topographical anatomy at Harvard Medical School.

Besides his medical practice and teaching duties, Dwight was outpatient surgeon at Boston City Hospital, visiting surgeon at Carney Hospital in South Boston and succeeded the stately Dr. Oliver Wendell Holmes as Parkman Professor of Anatomy and Physiology at Harvard Medical School. He also authored several books and wrote for both popular and professional medical journals. Dwight died in Nahant, Massachusetts in 1911.

Dyson, James

James Dyson was a Fall River policeman. Dyson, along with officers George Ferguson, Joseph Mayall, Philip Harrington and Patrick Doherty were assigned to guard the Borden house on August 4, 1892, the day of the murders, until 1:00 P.M. They were relieved by Officers Doherty and Harrington, who continued their investigation, as well as by John McCarthy, Joseph Hyde and Michael Reagan(see Joseph Hyde).

E

Eagan, Ellen T. (1857-1929)

Ellen T. Eagan is quite possibly the woman whom ice cream vendor Hyman Lubinsky claimed to have seen in the Borden yard near the barn at about the time Andrew Borden was murdered on August 4, 1892. At Lizzie's trial the defense used Lubinsky's claim to prove that the accused was not in the house at the time of her father's death and thus could not have been the murderer.

Eagan claimed she became sick that morning while walking north on Second Street in front of the Borden home. She said that she entered the Borden yard because she thought that it was the property of Dr. Michael Kelly, who, in fact, was the Bordens' next-door neighbor directly to the south. Eagan revealed this information while being questioned by Fall River police officers Patrick H. Doherty and Philip H. Harrington on August 11, 1892. She was not called as a witness at the trial.

Ellen T. (Hurley) Eagan was born in Ireland and came to the United States in 1874. She married Owen Eagan, a laborer, clerk and, later, owner of a variety store in Fall River, in 1885. The Eagans had five children before Owen died in 1901. Ellen Eagan passed away in Fall River and is buried in that city's St. John's Cemetery.

Eagan, John J.

John J. Eagan was listed as a possible witness on a memo handwritten by Hosea Knowlton and found among Knowlton's papers relating to the trial of Lizzie A. Borden. He was on Second Street the day of the murders and gave a statement to the police.

Eagan's name was on a list labeled, "As to escape." This possibly referred to the departure of the murderer from the Borden home, which Knowlton believed never happened, since the prosecutor suspected Lizzie of killing her father and stepmother. A letter "X" was put after his name, with no further explanation. Eagan did not testify at the trial.

Eagan was the son of Owen and Catherine Eagan. He was first mentioned as a Fall River resident in 1888. Eagan was employed as a clerk in 1892 for P.F. Millea, Provisions Dealer, located at 54 Spring Street. He was last listed in the Fall River directory in 1939 as an employee of A. Yoken and Sons, Grocers.

Earle, Thomas B.

Thomas B. Earle of Westport, Massachusetts was present for jury duty on the Borden trial but was not questioned and did not serve.

Eddy, Francis Wilmarth (1831-1898)

Francis W. Eddy was on District Attorney Hosea M. Knowlton's handwritten list of potential witnesses. He was listed as "Frank" Eddy under the label "miscellaneous." Eddy was a hack driver and may have been in the vicinity of the Borden house at the time the murders occurred. He was not called to testify at the trial.

Eddy was a Fall River native. He married Sarah J. Gardner and was employed by Charles T. Kirby and Company, Stables. He remained in that occupation until his death.

Eddy, James C.

James C. Eddy was a well-to-do financier and property owner in Fall River. He served as one of the pallbearers for Abby Borden at the double funeral for the victims that took place on Saturday, August 6, 1892.

The other pallbearers for Mrs. Borden were Henry S. Buffinton, John H. Boone, J. Henry Wells, Simeon B. Chase and Frank L. Almy.

Eddy, William

William Eddy was the manager of farm property in lower Swansea owned by Andrew Borden. After the murders, policeman Patrick H. Doherty questioned Lizzie Borden as to whether Andrew had any Portuguese in his employ on the Swansea farms. Lizzie mentioned Eddy and Alfred C. Johnson as Andrew's only Swansea employees. Lizzie told Doherty that Eddy was ill and neither man was in Fall River that day. She added, "neither Mr. Eddy nor Mr. Johnson would hurt my father."

Edson, Francis L. (1855-1906)

Francis L. Edson was a Fall River policeman. He was present at the investigation of the Borden murders on the evening August 4. He helped search the Borden home the following day and again on Mon-

Officer Edson.

day, August 8, 1892. He testified at the Borden trial as to what he observed during these examinations.

On the sixth day of the trial, June 10, 1893, Edson testified that he was involved in an organized search of the Borden home on the day after the murders. During that search, two wood axes, one hand ax and one small shingle ax were found in the cellar. Edson gave them to City Marshal Rufus B. Hilliard as evidence. The "handleless hatchet" was not among the axes discovered during this search.

On the stand, Edson testified that on Monday, August 8, he participated in the second search of 92 Second Street. With him were police officers Dennis Desmond, Patrick Connors, William H. Medley, Martin Quigley, Borden attorney Andrew Jennings and Pinkerton detective O.M. Hanscom. Edson remembered that Providence, Rhode Island private detective Edwin D. McHenry was also present at the second search, although he did not know who McHenry was at the time. McHenry would later play a brief but spectacular role in the Borden case (see Edwin D. McHenry and Henry G. Trickey).

Edson was born in Fall River to Daniel and Susan Edson. He gained employment as a roll coverer and was accepted for a position with the police department in 1883. At the time of the murders, Edson held the rank of sergeant. He was promoted to lieutenant in February 1893 and to captain in December of that year. He married Bertha C. Perkins and was involved in many fraternal and professional organizations. He died in Fall River.

Eldridge, Washington A.

Police officer Washington A. Eldridge was on guard duty at the New Bedford courthouse with George Gendron and Special Officer A.J. Smith during the Borden trial. They were all posted at the front entrance because so many people wanted to view the proceedings firsthand.

Emery, Mrs. Daniel

Mrs. Emery was questioned by police officer William H. Medley, who was checking the alibi of suspect John Vinnicum Morse, the uncle of Emma and Lizzie Borden. Mrs. Emery confirmed Morse's claim that he was at the Emery home visiting with his niece Annie at the time of the murders and that he left to return to 92 Second Street at about 11:20 A.M. Her husband Daniel was the cousin of John Vinnicum Morse.

Emery, William N.

Emery reported on the Borden trial for the *New Bedford Evening Journal*. He also built a massive scrapbook of newspaper articles concerning the Borden murders and trial that is still a valuable primary source of information today.

F

Feenan, Henry

Henry Feenan of Westport, Massachusetts, served on the grand jury that indicted Lizzie Borden on December 2, 1892 for the murders of her father and stepmother, Andrew and Abby Borden.

Feeney, Martin

Martin Feeney was a Fall River police inspector. He was briefly mentioned in the *Fall River Herald* as having "hunted down some good clues." His efforts were most likely less than spectacular, for he was never again mentioned anywhere in connection with the Borden murders and was not called upon by the defense or prosecution at any of the formal proceedings related to the crimes.

Ferguson, George

George Ferguson was a Fall River policeman at the time of the Borden murders. He and James Dyson, Patrick Doherty, Philip Harrington, Joseph Mayall and Joseph Hyde were assigned to watch 92 Second Street from about 11:30 A.M. until 1:00 P.M. on the day of the killings. They were relieved at 1:00 P.M. by Patrick Doherty and Philip Harrington, who continued their investigation, John McCarthy, Joseph Hyde and Michael Reagan. Hyde, in testimony given at the trial, said he and Ferguson were at the Borden house at 11:00 P.M.; a report in the *Fall River Herald* has him relieved ten hours earlier at 1:00 P.M. Hyde's testimony, as printed verbatim in the *New Bedford Evening Standard*, is probably the more accurate account.

Finn, John C.

John C. Finn was one of the potential jurors who was questioned and accepted for the Borden trial. He sat on the jury and helped acquit Lizzie Borden of all charges on June 20, 1893.

Finn was the youngest of all the jurors. He had served for a time before the trial on the common council of Taunton, his hometown. Finn was described as dependable and reputable. He was a Catholic and a registered Democrat with a wife and children. At his questioning for the jury, Finn expressed no opinion as to Lizzie's guilt or innocence. The *New Bedford Evening Standard* said of Finn on June 6, 1893, "Judging from his countenance, he will render a verdict strictly in accordance with the evidence presented to him, and having once formed his opinion, it will be useless for his associates to attempt to win him over in case of a disagreement."

Fish, George B. (?-1894)

George B. Fish was the husband of Abby's sister Priscilla. He and his wife lived in Hartford, Connecticut. Fish stated and had published his belief that John Vinnicum Morse hired someone to kill Andrew and Abby Borden. His death occurred on January 4, 1894, only twenty-one days before that of his wife, Priscilla (Gray) Fish.

Fish, Hannah

Hannah Fish was mentioned in the fake news story known as the "Trickey-McHenry" hoax (see Henry G. Trickey and Edwin D. McHenry). According to the story, Hannah Fish was to be an important prosecution witness. She was from Hartford, Connecticut. No more was ever heard of her after the newspaper article was exposed for the fake it undoubtedly was.

There was a woman named Fish from Hartford who was briefly mentioned in the newspapers, but it was Priscilla Fish, half-sister of Abby and husband of George B. Fish. Most likely, Hannah Fish never existed, or reporter Trickey simply got the name wrong.

Fish, Priscilla (Gray) (1820-1894)

Priscilla Fish, daughter of Oliver Gray, was the half-sister of both Sarah (Gray) Whitehead and Abby Borden. She owned a one-fourth share of the Gray's Ferry Street house after Oilver Gray died. This was the house that caused hard feelings between Emma and Lizzie on the one hand and Abby and Andrew on the other when Andrew purchased the remaining shares of the house and gave it to Sarah Whitehead.

Priscilla and her husband played no other part in the Borden murder case. After Abby's death was determined to have preceded Andrew's, Emma and Lizzie received equal shares of the Borden wealth. Priscilla and Sarah received only Abby's personal estate, which was a bank account containing $1,626.05, and $90.00 in cash. She died on January 29, 1894, just three weeks after her husband George.

Fish, Winifred

The name Winifred Fish was mentioned in the scandalous and embarrassing story printed in the *Boston Globe* and known as the "Trickey-McHenry" hoax. She was, according to the story, the daughter of Priscilla Gray Fish, sister of Sarah Whitehead and half-sister of Abby Borden.

In the article, Medical Examiner Dr. William A. Dolan found a slip of paper in the pocket of Andrew Borden that detailed the clauses in a will he had recently written. In this will, which was never found, he left 10 shares of "the new mill" stock and $2,500 in cash to Winifred Fish (see Henry G. Trickey and Edwin D. McHenry).

Fisher, David

David Fisher from Mansfield was a potential Borden trial juror. On the stand he admitted that he harbored an opinion that would prevent him from bringing in a guilty verdict and was excused.

Fleet, John (1848-1916)

John Fleet was Assistant City Marshal of Fall River and as such was in charge of the investigation of the Borden murders. He participated in almost every aspect of the Borden case and arrested Lizzie Borden for the murders of her father and stepmother on August 12, 1892. Fleet was a strong witness for the prosecution at the trial in New Bedford.

When City Marshal Rufus B. Hilliard received the telephone call informing him of the Borden murders, he sent policemen Fleet, William Medley and Charles Wilson to 92 Second Street. These three arrived at the scene at 11:45 A.M., a few minutes after officers Francis Wixon, Michael Mullaly and John Devine entered the house.

At the trial, Fleet said that when he entered the Borden home he saw John Vinnicum Morse, Bridget Sullivan and Alelaide Churchill in the kitchen, viewed both bodies and then went down into the cellar. He saw Mullaly and Devine there. Mullaly had two axes and two hatchets with him. Fleet then left the cellar and interviewed Lizzie in her bedroom.

Deputy Marshall John Fleet.

Lizzie told Fleet that she was ironing in the kitchen when Andrew Borden came home. She helped Andrew to the couch to take a nap, then went up to the barn loft for between twenty and thirty minutes seeking lead sinkers for a fishing trip while her irons in the kitchen were reheating. Lizzie then re-entered the house and discovered Andrew's mutilated body on the couch in the sitting room. She called up to Bridget, who was lying down in her room, and told her to go across the street and bring Dr. Seabury Bowen because someone had killed her father.

Fleet asked Lizzie other questions and it was to Fleet in this interview that Lizzie emphatically said Abby was not her mother but her stepmother. She also told Fleet about a stranger who had argued with Andrew at their door two weeks earlier and that Abby was not at home, for she had received a note and had left the house to aid a sick friend.

After finishing his talk with Lizzie, Fleet again went down to the cellar where Officers Mullaly and Devine and Dr. William A. Dolan had found two other suspicious looking hatchets. One had what appeared to be a freshly broken handle; the head of the hatchet was covered with ashes and most of the handle was missing. The hatchet head was left in the cellar until the following Monday, when it was wrapped and sent to the City Marshal.

On Saturday, August 6, while the family was at Oak Grove Cemetery for the funeral service of Andrew and Abby Borden, Fleet participated in yet another search of the house with City Marshal Hilliard, Officer Dennis Desmond, Massachusetts State Policeman George F. Seaver and Borden lawyer Andrew Jennings. They looked closely at all of the dresses found in the house but found no dress with blood or paint on it. Fleet also inspected the barn and found no new evidence.

Fleet was born in Ashton-under-Lyne, Lancashire, England. He came to the United States as a young man and worked for the American Linen Co. in Fall River. He served seventeen months in the navy during the Civil War and returned to Fall River where he held several jobs before gaining an appointment on the Fall River police force in 1877. He rose up through the ranks from patrolman to succeed Rufus B. Hilliard as City Marshal. Fleet retired from the force in 1915 and died in Fall River.

Flint, Samuel W.

After the double murders were discovered, Lizzie Borden asked Dr. Seabury Bowen to go to the telegraph office and send a message to her sister Emma, who was vacationing with friends in Fairhaven, Massachusetts, and inform her of the deaths of Andrew and Abby Borden. Dr. Bowen sent the message and then went into Baker's Drug Store where he spent a few minutes conversing with Flint. Bowen then left the drug store and drove directly back to the Borden home.

Flynn, Dominick

Dominick Flynn was the subject in a crank letter sent to City Marshal Rufus B. Hilliard shortly after the murders of the Bordens. The writer of the letter, one John S. Adams of Boston, named Flynn as the murderer. Hilliard did not investigate Flynn.

Foley, ??

Foley was a reporter who covered the Borden trial for the Associated Press news service.

Folger, Charles F.

Charles Folger of New Bedford was questioned as a potential juror in the trial of Lizzie Borden. He was listed in the *New Bedford City Directory* as having no job and was possibly retired. He said he was not prejudiced in the case and had no opinions. Folger was challenged by Lizzie Borden and did not become a member of the jury.

Foreman, Victoria A. (Banks) (1856-1896)

Victoria A. Foreman ran a boarding house in Albany, New York, and provided confirmation for the alibi of Joseph Carpenter, Jr. (see Joseph Carpenter, Jr.). Foreman swore that Carpenter was in Albany when the murders occurred because Carpenter paid his rent on time each week or in advance for the period July 8–August 13, 1892.

Foreman was born in Canada. She was living in Albany, New York in 1892 and supported herself by taking in boarders. She rented out property at numbers 33 and 35 Maiden Lane in the New York State capital. One room had been rented to Carpenter. Foreman was closely questioned by Fall River policeman Philip H. Harrington, who believed her story.

Forrester, Charles F.

Charles F. Forrester was a jeweler from Attleboro, Massachusetts. He showed up for jury duty in New Bedford but was questioned and did not serve on the jury that acquitted Lizzie Borden.

Francis, Edith A. (1870-1944)

Edith A. Francis was listed as a witness on District Attorney Hosea M. Knowlton's handwritten notes under the heading "Miscellaneous." After her name was the notation "no good." She was summoned as a witness at the trial but did not take the stand. Because she had been Charles C. Cook's bookkeeper, prosecutor Hosea Knowlton hoped she knew of a will Andrew Borden had made. She did not (see Charles C. Cook).

Francis was born in Fall River and employed as a clerk for the firm of Charles C. Cook and Sons. She later became a bookkeeper for John P. Slade and Son. She was an active member of the Third Baptist Church and served the church as a deaconess and superintendent of the primary department of the church's Sunday school. She was also active in the Women's Christian Temperance Union, the World Wide Guild Home Worker's Society and the Fall River Historical Society.

Francis, Ezekiel P.

Ezekiel Francis, a farmer from Taunton, was questioned as a potential juror and challenged by Lizzie Borden. He was excused.

Francis, Frank W.

Frank W. Francis was another citizen called to the New Bedford courthouse for jury duty. Francis was a cigar manufacturer and dealer in that city. He claimed to have served as a juror in Fall River in 1890 but could not produce any evidence to confirm that statement. In spite of that, he was excused.

Frazer, Isabel J. (1863-1936)

Isabel J. Frazer was one of a group of five friends who Lizzie Borden was planning to see in Marion, Massachusetts during a vacation. The others were Elizabeth M. Johnston, Louise Remington, Anna C. Holmes and Mary L. Holmes. The murders of Andrew and Abby Borden prevented Lizzie from going on that vacation.

Fuller, Everett

Everett Fuller worked as a cashier at the First National Bank in Fall River. He testified on August 26, 1892 at the preliminary hearing. Fuller stated that Andrew Borden entered the bank at 9:45 A.M. the day he was killed and left that establishment about fifteen minutes later.

G

Gadsby, Baker

Baker Gadsby was named in an article about the Borden murders that was published in the *Fall River Herald* on August 5, 1892. According to the article, Gadsby was a businessman who had recently vacated a store he was renting in the Borden Building, which was owned by Andrew Borden. That store was probably rented by Andrew to Jonathon Clegg, a hatter.

Lizzie had described an argument between her father and an unknown man about two weeks before the murders to Officer Philip Harrington, according to the *Herald*. This man, who was not from Fall River, was interested in renting the empty store, but Andrew refused to let the space for the purpose the stranger wanted to use it. After the argument, Andrew told the man he would think it over and let him know.

In the meantime, Andrew rented the property to Jonathan Clegg (see Jonathan Clegg). The *Herald* speculated that the stranger wanted to open a saloon in the rental area. The Fall River police did not follow up on this newspaper lead.

Gallagher, Mary R.

Bookkeeper Mary Gallagher of Fall River saw Andrew J. Borden walking past McManus' store the morning of the murders at 10:15 A.M. with a package in his hand. The package was probably the broken lock Andrew wrapped in a piece of paper while talking to carpenters Joseph Mather and Joseph Shortsleeves. Some people speculate that the paper was actually Andrew Borden's will. Gallagher was interviewed by policemen Patrick Doherty and Philip Harrington on August 6, 1892, but she gave no helpful information to the two officers (see Joseph Mather and Joseph Shortsleeves).

Gardner, Arnold D.

Arnold D. Gardner, a resident of Swansea, Massachusetts, was a member of the grand jury that indicted Lizzie Borden for the murders of her father and stepmother.

Gardner, Charles E.

Charles E. Gardner owned the stables where defense witness Hyman Lubinsky kept his team of horses and began his travels down Second Street between 11:05 A.M. and 11:10 A.M. on the day of the Borden murders (see Hyman Lubinsky). At the trial, Gardner stated that he was certain of the time Lubinsky left the stables because Gardner wanted to be prompt for a meeting with travelling salesman Charles V. Newhall.

Newhall had hired Gardner to drive him to several appointments the salesman had in Fall River that day and then to the railraod station so

Charles E. Gardner.

Newhall could catch the 11:50 A.M. train to New Bedford. Both Gardner and Newhall testified at the trial of Lizzie Borden for the defense.

Gardner, Orrin Augustus (1867-1944)

Orrin A. Gardner was a school teacher and principal in Fall River. He was summoned to appear at the Borden trial as a witness but was never called upon to testify.

In a newspaper article dated December 10, 1896, the *Boston Globe* announced that Lizzie Borden planned to marry a Mr. Gardner, who taught school, at Christmastime. It was possible that the Mr. Gardner referred to in the article was Orrin Augustus. Lizzie, of course, never married. Lizzie left Orrin Gardner $10,000 in her will.

Some speculated that either the newspaper publicity made Gardner shy away from marriage or that Lizzie did not want to submit him to the inevitable negative public exposure. Others believed that the entire story was simply fabricated.

Garvey, Thomas

Thomas Garvey was a member of the Fall River Police Department. He and Officer John J. Devine searched for suspects in the Borden murders. Garvey and Devine were sent by Assistant City Marshall John Fleet to look for clues in the Stafford Road area of Fall River.

Gay, George Washington (1842-1931)

George W. Gay was the personal physician of Massachusetts Attorney General Albert Enoch Pillsbury. Gay recommended to Pillsbury that Dr. Henry Harris Aubrey Beach would be an effective medical expert for the prosecution at the Borden trial. Beach was not used.

George Gay was born in Swanzey, New Hampshire and, after a two year apprenticeship with Dr. George B. Twitchell, entered Harvard Medical School. He probably studied under Dr. David W. Cheever (see David W. Cheever). He became surgical house officer at Boston City Hospital in 1867 and finished his medical degree at Harvard Medical

School the following year. He taught medicine at Harvard Medical School, established his own practice in Boston and became senior surgeon at Boston City Hospital. Gay received an honorary Masters of Arts from Dartmouth College in 1895 and published numerous books and articles, including *The Use of Opium in Senile Gangrene.*

Geagan, Henry

At the request of City Marshall Rufus B. Hilliard, police officer Henry Geagan dispersed a large crowd at the Fall River police station on the last day of the formal inquest into the murders of Andrew and Abby Borden. Geagan repeatedly cracked a bullwhip, which made the crowd move away from an arriving carriage that carried Lizzie Borden, her sister Emma and friend Mary E. Brigham.

Gendron, George

George Gendron was a Fall River policeman who was fluent in French. He was the interpreter for witness Joseph Lemay when Lemay took the stand at the Borden trial on June 15, 1893.

Gendron was also on guard duty with police officers Washington A. Eldridge and A.J. Smith at the entrance to the New Bedford courthouse because so many people demanded to view the proceedings.

Gifford, Charles H.

Charles H. Gifford was listed by Borden historian David Kent as a manager of one of the Swansea farms owned by Andrew Borden.

Gifford, Charles H.

This Charles H. Gifford was mentioned in the *New Bedford Evening Standard* of June 13, 1893 as a Taunton policeman stationed at the New Bedford courthouse front door along with officers Joseph Mather and A.J. Smith (see Charles H. Gifford above).

Gifford, Charles N.

Charles N. Gifford testified for the defense at the trial of Lizzie Borden. He rented a house on the west side of Third Street, next to the home owned by Dr. Jean Baptiste Chagnon. Gifford worked as a clerk in a clothing store.

Gifford claimed that he saw a strange man asleep on the side steps of his house at 11:00 P.M. the night before the murders. He said he awakened the man and chased him away. Gifford's testimony and similar statements by others at the trial were used by the defense as proof that there were strangers in the area shortly before the murders and any one of a number of persons could have killed the Bordens.

Uriah Kirby, who owned the house, was with Gifford at the time and also testified to seeing the sleeping stranger. It was possible that the unidentified man could have been town drunk Michael Graham, also known as "Mike the Soldier."

Gifford, Ellie M.

Ellie Gifford was interviewed by police officers Philip Harrington and Patrick Doherty on August 8, 1892. She said that she knew nothing about the murders but had heard rumors that were quickly discounted by the police. She lived on Franklin Street at the same address as Hannah H. Gifford. She was related to Arthur L. Gifford, a Fall River watchmaker and jeweler (see Hannah H. Gifford).

Gifford, Hannah H. (1836-1912)

Hannah H. (Borden) Gifford was a seamstress who occasionally made clothes for Abby, Emma and Lizzie Borden. She was a witness at the inquest and at the final trial. Her testimony concerned the relationship between Lizzie and her stepmother Abby Borden.

At the trial in New Bedford, Gifford said that she had made clothes for the Borden women for six or seven years. All of the work was done at her shop on Franklin Street in Fall River; Gifford never visited 92 Second Street.

On August 8, Gifford specifically related the details of a conversation she had with Lizzie in March 1892 to police officers Patrick Doherty and Philip Harrington. When the seamstress referred to Abby as her mother, Lizzie replied, "...she is a mean good-for-nothing." The prosecution used Gifford's testimony as an example of Lizzie's ill feelings for Mrs. Borden.

Hannah H. Gifford, a Quaker, was born in Fall River to Joseph and Hannah (Westgate) Borden. She was related to Andrew through a common great-grandfather. She married Perry Gifford, a dealer in dry and fancy goods and was widowed in 1898. Mrs. Gifford moved to Hanson, Massachusetts in 1904 and died there eight years later.

Gifford, Oliver E.

Oliver E. Gifford was a painter from New Bedford. On the stand as a potential juror in the Borden trial, he said that he was distantly related to the defendant. This statement made Lizzie gasp in surprise since she had never seen him before. Gifford, Lizzie Borden's uncle by marriage, was excused.

Gilmore, Abiel P.R.

Abiel Gilmore of Acushnet, Massachusetts was a member of the grand jury that indicted Lizzie Borden for the murders of Andrew and Abby Borden.

Gillon, Patrick

Gillon was a policeman in Fall River. At the preliminary hearing City Marshal Rufus B. Hilliard, on the stand as a witness, testified that Gillon was with officers Patrick Doherty, Michael Mullaly, William Medley, Charles H. Wilson and others he did not remember at the Borden house on the day of the murder. Since no other mention has ever been made of Officer Gillon in connection with the Borden murder case, Hilliard could have been in error when giving his testimony on August 31, 1892.

Godfrey, Gordon H.

Gordon H. Godfrey, from Taunton, said he had a prejudiced opinion in the Borden case and was excused from serving on the jury. Godfrey worked as a tackmaker.

Goff, Dexter

Dexter Goff appeared for jury at the Borden trial but was not questioned and did not serve on the jury.

Gorman, Augustus P. (1860-1933)

Augustus P. Gorman owned a paint and wallpaper store on the corner of Borden and Second Streets. He took the stand as a witness at the trial on June 10, 1893. Reporter John J. Cunningham telephoned the news about the murders to the police from Gorman's store at approximately 10:50 A.M. He could not be more specific, Gorman said at the trial, because his shop's clock "didn't keep very good time."

Augustus P. Gorman

Gorman was born in Fall River on August 28. He worked as a youth in a Fall River woolen mill until he was injured on the job. He then entered the paint trade and became successful. Gorman was elected to the Massachusetts state legislature in 1884 and 1885. He was the youngest member of the lower house at that time. Gorman was on the Fall River city council for five years beginning in 1890 and ran unsuccessfully for mayor of Fall River in 1895.

Gormley, Elizabeth A. (1870-1902)

Elizabeth Gormley was on Hosea M. Knowlton's handwritten list of witnesses under the heading, "As to not seeing prisoner escape," which probably referred to not seeing anyone leave the Borden property at the time of the murders. She had told the police that she was at the Churchill house on Second Street next door to the Bordens and Mrs. Churchill ran through the house and told her that Andrew had been killed. Gormley was summoned to appear at the trial but was not put on the stand.

Mrs. Gormley was born in Providence, Rhode Island to John and Eliza Bryne. She married John H. Gormley and held many different jobs. Her husband was a saloon keeper. The Gormleys lived at 122 Third Street. Elizabeth died at her home in Fall River.

Goss, Henry M.

Goss, from Attleboro, appeared for jury duty in New Bedford at the Borden trial. He was questioned and did not serve on the jury. Goss is listed in some articles as Henry M. Gross, and this could indeed be his real name.

Graham, Michael

Michael Graham was also known around Fall River as "Mike the Soldier." Graham was a weaver by trade. He was employed at Borden City Mill No. 2. A heavy drinker, Graham was spotted near 92 Second Street at about 10:00 A.M. on the morning of the murders. He showed up drunk at the mill shortly after 10:00 A.M. and was not allowed to work. He could not have been in the Borden home at the times Abby and Andrew were killed and still have returned to the mill when he appeared there in an alcoholic haze.

Graham seemed to fit the description of Dr. Benjamin Handy's "wild-eyed man" and also of Charles N. Gifford and Uriah Kirby's description of the man asleep on the front steps of Kirby's house on Third Street the night before the murders (see Dr. Benjamin Handy, Charles N. Gifford and Uriah Kirby).

Grant, Louis F.

Grant was a staff artist for the *Boston Globe*. He accompanied reporter John Carberry and fellow staff artist Bert Poole to New Bedford in June 1893 to cover the Borden trial for the *Globe*.

Graves, William (1825-?)

Graves was a potential juror at the Borden trial from Mansfield, Massachusetts. He said he had no opinion in the case and was not prejudiced. Although he was sixty-eight years old, he expressed a willingness to serve on the jury. Lizzie Borden approved of him, but Graves was challenged by the prosecution.

Gray, Elizabeth Ann (Howard) (1833-1907)

Elizabeth Ann Gray was the mother of Annie Howard (Gray) Howland. Her brother-in-law, Captain James C. Stafford suggested her as a possible source of information on the Borden and Morse families because in 1857, her widowed mother lived at 9 Ferry Street and was a neighbor of Andrew Borden and his first wife Sarah. Mrs. Gray did not appear as a witness at any of the hearings or trials.

Mrs. Gray was born in Amesbury, Massachusetts, to James and Ann Howard. She married Nathaniel P. Gray, an experienced sailor from Fall River. She and her husband lived in Fall River and shared a house with Gray's sister and brother-in-law, the Staffords. Elizabeth Gray and her husband relocated to New Bedford in 1870 and Nathaniel P. Gray died there nine years later. She moved in with her daughter Annie Howland in New Bedford in 1893 and lived there until her death at the age of seventy-four.

Gray, Ida P.

Ida P. Gray was a dressmaker who lived at 27 Whipple Street in Fall River. She told policemen Patrick Doherty and Philip Harrington on August 8 that on Friday evening, the day after the murders, she overheard two women whom she did not know say that they heard Lizzie Borden say that her stepmother "was of the kind that never die."

Gray, Jane B. (Negus) (1829-1917)

Jane B. Gray had known Lizzie Borden for many years and gave a statement to the police about incidents in Lizzie's life before the murders that Gray personally remembered. Mrs. Gray lived at 188 1/2 Second Street in 1892. She was summoned to appear in court at the trial but was not asked to testify.

Jane B. Gray was born in Massachusetts to Benjamin and Betsey Negus. She married Ellery Gray, a Fall River mariner and was widowed in 1865. She died in Fall River in her eighty-eighth year.

Gray, Jane E.D. (Baker) Eldridge (1826-1916)

Jane E.D. Gray was the widow of Oliver Gray and the father of Abby's half-sister, Sarah (Gray) Whitehead. It was to Jane Gray that Andrew gave $1,500 in exchange for her quarter-share of the Fourth Street house where she lived. Andrew then gave his share to Abby, who also inherited a quarter-share when Oliver Gray died. Sarah Whitehead, who had her own quarter-share, lived in the house with her mother. The last fourth was owned by Priscilla (Gray) Fish of Hartford, Connecticut. Andrew and Abby gave their shares to Sarah Whitehead.

Andrew did this at Abby's urging in 1887 so that Sarah, beloved by her older sister Abby Borden, would always have a home. This caused strong resentment of Andrew and Abby by his two daughters, Emma and Lizzie. Many people, then and now, see in this act of benevolence on Andrew's part a motive for murder (see Sarah Gray Whitehead).

Gray, John Windsor

John W. Gray owned a paint store at 103 Second Street. His sister Sarah J. Gray stopped in the shop on the morning of the murders and later gave a statement to the police.

Gray, Lizzie

Lizzie Gray told Fall River authorities that she saw Andrew J. Borden while she was standing at the corner of Spring and Second Streets. She said Andrew walked up Spring and turned north at Second to go home. Gray stated that this occurred between 10:00 A.M. and 11:00 A.M. on the morning Andrew was killed. Gray's statement added to the information authorities were seeking about Andrew's travels before he returned home for the final time.

Gray, Oliver (1800-1878)

Oliver Gray was the father of Priscilla Fish, Sarah Whitehead and Abby Borden. He and his family lived on Fourth Street in a part of Fall River that the local gentry did not hold in high esteem. Gray was a tin peddler who sold china, sundries and household goods from a pushcart on the streets of town. He was far below Andrew Borden on the social scale. Abby was the daughter of Gray and his first wife Sarah (Sawyer) Gray. Sarah Gray Whitehead was born thirty-five years later to Oliver and his second wife Jane E.D. (Baker) Eldridge Gray.

Gray, Sarah J. (1855-1934)

Sarah J. Gray was in her brother John's paint store at 103 Second Street and gave a statement later to Fall River policemen. Her statement probably related to something out of the ordinary that she might have seen on Second Street that morning. Sarah Gray was born in England to John and Sarah A. (Crowther) Gray. She lived in Fall River for a large part of her life.

Gray, Sarah (Sawyer) (1794-1860)

Sarah (Sawyer) Gray was the first wife of Oliver Gray and the mother of Abby Durfee (Gray) Borden. After she died, Oliver married Jane E.D. Baker, the mother of Sarah (Gray) Whitehead and Priscilla (Gray) Fish.

Green, Minnie (c.1867-?)

Minnie Green was a friend of Bridget Sullivan who came with her to the United States from Ireland sometime around the year 1886. Years after the killings, when both Sullivan and Green were living in Montana, Bridget seemed ready to confess something to Minnie, but at the last minute changed her mind.

According to writer Edward D. Radin, Bridget was seriously ill in Anaconda, Montana, where she was living in 1942. She thought that she was dying and called for Minnie Green to come to her bedside and hear a secret she had kept to herself for decades. By the time Green arrived in Anaconda from her home in Butte, Montana, Bridget had recovered and decided not to tell her secret. Some students of the Borden mystery speculate that Bridget knew who had killed Abby and Andrew and was going to tell Green. Author Edwin D. Radin believes Sullivan was going to make a confession of her own guilt.

Green, Olney

Olney Green from Seekonk, Massachusetts was described by the *New Bedford Evening Standard* as youthful. He was called to jury duty but was challenged by the prosecution. He did not serve on the Borden jury.

Greene, Chester Washington (1811-1896)

Greene was questioned as part of the "sanity survey" commissioned by District Attorney Hosea M. Knowlton to seek evidence that members of the Borden or Morse family had displayed signs of insanity. It was conducted by Moulton Batchelder and the results of the survey did not satisfy Knowlton (see Moulton Batchelder).

Greene said that he knew the Bordens and the Morses but not too well. He stated that he never heard anyone mention their names in connection with insanity.

Greene was born in Coventry, Rhode Island. He lived in Illinois and relocated to Fall River in 1844. He became a successful businessman and was involved in insurance and real estate with his son. Greene served for a time as postmaster of Fall River. He died there at the age of eighty-five.

Greenough, W.F.

W.F. Greenough was a reporter for both the *New Bedford Evening Standard* and the *Taunton Gazette*. He covered the Borden trial for these newspapers.

Griffiths, Edward L.

Edward L. Griffiths reported seeing a strange man on the morning of the Borden murders, August 4, 1892. His story was published in the *Fall River Herald* the day after the Bordens died.

According to the *Herald*, Griffiths and his brother Robert P. were carpenters on Anawan Street. As they drove up Pleasant Street about 11:00 A.M. they saw a man walking with unusual haste in front of "Flint's building." The stranger was carrying a cleaver with the handle facing down towards the street. Edward Griffiths described it as looking like a tool carried by fish mongers. It was rusty and appeared not to have been used in quite a while. The strange man was described as short in stature, poorly dressed and clean-shaven. Griffiths suspected that the cleaver could have been the murder weapon used on the Bordens.

Griffiths, Robert P.

Robert P. Griffiths, a carpenter, was with his brother Edward L. Griffiths when he saw a strange man in town the day the Bordens were killed (see Edward L. Griffiths).

Grinnell, Eben S.

Eben S. Grinnell of Freetown, Masachusetts, was questioned as a potential juror for the Borden trial. He said that he was against capital punishment and was excused.

Gross, Henry M.

See Goss, Henry M.

Grouard, John W.

John W. Grouard was a professional house painter. He was a witness for the defense at the trial and related that he was commissioned to paint the Borden house at the same time that Mrs. Mary A. Raymond, a seamstress, was making a dress for Lizzie Borden. Grouard was using the same shade of brown paint on the Borden house that Lizzie claimed was on the dress she burned in the kitchen stove on the Sunday morning after the murders. The prosecution tried to convince the jury at the trial in New Bedford that the dress was stained with the blood of the murder victims, not the paint of John Grouard.

Grouard took the witness stand for the defense on June 15, 1893. He said that when he first arrived at the Borden home, Lizzie did not like the shade of brown he had chosen. Grouard exchanged the paint

John Grouard and Charles Gifford.

and returned the following day and mixed the colors to suit Lizzie's taste. The painting began on May 9, 1892. Grouard testified that Lizzie was near the paint tube by the north (side) door and that was how her dress became soiled. "We (Grouard and Lizzie) commenced painting right away," Grouard stated at the trial. He described the job as coloring the house a "dark drab with darker trimmings."

Grundy, James

James Grundy was a glassmaker from New Bedford. Summoned to jury duty for the Borden trial, Grundy said he had formed no opinion about Borden's guilt or innocence. In spite of this, he was challenged by Lizzie and not assigned to the jury.

Guild, Jason T. (1824-?)

Jason T. Guild, who appeared for jury duty in the Borden trial, was from North Attleboro. He was excused because of old age. Guild was sixty-nine at the time of the trial.

Gunning, Augustus

Gunning's name was mentioned in the story that was soon called the "Trickey-McHenry" hoax (see Henry G. Trickey and Edwin D. McHenry). According to the *Boston Globe* story, Gunning was a boarder at the Churchill residence next door to the Borden house and he was prepared to testify that he saw a "hooded Lizzie" at the window of the guest room where Abby Borden died. Most likely, Augustus Gunning was invented by reporter Trickey and never existed. He certainly never boarded at the Churchill residence (see Adelaide Churchill).

Gunning, Thomas (?-1931)

Dr. Thomas Gunning assisted Medical Examiner William A. Dolan and Drs. Albert C. Dedrick, John W. Coughlin, John H. Leary, Emmanuel C. Dutra, J.Q.A. Tourtellot, Anson C. Peckham and Seabury Bowen in the first autopsy of the Bordens on the dining room table at 92 Second Street at 3:00 P.M. on the day of the murders. Gunning died on March 17, 1931 in Fall River. He was he last survivor of the physicians who were present at the Borden autopsies.

Gushee, Edward

Edward Gushee of Raynham, Massachusetts, was challenged by Lizzie Borden during the questioning of prospective jurors and was excused.

H

Hacking, William L. (1863-1939)

William L. Hacking was on District Attorney Hosea M. Knowlton's handwritten list of witnesses beside the label "As to escape," meaning whether he or anyone else under that label saw the murderer flee the Borden house after Andrew and Abby were killed. Those prosecution witnesses who testified said they did not see any person come in or go out of 92 Second Street when the murders occurred, thus making Lizzie Borden the only suspect with an opportunity to kill.

Hacking was sitting on the front steps of the Buffinton House, the home of Mrs. Adelaide Churchill and her family with Charles Cook, George Douglas and Oliver H. Perry Durling on the morning when the Bordens were killed. Hacking testified at the preliminary hearing and before the grand jury that he saw no one enter or leave the Borden premises during the time the murders occurred. Hacking was summoned to appear at the final trial in New Bedford but was not called to the witness stand to testify.

William Hacking was born in Fall River. He worked as a lineman and later a motor inspector and wireman for the firm of Potter and Earle, electrical contractors. He was first hired by Potter and Earle in 1905 and remained with the company for thirty years. He relocated to Somerset, Massachusetts, in 1909 and remained there until his death.

Hall, Augustus O.

Hall was a jeweler from North Attleboro who was called to serve as a potential juror in the Borden case. He said he had not followed the case and had no interest in it. Hall was challenged by the prosecution and did not sit on the jury.

Hall, Louis L.

Louis L. Hall was interviewed on September 25, 1892 by Fall River police officers Patrick Doherty and Philip Harrington. He was on District Attorney Hosea Knowlton's handwritten list of witnesses who would say on the stand that they were in a position to see the comings and goings at the Borden house during the morning the murders occurred. He saw no one enter or leave 92 Second Street. Hall, however, was not called to testify at the Borden trial in June 1893. He moved from Fall River to Taunton in 1895.

Hall operated L.L. Hall and Company-Livery, Boarding, Sale and Exchange Stable at 129 Second Street, to the south of the Borden home and resided at 81 Second Street, just north and on the opposite side of the street of number 92.

He told the Fall River police that he was "in view of" the Borden residence for "some time" before 11:00 A.M. that morning and saw nothing out of the ordinary. It was at Hall's establishment that Mrs. Adelaide Churchill found her handyman Tom Boulds and told him to call for a doctor to rush to the Borden house. John Cunningham, also there, overheard the conversation and alerted the local newspapers and the police (see John J. Cunningham and Thomas Boulds).

Hall, Norman

Norman Hall was one of the pallbearers at the funeral of Lizzie Borden the Saturday after she died at the age of sixty-eight. The other pallbearers were Fred Coggeshall, Ernest Terry and Edson Robinson. The funeral took place in Oak Grove Cemetery. Hall, who lived in Swansea, was Lizzie Borden's gardener at Maplecroft.

Hammett, John F.

John Hammett, from Acushnet, Massachusetts, stated as a potential juror at the Borden trial that he could never vote "guilty" in a case of this kind. He was excused.

Hammond, John Wilkes (1837-1922)

John Wilkes Hammond was a Massachusetts superior court judge. Lizzie Borden appeared before him at her arraignment in New Bedford on May 8, 1893. In what was described as a strong voice, Lizzie pleaded "not guilty" and her trial was set for June 5, 1893 in New Bedford.

Hammond was born in Mattapoinsett, Massachusetts. He graduated from Tufts University in 1861 and became a teacher for a brief period of time. After serving his country in the Civil War, Hammond returned to teaching, then began to study law in the Boston offices of Messers. Sweester and Gardner. He also attended Harvard Law School and was admitted to the Middlesex bar.

John Hammond began to practice law in Cambridge, Massachusetts, and was City Solicitor there from 1873-1886. He resigned to accept an appointment to the Massachusetts superior court as a judge and as such presided over the arraignment of Lizzie Borden. He resigned from the superior court in 1898 to become a justice of the Supreme Court of the Commonwealth of Massachusetts.

Handy, Benjamin Jones (1849-1929)

Dr. Benjamin J. Handy reported that he saw a suspicious looking stranger near 92 Second Street at about 10:30 A.M. on the day of the Borden murders. He testified at the preliminary hearing and at the final trial. The person Handy claimed to have seen was dubbed "Dr. Handy's wild-eyed man" by the press.

Handy told the Fall River police that he was driving in his carriage down Second Street at about 10:30 on the morning of August 4 and

Dr. Handy, author of the "wild-eyed man theory."

saw a strange man pacing between the Borden house and the Kelly residence which was directly south of the Borden home. According to Handy, the stranger did not act drunk but did appear to be waiting for someone. Many people reported sighting strangers near the Borden house that day, but because Dr. Handy was a respected and well-known member of Fall River society, the police took his claim quite seriously.

Handy described the man he saw as being about thirty years old and 5'5" tall; the man's weight he guessed to be 130 pounds. The stranger wore light gray clothes and a hat that was made either of straw or of felt. Handy said the man's features were very pale, almost white, and he looked like someone who almost never went outside in the sun. Handy guessed that perhaps the man worked in a dark cellar or had recently been released from prison. The police searched the city but could find no one matching Handy's description. After Handy's sighting was reported in the local press the police were strongly criticized for not making an arrest. This unknown person was called "Dr. Handy's wild-eyed man" because Handy said the stranger's eyes were always on the sidewalk, and "he was acting differently from any person I ever saw on the street in my life—he was agitated and seemed weak." Ironically, Handy never remarked about a strangeness in the man's eyes or that they were in any way wild.

Two of the major Fall River newspapers differed in their description of the man Handy saw. The *Fall River Herald* gave the description mentioned above. The *Globe* on the other hand described him as 5'4", of medium weight, with a dark moustache upon a white face and a "round and full" figure. The *Globe* guessed the man's age to be twenty-four.

Handy was born in Marion, Massachusetts. He received a Doctor of Medicine degree from Harvard Medical School in 1871 and had a successful practice in Fall River from 1874-1913. In that year Handy returned with his wife, the former Susan E. Holmes, to Marion where he died at the age of eighty.

Hanscom, Oscar M.

O.M. Hanscom was the superintendent of the Boston office of the Pinkerton Detective Agency. He was hired by Lizzie Borden's lawyer Andrew Jennings during the weekend after the double murders of Andrew and Abby Borden. It was to Hanscom that Alice Russell first related the news that Lizzie had burned a dress on Sunday morning, August 7, 1892.

Hanscom was hired by Jennings to investigate the Borden slayings. He discussed the case with the Fall River police and was present when they searched the Borden home on the Saturday, Sunday and Monday after the murders. After the search on Sunday, Hanscom played almost no role in the case. He never found any new evidence in Fall River. Jennings eventually sent him to Hastings, Iowa to investigate the life of John Vinnicum Morse prior to Morse's return to Bristol County about two years before the murders.

On Sunday morning, August 7, Alice Russell saw Lizzie burn a dress in the kitchen stove. The following day, Russell told Lizzie that she had spoken with Hanscom and told Lizzie that burning the dress would make it appear that the murderer was destroying evidence. "It was the worst thing you could have done," she told Lizzie. Russell had informed Hanscom of the dress because earlier he had asked Russell if all of the dresses Lizzie owned were still in the house. Russell had answered in the affirmative, forgetting about the one Lizzie destroyed. When Russell realized later that she had given Hanscom false information, she felt guilty and approached Hanscom to correct herself.

Another reason O.M. Hanscom was hired by Andrew Jennings was because the lawyer was fearful the police might place false evidence in the Borden home to assure her arrest and conviction and thereby placate a demanding press and public that insisted upon a quick arrest.

The Fall River police were aware of Hanscom's co-operation with Lizzie. City Marshal Rufus B. Hilliard hired Providence, Rhode Island private detective Edward D. McHenry, later involved in the so-called Trickey-McHenry hoax, to keep an eye on Hanscom. When McHenry noticed Hanscom eavesdropping on a conversation between Hilliard and state policeman George F. Seaver by the rear window of Hilliard's house, McHenry chased Hanscom around the building and away from the dwelling.

One reason Jennings sent Hanscom to Hastings, Iowa was that by law Hanscom could not keep any legal evidence he might have discovered a secret; he had to inform the police. This put Hanscom and Jennings in an uncomfortable position: Hanscom was hired to work for Lizzie Borden but his information about the dress would put Lizzie in a poor light. The answer seemed to be to get Hanscom far enough away from Fall River so the Pinkerton man could not talk to the Fall River police. This plan worked; knowledge about the dress burning did not come out until Alice Russell decided to tell the story to the grand jury in November, 1892.

Harland, ??

Harland was in A.J. Smith's drug store with Eli Bence and Frank H. Kilroy when Lizzie entered the store and attempted to purchase ten cents worth of prussic acid, according to the testimony of druggist Bence at the preliminary hearing. Since no evidence relating to the acid was allowed in the final trial, Harland never took the stand as a witness in New Bedford.

Harrington, Hiram C. (1829-1907)

Hiram C. Harrington became the brother-in-law of Andrew Jackson Borden when he married Borden's only sister Laurana (or "Lurana" as it was sometimes spelled) and thus was the uncle of Emma and Lizzie Borden. The Borden sisters loathed their Uncle Hiram but were quite fond of their Aunt Laurana and maintained a relationship with her until the murders of Andrew and Abby Borden. At the inquest, held August 9-11, 1892, Lizzie mentioned her uncle as a possible suspect in the murders. Harrington was also called as a witness at the inquest, but no record of his remarks is currently available. He was summoned to the final trial but was not put on the stand.

Hiram and Andrew had feuded for years before the murders, although no one seemed to know why. Andrew disapproved of Hiram's marriage to his sister because he felt Hiram Harrington, content with his occupation as a blacksmith, lacked ambition. Harrington was not welcome at the 92 Second Street house, and Andrew never visited his sister unless he knew Hiram was not at home.

In an interview with the *Fall River Herald*, Hiram called Andrew a very hard man with money. He stated that he believed the motive in the killings was Andrew's estate, which Hiram said was worth over $500,000. Harrington also expressed surprise at Lizzie's statement that she did what she could to make Andrew comfortable after he arrived home on the morning of his death because, according to Harrington, she apparently displayed a kindness, "that I never suspected was a part of her nature or custom before."

Harrington also stated in the interview that there had been angry disputes in the Borden household for the past ten years but they were always kept quiet. Andrew, he said, tried to soothe the resentment his daughters felt over the Fourth Street house (see Jane E.D. Gray and Sarah Whitehead) by giving Emma and Lizzie money and stocks, but the sisters remained angry.

He described Emma as quiet and Lizzie as "haughty and domineering." Lizzie was, Harrington continued, "of a repellant disposition, and would become sulky." He had heard Lizzie speak many times in a critical tone about Andrew's miserliness and sympathy for Abby's family over his own. He strongly hinted that Lizzie was the killer.

Hiram Harrington was born in East Greenwich, Rhode Island. He moved to Fall River and married Laurana Borden in 1854. Harrington worked as a blacksmith at Fourth and Borden Streets, only two blocks from the Borden residence. He served on the Fall River City Council for two terms, in 1860 and 1864, and was also an active Mason. Hiram Harrington died at his home on Turner Street in Fall River.

Harrington, Laurana (Borden) (1826-1898)

Laura Ann, or Laurana as she became known, was the daughter of Abraham and Phebe (Davenport) Borden of Fall River. She was the only sister of Andrew Jackson Borden and the aunt of Emma and Lizzie Borden.

Lizzie, like Andrew, loved Laurana while scorning her husband Hiram Harrington. Harrington, in giving his opinion of the Borden family to the *Fall River Herald* was quoted as saying, "My wife, being an only sister, was very fond of Mr. Borden and always subservient to his will, and by her intimacy with his affairs I have become acquainted with a good deal of the family history."

Harrington, Patrick

Patrick Harrington was a cousin of Borden maid Bridget Sullivan. After Bridget appeared at the inquest at the Fall River police station she was escorted by policeman Patrick H. Doherty to the Borden home to collect her belongings according to Edwin H. Porter, the Fall River newspaper reporter who in 1893 wrote the first book on the Borden murders. Doherty then accompanied Sullivan to the home of her cousin Patrick Harrington at 95 Division Street where she spent the night.

Harrington, Philip H. (1859-1893)

Philip Harrington was a sergeant on the Fall River police force in 1892 when the Bordens were killed. Later that same year, Harrington was promoted to the rank of captain. Harrington participated in searches of the Borden property, questioned Lizzie Borden personally,

Captain Philip Harrington, c.1892.

interviewed Eli Bence concerning Lizzie's attempt to purchase prussic acid and was a witness for the prosecution at the preliminary hearing and at the final trial.

Harrington explained at the trial as a prosecution witness that he arrived at 92 Second Street at 12:20 P.M. on the day of the murders with policemen John Fleet, William H. Medley and Charles Wilson. He stayed on duty until about 6:00 P.M. that evening. Harrington inspected both bodies and then went upstairs to question Lizzie in her room. Lizzie told him essentially the same story that she previously related to Assistant City Marshal John Fleet. She described Andrew's angry argument with a prospective renter two weeks before the murders, what happened when Andrew first returned home that morning, and her trip to the barn and return into the house to find her father dead. Officer Harrington recalled that Lizzie never showed any emotion during the interview and that she was wearing a pink wrapper while in her room.

Officer Harrington then went downstairs to the kitchen and saw Dr. Seabury Bowen with a cylindrical roll of paper about twelve inches long and less than two inches wide. When Harrington asked the physician what he was in his hand, Bowen said it was nothing and threw it into the stove. Harrington noticed one word on the burning scroll, the name "Emma."

Harrington later that day guarded the axes and hatchets he received after Dr. William A. Dolan's search of the cellar. He then went into the barn with Dolan, examined the hay pile in the loft and said that it was extremely hot in the barn, "very dusty, very uninviting." They saw no footprints in the loft. This testimony was meant to show that Lizzie was not in the loft as her father was being murdered.

The following day, Friday, August 5, Harrington interviewed Eli Bence at D.R. Smith's drug store about Lizzie's attempt to purchase prussic acid. That afternoon he again searched the Borden home with Dr. Dolan. City Marshal Rufus B. Hilliard, Fleet, State Detective George Seaver and Captain Dennis Desmond were also there. During this search, Harrington later recalled, Lizzie was "phlegmatic" and "extremely matter-of-fact."

Although nothing was found during the search to implicate anyone as the killer, Harrington and Fleet wanted Hilliard to order the arrest of Lizzie Borden. Hilliard refused to do so because neither a bloody dress nor a murder weapon was discovered; Hilliard wanted at least some solid evidence before he committed himself.

While the inquest was in session Harrington and Hilliard accompanied carpenter Maurice Daly to the Borden home and took pieces of wood from door frames and windows that were stained with the victims' blood. The next day, Saturday, August 13, Harrington and Officer John Minnehan searched some nearby woods for a stranger reportedly observed by farmer Joseph Lemay (see Joseph Lemay).

Philip H. Harrington was born in Fall River to James and Mary (McCue) Harrington. His college education at St. Lawrence University in Canton, New York was left unfinished because his father suffered some serious business setbacks. He worked at numerous jobs and at one time did some carpentry work for Andrew Jackson Borden. Harrington joined the police department's night patrol until Marshal Hilliard assigned him to day work. He eventually became a captain on the force and was a clerk for the Fall River Police Beneficial Association. He died unexpectedly in Newport, Rhode Island.

Hart, Abraham Gifford (1831-1907)

Abraham G. Hart was the treasurer of the Union Savings Bank in Fall River. He was also a pallbearer of Andrew Borden, along with Richard C. Borden, George W. Dean, Jerome C. Borden, James M. Osborne and Andrew Borden. He testified at the preliminary hearing and the final trial about Andrew Jackson Borden's whereabouts on the morning he was murdered.

Hart said that Borden entered the Union Savings Bank at 9:30 A.M. on Thursday, August 4 and stayed about five minutes. Hart thought that Borden appeared tired and frail. The banker said on the witness stand that a circulating rumor hinting Andrew had talked with him about a will was a lie and that a will was never mentioned in conversation between the two.

Hart was born in Fall River to Jonathan and Susan (Gifford) Hart. He went through the Fall River public school system and was a machinist in the shop of Marvel and Davol for twenty years. He was active in state and local politics and became treasurer of the Union Savings Bank where Andrew Jackson Borden was a director. Hart was active in church affairs and belonged to several fraternal organizations. He was also the first president of the Fall River Veteran Fireman's Association. He died in his hometown.

Hart, Frederick Bradford (1870-1941)

Frederick B. Hart was working as a drug clerk along with Eli Bence at D.R. Smith's drug store when a woman Bence claimed to be Lizzie Borden tried to buy prussic acid. Hart was a witness at the inquest and the preliminary hearing. He was summoned to appear at the final trial to relate what he saw in the drug store that Wednesday before the murders but was not called because the court ruled that no evidence related to prussic acid could be used by the prosecution.

Although Hart swore that it was Lizzie who entered the store, he could not remember what she was wearing that day or what time she entered, except that it was after 10:00 A.M. and before 11:00 A.M. on Wednesday, August 3. At the inquest, Lizzie was overheard telling her friend Mary Brigham that she had never been in Smith's store in her life.

Frederick B. Hart, a descendant of the colonial Massachusetts governor William Bradford, was born in Fall River to William and Betsey (Briggs) Hart. After he left the employ of Smith's drug store, Hart became a salesman and collector for the Enterprise Brewing Company in Fall River. He worked for that company until his death.

Hart, Sarah B.

Sarah B. Hart testified at the Borden trial about a strange man she saw while she walked down Second Street to catch the trolley car on Main Street. Walking with her was Delia S. Manley, her sister-in-law.

While walking by the Borden house, at about 9:45 A.M. on the day of the murders, Hart and Manley stopped to talk to Hart's nephew Ezra P.B. Manley, who was riding by in a carriage. While talking, Hart and Manley noticed a stranger leaning on the front gate post of the Borden house. He was, Hart said at the trial, "elderly" and neither woman recognized him.

At the trial, Hart said that she had lived in Fall River for "15 or 20 years" before moving away in 1892. Her sister had once lived for two or three years in the house on Second Street owned in 1892 by Dr. and Mrs. Michael Kelly. She was, therefore, familiar with Second Street and knew Andrew Borden by sight. The older man near the gate post was not Andrew, Hart testified (see Delia Summers Manley).

Hartley, James W.

James W. Hartley was a Fall River doctor. At the preliminary hearing, Dr. William A. Dolan said that he entered 92 Second Street the morning of the murders with fellow physicians Hartley and J.Q.A. Tourtellot and examined the guest room.

Harvey, J. Herbert

Norton, Massachusetts resident J. Herbert Harvey was a member of the grand jury that indicted Lizzie Borden on December 2, 1892 for the murders of Andrew and Abby Borden.

Haskell, William H.

William H. Haskell of Boston was an assistant to Norfolk County court reporter Frank Hunt Burt. Burt's other assistants were C.E. Barnes and William B. Wright (see Frank Hunt Burt).

Haskell, Mrs. William H.

Mrs. Haskell was one of four official type writers who typed the dictated stenographic notes of the Borden trial taken by Annie M. White. The other official type writers were A.M. Dollard, Florence D. Ross and Florence W. Cushing. All were from Boston.

Hastings, Isaac

Mistakenly described in Victoria Lincoln's book, *A Private Disgrace, Lizzie Borden by Daylight* (1967) as the man with whom John Vinnicum Morse lived in South Dartmouth, Lincoln was describing to Isaac C. Davis (see Isaac C. Davis).

Hatch, Joseph W.

Joseph W. Hatch was a tinsmith from New Bedford. He presented the court with a certificate to excuse him from jury duty. The certificate was not sworn to and was ruled inadmissible. In spite of this legal technicality, Hatch was excused from jury duty.

Hathaway, Andrew J.

Andrew J. Hathaway of Dighton, Massachusetts, served on the grand jury that indicted Lizzie Andrew Borden for the murders of her father and stepmother.

Hathaway, Charles F.

A prospective juror from Swansea, Hathaway was challenged by the prosecution and excused.

Hathaway, Franklin L.

Frank Hathaway was a police inspector from New Bedford. Along with fellow New Bedford inspector John Parker, Hathaway investigated the murders of Andrew and Abby Borden for the Fall River police, especially the theory that a dispute over real estate caused the killings. Their investigations were chronicled in the *Fall River Globe*.

According to the *Globe* issues of August 17 and 18, 1892, Hathaway and Parker were at the Borden home at 92 Second Street and the home on South Mill Road in South Dartmouth where John Vinnicum Morse was living. They also investigated a trip Emma Borden supposedly made to South Dartmouth and Morse's journeys into Fall River in the months before the murders.

The two detectives worked on the case for two weeks and came up with nothing new. Hathaway and Parker were never called to testify at any inquest, hearing or trial and were not heard from after that time concerning the Borden case, except for a mention in the Trickey-McHenry articles (see Henry G. Trickey and Edwin D. McHenry).

Hathaway, George E.

George E. Hathaway was a prospective juror in the Borden trial. He was from Taunton and the *New Bedford Evening Standard* described him as looking about thirty-five years old. He told the court that he did have an opinion concerning the case but did not consider himself prejudiced and was not against the death penalty. He was challenged by the prosecution and did not serve on the jury.

Hathaway, George W. (1843-1925)

George W. Hathaway appeared before the grand jury in November 1892. He was summoned to testify at the trial in New Bedford but was never called as a witness. He told Orrick Smalley that Andrew Borden had told a friend of Hathaway that he, Borden, was having family problems at home (see Orrick Smalley). This was only hearsay evidence, but in a grand jury proceeding hearsay is allowed, in contrast to a "petit" or 12 person jury which meets to hear evidence and decide whether the accused is "guilty" or "not guilty."

George W. Hathaway was born in Freetown, Massachusetts. He was a commercial salesman and settled in Fall River in 1882 with his wife Emily. Hathaway remained a resident of that city until 1917 when he relocated to Assonet, Massachusetts, a town close to Fall River. George W. Hathaway died at the home of his son in 1925 in the city of Fall River.

Hathaway, Joseph W.

Joseph W. Hathaway of Taunton arrived in New Bedford for jury duty but was not questioned or picked.

Hathaway, Nathaniel

Nathaniel Hathaway was an analytical chemist with a degree from Columbia University. He was called upon to testify on the tenth day of the trial, June 15, 1893, as to the uses of prussic acid to clean furs, kill humans and apply as an insecticide. Also testifying as to the uses of prussic acid were fur dealer Henry H. Tillson and pharmacist Charles Henry Lawton, both from New Bedford.

Hathaway stated that prussic acid had no use in the care of furs. His testimony, along with that of all witness who spoke of prussic acid, was thrown out by the court on June 16 due to protests by the defense (see George Dexter Robinson).

Hathaway, Stephen A.

Stephen A. Hathaway of Freetown, Massachusetts, was a prospective juror in the Borden murder case. He was neither questioned nor chosen to sit on the jury.

Heap, Joseph M.

Joseph M. Heap was a Fall River policeman at the time of the Borden murders. He interviewed numerous people about the killings, none of whom provided any solid leads for the local authorities.

All of Officer Heap's interviews concerned an incident that occurred on Jencks Road involving wagon driver Romauld St. Amant and a stranger wanting a ride into New Bedford (see Romault St. Amant, Exentive St. Amant, Jean St. Laurant, Francois Charrete, Joseph Michaud and Alexander Côté).

Hendry, F.

F. Hendry was a sketch artist for the *Boston Journal* and drew pictures of some of the participants in the Borden trial.

Hickey, Thomas F.

Thomas Hickey was a reporter who testified at the trial concerning an argument at the Taunton jail between Lizzie Borden and her sister Emma and witnessed by jail matron Hannah Reagan. Hickey testified on June 16, 1893 at the final trial that he represented three newspapers: the *Boston Globe*, the *Fall River Globe* and the *Boston Herald*. Hickey stated that after the story of the argument appeared in the *Fall River*

Globe, he questioned Reagan about the truth of the article and Reagan said the story was a lie and that there was never a disagreement between the two sisters.

Hill, Edmund E.

Hill, a prospective juror on the Borden trial, apparently gave satisfactory answers, so far as the prosecution was concerned, but he was challenged by Lizzie Borden and did not serve on the jury.

Hilliard, Rufus Bartlett (1850-1912)

Rufus Bartlett Hilliard was the City Marshal of Fall River at the time of the Borden murders. As such, he was the main law-enforcer in the city. One may compare the office of city marshal with the modern-day position of chief of police.

It was Marshal Hilliard who received the telephone call from reporter John Cunningham at 11:15 A.M. on Thursday, August 4, 1892 that there was "trouble" at the Borden house . He immediately ordered

City Marshall Rufus Hilliard.

Officer George A. Allen to rush to the Borden residence and check out the problem. Hilliard was involved in many aspects of the Borden investigation and testified at the inquest and at the final trial. Marshal Hilliard did not personally enter the Borden home until about 3:00 P.M. that afternoon. When he arrived at 92 Second Street, he made a quick search of the house and then rushed to the barn where he found the door closed and the barn, when he entered, very hot.

The following day, Friday, August 5, Hilliard and Fall River mayor Dr. John William Coughlin hired private detective Edwin D. McHenry to help the police solve the murders (see Oscar M. Hanscom and Edwin D. McHenry). The findings of McHenry would prove less than satisfactory to those who felt Lizzie Borden was the killer.

On Saturday, August 6, the day of the double funeral at Oak Grove Cemetery, Hilliard again searched the Borden house and requested from Andrew Jennings, Lizzie Borden's lawyer, the dress Lizzie wore on the day of the murders. He got the dress from Jennings and gave it to Dr. William A. Dolan, the Fall River Medical Examiner.

Later that day, Hilliard accompanied Officer Philip Harrington and local carpenter Maurice Daly to the Borden house where Daly removed pieces of bloodstained wood from areas where the Bordens were killed. At about 7:45 P.M., Hilliard and Mayor Coughlin made a major mistake which would greatly hurt the prosecution's case at the trial the following year. They went to the Borden home without an arrest or search warrant to talk with Lizzie, her sister Emma and her Uncle John Vinnicum Morse. During the conversation Coughlin told Lizzie that she was a suspect in the murders.

This mistake had the effect of making her later inquest statements, some of which were confusing and contradictory, inadmissible during the final trial since she had not been advised of her Fifth Amendments rights. More precisely, the court ruled that Lizzie's statements were not voluntary when made at the inquest because she was technically under arrest at the time (see Robert Sullivan's *Goodbye Lizzie Borden* (1974) for a more complete discussion of the legal issues involved in the exclusion of Lizzie Borden's inquest statements).

After Lizzie was finally arrested on Thursday, August 11, Hilliard had her committed to the matron's room at the jail because it had facilities to accommodate females. Here another incident took place that would involve Hilliard. Apparently, Lizzie had an argument in her room with her sister Emma, who had come to visit her on August 24, 1892.

This discussion was overheard by Hannah Reagan, the jail matron. When the story of the argument was published in the *Fall River Globe*, Lizzie's lawyer Andrew Jennings wanted Reagan to sign a statement that no argument had ever occurred. Jennings claimed that Reagan was willing to sign the document, but her superior, City Marshal Hilliard, was quoted as saying to her, "If you sign that paper, it will be against my express orders," or "You do it in direct violation of my orders." On the witness stand, Mrs. Reagan testified that she never said she would sign any paper about the conversation Lizzie had with Emma.

When the jury acquitted Lizzie Borden on June 20, 1893, City Marshal Hilliard officially closed the Borden case and all further official investigations ceased. The case remains, of course, unsolved to this day.

Rufus B. Hilliard was remembered as having a somewhat round face with a crimson handlebar moustache. He was a quiet man who rarely lost his temper. The City Marshal was born in Pembroke, Maine. After attending school in Newburyport, Massachusetts until the age of 15, he enlisted in the army during the Civil War.

Hilliard arrived in Fall River in 1872 and was employed at the American Printing Company until his appointment to the Fall River police department. He received several promotions and became City Marshal in 1886. After the Borden trial ended in acquittal, Hilliard played a decisive role in the Bertha Manchester axe murder in which a suspect was arrested and convicted (see Bertha Manchester).

Hodges, Alfred B.

Hodges was a Taunton deputy sheriff who, with fellow deputies E.C. Brown George H. Arnold and John W. Nickerson, accompanied the Borden jury on the second day of the trial to 92 Second Street to view the murder scene at the request of prosecutor Hosea M. Knowlton.

Hodges, Henry A.

Henry A. Hodges was a music teacher from Taunton who was called to jury duty for the Borden trial. He did not show up at the New Bedford courthouse.

Hodges, Louis Bradford (1834-1905)

Louis D. Hodges was the seventh juror chosen in the Borden case. He is best remembered today for almost fainting at the sight of the gruesome photographs of Andrew Borden's face on June 13, the eighth day of the trial. He was revived when a fellow juror fanned him and another juror brought him a glass of water. There was a five minute recess and Hodges was taken out of the court room and into the hall where he was given smelling salts. He then returned to his seat and heard six more hours of testimony that day.

Hodges was described as "elderly looking" with "snowy white locks — an overhanging brow" and "strongly set features" that displayed a "firmness of character." When questioned as a prospective juror on June 5, he stated that he had little interest in the case but did not think his opinion would interfere with rendering a fair decision.

Hodges was born in Taunton, married Hannah Elizabeth Godfrey in 1861 and joined the United States Army to fight in the Civil War the next year. He was an iron moulder by profession and was active in local civic affairs, including membership in Taunton's Common Council. He died in that city at the age of seventy-one.

Holland, Mrs.

See Howland, Anne Howard (Gray).

Holmes, Anna Covell (1861-1943)

Anna C. Holmes was one of a group of five women who Lizzie Borden had planned to meet in Marion, Massachuetts, during the first week of August 1892. The murders of Lizzie's father and stepmother resulted. in a cancellation of that vacation. The other women were Mary L. Holmes, Elizabeth M. Johnston, Isabel J. Frazer, and Louise Remington. Anna Holmes and her sister Mary were the daughters of Mary Anna and Charles Jarvis Holmes, a strong supporter of Lizzie during the trial.

Holmes, Charles Jarvis (1834-1906)

Charles J. Holmes was a prominent Fall River banker. He and his wife Mary were strong supporters of Lizzie from the time of her arrest. Charles and Mary Holmes were two of the mourners allowed to attend the funeral services at 92 Second Street of Andrew and Abby Borden, along with Abby's two sisters, Sarah Whitehead and Priscilla Fish, Dr. Seabury Bowen and his wife Phoebe, Frank Almy, Adelaide Churchill, Alice Russell, Emma and Lizzie Borden and John Vinnicum Morse. The Reverends Edwin A. Buck and Thomas Adams conducted the service. Holmes also testified as to the veracity of the story that Emma and Lizzie had an argument while Lizzie was staying in the matron's room at the Fall River jail.

Before the Borden murder trial began, all of Fall River heard about a similar crime involving the ax murder of Bertha Manchester, which had disturbing similarities to the Borden killings. Holmes and his wife made many statements to the press on Lizzie's behalf, especially how the crimes were so alike even though Lizzie was in jail at the time Manchester was killed (see Bertha Manchester and José Correira).

At the trial, Charles J. Holmes testified that Hannah Reagan wanted to sign a statement to the effect that the much-publicized spat between Lizzie and Emma Borden in Lizzie's jail cell never occurred but her boss, City Marshal Rufus B. Hilliard, would not allow it. Hannah Reagan had denied she wanted to sign the paper and said the fight did indeed take place.

On the evening of Lizzie's acquittal, June 20, 1893, a party was held in her honor at 67 Pine Street, Charles Holmes's house. There, Lizzie gave to the *Fall River Globe* what would be one of her very last interviews.

Charles Jarvis Holmes was born in Rochester, Massachusetts. He first came to Fall River as a youth and upon graduation from high school began his long career in banking. In 1855, at the age of twenty-one, he was appointed treasurer of the Fall River Five Cents Savings Bank. He remained with that institution until his death. Three years after becoming treasurer, he married Mary Anna Remington.

Holmes also had other public interests. He was a manager of many textile-manufacturing companies, served in the state legislature, was a public school trustee for sixteen years and became an officer of the Fall River Public Library.

Holmes, Mary Anna (Remington)

Mary Anna Holmes testified at the Borden trial as a witness for the defense just before her husband took the stand on June 16, 1893. Mrs. Holmes said basically the same things that her husband said as the next witness (see Charles Jarvis Holmes). Mrs. Holmes was also at 92 Second Street on the afternoon of the murders when the police arrived to question Lizzie and was present at the Borden home for the funeral of Andrew and Abby on Saturday, August 6, 1892. After Lizzie was acquitted, Mary Anna and Charles Holmes threw Lizzie a celebration at their house.

Sometimes called Marianna, Holmes was the wife of banker Charles Jarvis Holmes and an acquaintance of Lizzie Borden. Mrs. Holmes had known Lizzie since childhood and Lizzie went public school with Holmes's daughter, Anna G. Holmes, one of the friends Lizzie had planned to meet in Marion, Massachusetts, before the double murders changed her plans. She was also the mother of Mary L. Holmes, another of the friends whom Lizzie planned to see in Marion.

Mrs. Charles J. Holmes of Fall River.

Holmes, Mary Louisa (1859-1934)

Mary L. Holmes was one of a group of five friends who were supposed to meet Lizzie Borden for a vacation in Marion, Massachusetts, during that first week in August. The deaths of Lizzie's father and stepmother cancelled those plans. The other friends were Anna C. Holmes, Louise Remington, Isabel J. Frazer and Elizabeth M. Johnston. Mary L. Holmes was the sister of Anna C. Holmes and the daughter of Charles Jarvis and Mary Anna Holmes (see Anna Covell Holmes and Charles Jarvis Holmes).

Hopkins, Harold V.

Harold V. Hopkins from Attleboro was a youngish-looking man who was questioned for duty on the jury in the Borden trial. He worked for William Coupe and Company. Hopkins said he had no pre-formed opinion as to the guilt or innocence of the defendant but was against capital punishment. Hopkins was challenged by the prosecution and did not serve on the jury.

Horton, Charles M.

Andrew Borden had a discussion with Charles M. Horton on the steps of the Fall River post office near Second Street on the morning he and his wife Abby were killed. Andrew finished his discussion with Horton at about 10:30 A.M. and then walked towards S. Main Street. Horton was not asked to appear at the trial of Lizzie Borden as a witness.

Horton, Dexter D., Jr. (1868-?)

Dexter D. Horton, Jr., 25 years of age, was against capital punishment and excused from serving on the Borden trial. He was from Rehoboth, Massachusetts.

Horton, Gilbert M. (1827-?)

Gilbert Horton expressed his desire to serve on the Borden jury. He stated that he had formed no opinion of the case. He was, however, challenged by Lizzie Borden and excused.

Horton, Josiah G.

Josiah G. Horton was described in the *New Bedford Evening Standard* as a "sunburnt farmer" from Dighton, Massachusetts. He was questioned as a potential juror at the Borden trial and challenged by the prosecution. He was then sent home.

House, Morris

Morris House was an employee of the Tilden-Thurber art gallery in Providence, Rhode Island where Lizzie Borden was accused of shoplifting in 1897 (see William G. Thurber and Henry Tilden). He witnessed the signing of a document by Lizzie Borden admitting to the murders of her father and stepmother five years before. She signed the paper to avoid the embarrassment of being prosecuted for stealing two paintings on porcelain. Also present as witnesses were Tilden, Thurber, police detective Patrick H. Parker and Stephen O. Metcalf, a reporter.

Many Borden writers believed the confession with Lizzie's signature was a forgery, especially Edward D. Radin who pays the incident close attention in his book, *Lizzie Borden: The Untold Story* (1961). Radin believes that this event never took place.

Howard, Joseph, Jr.

Joe Howard has been called journalism's first syndicated columnist. He represented many of the nation's top newspapers, including the *Boston Globe*, the *New York Recorder*, the *San Francisco Chronicle*, the *Chicago Tribune* and Joseph Pulitzer's *New York World*, at the Borden trial.

He was a strong believer in Lizzie Borden's innocence and has been described as a "stand-out performer," "voluble" and "robust." The whole country read with interest Howard's colorful descriptions of the trial and of the local citizens. "There were two or three very pretty girls from Boston [watching the Borden trial]," Howard wrote, "but a

Joseph Howard, Jr.

large majority were vinegar-faced, sharp-nosed lean-visaged and extremely spare in physique...[with] a host of unkempt and unattractive females." Descriptions such as this kept up interest around the nation during and after the trial.

Joe Howard was born in Brooklyn, New York. As a boy, Howard was inspired by the colorful sermons and public talks of America's most famous mid-nineteenth century religious leader, Henry Ward Beecher. Howard could always be recognized by his trademark red beard and wide-brimmed straw hat cocked at a jaunty angle. Howard was always accompanied by a beautiful blonde stenographer.

One of Howard's early stories affected the progress of the Civil War. In 1862 he invented a story that the government was going to initiate the first military draft in American history because so many soldiers had been killed or wounded in battle. What Howard did not know was that the government really did plan a draft, which had to be postponed because of the riots of protest that followed the publication of his story. As a result, Howard was arrested and spent some time in jail.

Howard was famous for his P.T. Barnum-like style and what Borden scholar Robert Sullivan described as "an excessive use of adjectives to the point of being euphistic." After the Civil War ended, it was Joe Howard who first broke the famous Credit Mobiliér scandal that almost ruined President Ulysses S. Grant's first administration.

Howard was just as colorful and cynical in reporting the Borden trial as he was describing government scandals. Even though he believed in Lizzie's innocence, he criticized Judge Justin Dewey's controversial instructions to the jury before they began deliberation: "With matchless clearness, he [Dewey] set up the case of the prosecution point by point and, in the most ingenious manner possible, knocked it down." After the jury acquitted Lizzie Borden, she arose from her seat in the courtroom, went over to Howard and personally thanked him for his journalistic support. Lizzie later gave a reception in Howard's honor as a further token of appreciation.

Howe, ??

Howe lived in South Dartmouth and was a friend of John Vinnicum Morse. The *New Bedford Evening Standard* of August 8, 1892 reported that "Messrs. Davis and Howe," two acquaintances from South Dartmouth paid Morse a visit on the day of the Bordens' funerals. The Davis mentioned was Isaac C. Davis.

Howe, George A.

George A. Howe worked as a solderer in New Bedford. He was called to appear for jury duty in the Borden trial. Howe was described as a young man and admitted he had formed an opinion and could not render a fair verdict. Howe was excused.

Howland, Annie Howard (Gray) (1861-1938)

Annie Howard (Gray) Howland participated in the "sanity survey" Moulton Batchelder conducted for District Attorney Hosea M. Knowlton (see Moulton Batchelder). Batchelder was looking for evidence of insanity among the Borden and Morse families. Howland told Batchelder that she knew of no insanity in either group but she stated, "I always have heard that [both the Bordens and Morses] were somewhat peculiar and odd."

Annie Howland was born in Fall River to Nathaniel P. and Elizabeth Ann (Howard) Gray. She was the niece of Captain and Mrs. James Coggeshall Stafford; Annie Howland's mother was Mrs. Stafford's sister (see James Coggeshall Stafford). Annie H. Gray moved to New Bedford in 1870 and married John J. Howland. She was active in the New Bedford Historical Society, the Women's Club and the Country Week Society before moving into the home of her daughter in South Dartmouth in 1934.

Howland, Ellis L.

Ellis L. Howland was a reporter for the *New Bedford Evening Standard* and covered the Borden trial in 1893.

Howland, Gideon

Gideon Howland was called to jury duty for the Borden trial. He stated on the stand that he was prejudiced and had an opinion and was then excused.

Hoxie, Henry F.

Henry F. Hoxie, at his jury call, said he was not biased and had no interest in the Borden case. He felt that he could render a fair verdict. He was, however, against capital punishment and was excused. There was no occupational listing for Hoxie in the *New Bedford City Directory*. He possibly was retired.

Humphrey, Daniel J.

Daniel J. Humphrey was a New Bedford policeman who was assigned the task, along with officers John C. Rooks and Milton A. Brownell, of keeping order while the trial of Lizzie Borden was in progress. On June 5, 1893, Humphrey, Rooks and Brownell dispersed a large crowd of people trying to enter the courtroom to view the trial. No one was allowed in that day because there were too many prospective jurors in the courtroom who needed to be questioned by the defense and prosecuting attorneys. Humphrey was later on duty at the rear entrance to the courthouse.

While in the courtroom trying to keep control in spite of the almost suffocating heat during the trial, he was, according to the *New Bedford Evening Standard*, always firm, yet courteous. He was commended for his kindness by the *Evening Standard*, especially for allowing people who came from a great distance to view the proceedings. Specifically mentioned were a lawyer from the state of Georgia and a Spanish merchant from New York who were able to get seats thanks to Officer Humphrey.

Hunt, Josiah A. (1845-1898)

Josiah A. Hunt was more commonly called "Keeper" Hunt in the local newspapers. Hunt was the jailkeeper, or "keeper" in New Bedford. After Bridget Sullivan left Fall River, she was employed by Hunt and his wife, possibly so they could watch her before she testified. Sullivan performed the same tasks at the Hunts' Court Street home in New Bedford that she did for the Bordens.

Hyde, Joseph (1845-1933)

Joseph Hyde was a Fall River policeman. He was one of a group of officers who guarded the Borden home on the afternoon and evening of the murders. Hyde testified at the final trial as a witness for the prosecution as to his observations while on patrol that night.

Hyde and officers Patrick Doherty, Philip Harrington, John McCarthy and Michael Reagan were assigned to watch the Borden house on the day of the killings from 1:00 P.M. until 11:00 P.M.. They relieved officers James Dyson, George Ferguson, and Joseph Mayall who had been on guard duty since approximately 11:30 A.M.

At the trial of Lizzie Borden, Hyde testified that he saw Lizzie and Alice Russell go down into the cellar at about 9:15 P.M. Russell carried a lamp and Lizzie was holding a slop pail. Lizzie was alone in the cellar for about two minutes. Later that evening Lizzie, now back in the house, went from the sitting room to the cellar washroom, again for about two minutes.

Hyde was born in England and found work as a laborer in Fall River. He applied for a position with the Fall River Police Department and became a day patrolman in 1879. He remained with the force until 1915. Hyde married Mary E. Burke of Fall River, who later became that city's first female lawyer. Hyde died in Fall River at the age of eighty-eight.

J

Jackson, James Frederick

James F. Jackson was a Fall River lawyer with the firm of Jackson, Slade and Borden and a former mayor of Fall River. He was hired by two of Abby Borden's sisters, Sarah Whitehead and Priscilla Fish. Jackson contended that if authorities could prove that Andrew died before his wife, Abby was the heir to the Borden fortune and all of the estate would go to Abby's relatives rather than to Lizzie and Emma Borden. When the autopsies showed that Abby preceded her husband in death by about ninety minutes, all attempts by Abby's survivors to claim Andrew's fortune were dropped.

Jelly, George Frederick (1842-1911)

Dr. George Frederick Jelly was a Boston alienist, or psychiatrist. District Attorney Hosea M. Knowlton wanted to use Dr. Jelly as a professional consultant in the Borden murder case. Jelly turned down Knowlton's request because he believed there was not enough information from Moulton Batchelder's "sanity survey" for him to express a professional opinion (see Moulton Batchelder). Perhaps that was why Knowlton was displeased with Batchelder's efforts.

Jelly was born in Salem, Massachusetts. He attended Brown University and received a B.A. and an M.A., the latter degree in 1864. He then went to Harvard Medical School and received a medical degree in 1867. He began his practice in Springfield, Massachusetts, as a general practitioner and later was a physician at the McLean Asylum for the Insane between 1869 and 1871. He remained there until 1879 as superintendent of the asylum, then relocated to Boston where he corresponded with Attorney-General Albert E. Pillsbury concerning the Borden case.

Jelly later served as Chairman of the Massachusetts Board of Insanity (1898-1908) and received an honorary Doctor of Science degree from Brown in 1907. Jelly was a respected expert in his field and was involved in several interesting cases for the Commonwealth of Massachusetts including one involving Mary Baker Eddy, the founder of the Christian Science religious movement. He retired to Wakefield, Massachusetts, shortly before his death.

Jenney, Henry P.

Henry P. Jenney was from New Bedford. He was excused from serving on the Borden trial jury because he said he was biased. The city directory of New Bedford did not list an occupation for Jenney. He possibly was in retirement.

Jennings, Andrew Jackson (1849-1923)

Andrew Jackson Jennings had been the Borden family lawyer for many years before the murders of Andrew and Abby. He continued in that position after their deaths by representing Lizzie Borden at the preliminary hearing and as a member of her defense team at the final trial. He made the decision to hire Pinkerton detective O.M. Hanscom of Boston and drafted the statement he wanted jail matron Hannah Reagan to sign denying that there was ever an argument in Lizzie's jail cell between her and Emma. He also made the opening statement at Lizzie's trial on June 6, 1893.

Jennings took an active role in most aspects of the trial and the following year, 1894, succeeded Hosea M. Knowlton as district attorney. As a token of thanks to Jennings for her acquittal, Lizzie and Emma named Jennings to the board of directors of the Globe Yarn Mill, in which they owned stock.

After Lizzie was arrested on August 12, Jennings decided to get another lawyer to help him. He chose Colonel Melvin O. Adams, the former assistant district attorney for Suffolk County, Massachusetts.

Adams was active during the preliminary hearing held between August 25 and September 1, 1892, questioning many of the witnesses.

That hearing began in controversy when Jennings objected to the decision of Judge Josiah C. Blaisdell to preside because Blaisdell had also presided at the inquest and issued the arrest warrant for Lizzie Borden. Blaisdell refused to recuse himself, and the preliminary hearing proceeded. It ended with Jennings making an impassioned plea to Judge Blaisdell not to find his client "probably guilty" of the murders of Andrew and Abby Borden. Blaisdell did so anyway and the case went to the grand jury. After the grand jurors heard the evidence against her, a trial date was set for June 5, 1893.

At the trial, held in New Bedford on June 5-20, 1893, Jennings helped defense team leader George Dexter Robinson choose the jurors. Jennings wanted as many jurors as possible from the New Bedford area and none from Fall River. After the jury was chosen, Jennings made the opening statement to the twelve jurors.

Instead of attempting to outline the defense argument, Jennings made a strong emotional plea expressing his own long personal regard for all of the Bordens, including the accused, and detailed Lizzie's close relationship with her father. He also stressed Lizzie's church and charitable volunteer efforts as well as what he called Lizzie's "domesticity." Jennings admitted that Lizzie might seem guilty if she had had the sole opportunity to kill but gave numerous examples of strangers who were seen around the Borden property the day of the murders. His opening statement took twenty-eight minutes.

In cross-examinations during the trial, Jennings made several telling points that probably impressed the jury. In his questioning of prosecution witness Thomas Kieran, a civil engineer who had measured all there was to measure at the Borden home, he got Kieran to admit he could not see Abby's body lying in the guest room from the second floor landing. This weakened the argument of prosecuting attorney William Moody. In his cross-examination of Hannah Reagan, the Taunton jail matron who claimed she heard Lizzie and Emma arguing in Lizzie's jail cell, Reagan told the jury she was never asked to sign a document about a fight between the two sisters.

When the defense had its turn to argue Lizzie's innocence to the jury on June 15, Jennings called and questioned Martha Chagnon, Mary Durfee, Charles Gifford, Uriah Kirby, Mark P. Chase, Joseph Lemay, Dr. Benjamin Handy, Delia Manley, Hyman Lubinsky and Sarah B. Hart. He called them to the stand to demonstrtae that there were strangers about the area shortly before and during the murders. He also called Everett Brown and Thomas C. Barlow ("Me and Brownie") to discredit testimony that Lizzie was not in the loft at the time of the murders. He questioned Charles Sawyer, Thomas Hickey, Mary and Charles Holmes, John Caldwell and Mary Brigham to weaken the testimony of prosecution witness Hannah Reagan. His most interesting witness by far was Emma Borden, who stated that it was she who advised Lizzie to burn the stained dress. Emma also undermined the testimony of Alice Russell under Jennings' skillful questioning.

After Lizzie was acquitted, Jennings would not talk about the trial or of Lizzie Borden's guilt or innocence for the rest of his life. He even refused to discuss the case with members of his own family. Jennings did, however, possess the only known copy of the preliminary hearing transcripts, which was made public after his death and is an invaluable primary source material for Borden scholars to this day.

Andrew Jackson Jennings was short with a thick body and heavy eyebrows over dark, intense eyes. He was able, intelligent and clever, but also, according to author Robert Sullivan, "taciturn...brusque (with an) almost antagonistic air of importance."

He was born in Fall River to Andrew M. and Olive (Chace) Jennings. He graduated from Brown University in 1872 and became a high school principal in Warren, Rhode Island. He began his study of the law in the offices of James M. Morton of Fall River, then attended Brown Law School, from which he received a degree in 1876. That same year Jennings was admitted to the bar in Bristol County. After forming two partnerships that failed, he practiced alone and served in the Massachusetts House of Representatives and in the state Senate.

Jennings was elected district attorney for the Southeastern District of Massachusetts and held that office from 1894-1898. He belonged to several professional organizations and was active in church and civic affairs. He was also president of the Fall River Bar Association and a director in several local businesses including the Globe Yarn Mills, the Stanford Spinning Company, the Merchants Manufacturing Company and the Union Savings Bank.

Johnson, Alfred C.

Alfred C. Johnson was the property manager of a farm Andrew Jackson Borden owned in Swansea, Massachusetts, referred to as the "upper Swansea farm" to distinguish it from the "lower" Swansea farm managed by William Eddy. When police officer Patrick H. Doherty asked Lizzie after the murders if Johnson or Eddy could have killed the Bordens, Lizzie said neither was capable of harming them and they were immediately dropped as possible suspects.

Johnson and Eddy did give statements to the Fall River police about their knowledge of any axes or hatchets at 92 Second Street. They were both summoned to appear at the trial of Lizzie Borden but were not called upon to testify.

Johnston, Elizabeth Murray (1858-1907)

Lizzie Borden was supposed to meet Elizabeth Johnston and four other friends, Anna C. Holmes, Mary L. Holmes, Isabel J. Frazer and Louise Remington in Marion, Massachusetts, for a vacation. The murders of the Bordens ended Lizzie's hopes of getting away from Fall River. Lizzie sent Johnston a letter in Marion on August 4, 1892, the day of the murders. Johnston appeared at the preliminary hearing and before the grand jury. She did not take the stand as a witness at the final trial in June 1893.

Johnston was born in Fall River to Thomas and Annie (Murray) Johnston. She attended Bridgewater Normal School and began her career as a teacher in Myricks, Massachusetts, then taught for another twenty-five years in Fall River. She eventually became principal of two schools in her home town. She was a member of several professional organizations. Johnston died suddenly at her home in Fall River at the age of forty-nine.

Elizabeth Jordan and Anna Page Scott of the New York World.

Jordan, Elizabeth Garver (1867-1947)

Elizabeth Jordan was a reporter with the *New York World* who, along with Anna Page Scott, covered the Borden trial for that Pulitzer-owned newspaper.

Jordan was born in Milwaukee, Wisconsin and was educated in Catholic schools. She originally wanted to become a nun, but her father objected to this and convinced Elizabeth to enter the field of journalism, at the time a profession dominated by men. She worked at the *St. Paul Page* and the *Chicago Tribune* in the late 1880s and became a reporter for the *New York World* in 1890. Later in life, Jordan was an editor, author and drama critic and was active in women's issues, especially the struggle for women's right to vote.

As a literary adviser to publishers Harper and Brothers, Jordan convinced the company to publish the first novel of the then unknown Sinclair Lewis. She died in New York City on February 24, 1947 and was buried in Florence, Massachusetts, where she kept a summer retreat.

Jubb, William Walker (?-1904)

William Walker Jubb was Lizzie Borden's pastor at the Central Congregational Church in Fall River, Massachusetts, when Andrew and Abby Borden were murdered. He was a strong and vocal champion of Lizzie and a firm believer in her innocence. Jubb gave a well-publicized service at the church on August 7, 1892, the Sunday after the murders. He frequently spoke in Lizzie's defense and supported her throughout the trial. In his August 7 sermon, Jubb rebuked the local newspapers for ruining an innocent woman's reputation "...by casting a groundless or undeserved insinuation that...may blacken and blast a life forever, like a tree smitten by a bolt of lightening, a life which has always commanded respect, whose acts and motives have always been pure and holy."

Jubb, along with City Missionary Edwin A. Buck, was constantly at Lizzie's side. A religious leader in the community, Jubb presented Lizzie in a favorable light to the people of Bristol County, twelve of whom would eventually judge her at trial and find her "not guilty." Borden scholar Robert Sullivan, in describing the cloying presence of both ministers, called them "almost sickening." Jubb was also in the forefront of those who criticized Judge Josiah C. Blaisdell for not recusing him-

Rev. W.W. Jubb and Rev. E.A. Buck in court.

self from the preliminary hearing after being the judge who presided over Lizzie Borden's inquest (see Andrew Jackson Jennings).

After the trial Jubb, like most of Fall River's upper class, had little to do with Lizzie Borden. He, as did much of the city, ignored her and silently let her know that she was not welcome as a member of Fall River's high society.

William Walker Jubb was born in Morsley, England. He succeeded the Reverend Eldridge Mix as pastor of the Central Congregational Church in 1882. When he left Fall River in 1897, he was succeeded by the Reverend William Knight. Although Jubb was Lizzie Borden's pastor, Andrew and Abby belonged to the First Congregational Church and had a different minister, Dr. Thomas Adams. In reality, however, Andrew and Abby rarely, if ever, attended services although they did rent a pew at the front of the church. William Walker Jubb died in Illesley, England, in 1904.

Julien, Matthew C.

M.C. Julien, a minister of the Trinitarian Congregational Church in New Bedford, offered the opening prayer on the first day of the Borden trial, June 5, 1893. He asked for God to guide the jury to a fair decision.

Rev. M.C. Julien

K

Kavanaugh, Patrick

Patrick Kavanaugh worked as a laborer in John Crowe's stone yard, which was located to the rear of the Borden residence on Third Street (see John Crowe). He was misidentified at the Borden trial by witness John Dinnie, a fellow laborer, as the man who sneaked onto the Borden property and stole pears from trees in the backyard on the morning Andrew and Abby Borden were murdered. The real forager of pears that morning was Patrick McDonald, another worker in the Crowe stone yard.

Keefe, David P.

David Keefe worked in Fall River as a mailman. The *New Bedford Evening Standard* reported on August 8, 1892 that Keefe and John Vinnicum Morse searched a hay pile in the Borden barn for the murder weapon and examined carriages and sleighs that were stored there. Morse later asked Keefe to bury Andrew and Abby's bloodstained clothes and towels in the Borden backyard even though Medical Examiner Dr. William A. Dolan ordered that nothing be touched.

Keefe wanted to charge Morse five dollars to bury the clothing and pieces of the victims' skulls, according to the *Fall River Daily Herald*. Morse protested the price and they eventually settled on a fee of three dollars.

Kelly, George H.

Although the only George H. Kelly mentioned in the *Fall River City Directory* of 1892 was listed as being in the restaurant business, a George H. Kelly, drawtender at Stone Bridge, is mentioned in Annie M. White's stenographic notes as being interviewed by Fall River policeman P.T. Barker on August 4, 1892. Kelly said that a Portugese man told him he wanted to travel to New York City. Kelly advised the man to first go to Newport, Rhode Island, and from there he could get transportation to New York. This conversation, according to Kelly, took place at 6:00 P.M. on the day the Bordens died. Could this have been the same man involved with incidents concerning Romauld St. Amant, Mark T. Vincent, S.R. Paquin, George Manchester or George Bentley (see entries for St. Amant, Vincent, Paquin, Manchester and Bentley)?

Kelly, Mary Caroline (Cantwell) (1861-1951)

Mary Kelly and her husband Dr. Michael Kelly were Andrew and Abby's next door neighbors directly to the south of the Borden property at 96 Second Street. Mrs. Kelly testified at the preliminary hearing and at the final trial.

Mrs. Kelly remembered seeing Andrew Borden return home as she was passing "down street" on the morning he was murdered. He was carrying a bundle or something wrapped in white paper about the size of "a small box." Most assumed that the box contained a broken lock that Andrew picked up off of the floor when he visited the shop Jonathan Clegg was preparing to rent. Others, however, believed that Andrew was holding a package that contained his will, presumably with his wife Abby replacing Lizzie and Emma Borden as the sole heir to Andrew's fortune. The prosecution at the final trial wanted to convince the jury that this will was the motive for the murders.

Mrs. Kelly testified that she was walking downtown for a dentist appointment and as she passed the Borden house saw Andrew walk from the side, or north, door to the front door and attempt to open it and enter the house. The front door was locked however, and Bridget Sullivan, the Borden maid, tried to open it from the inside. Bridget had trouble undoing the locks and uttered a mild curse, "Oh, pshaw!" in response to which Lizzie laughed from the second floor landing.

Mrs. Kelly did not hear Lizzie laugh, but Bridget Sullivan testified under oath that this had happened after Andrew tried to go into the house. This was important to the prosecution, for it placed Lizzie near the mutilated body of Abby before her murder was officially discovered.

Mary Caroline Kelly was born in Peoria, Illinois, and moved to Providence, Rhode Island. She married Dr. Michael Kelly there in 1891, and soon after the couple moved to Fall River.

Mary Kelly was active in the Catholic Church. She helped found the Queen's Daughters, a Catholic organization that provided nursing aid to the poor. She was a member of the first American pilgrimage to the Holy Land, an area previously off-limits to Christians. Later in life, Mary Kelly moved to Passaic, New Jersey, to live with her daughter after her husband died in 1916. Kelly died there at the age of ninety.

Kelly, Michael (1856-1916)

Dr. Michael Kelly, perhaps because of anti-Irish sentiment, was not called upon to assist in the Borden murder case in any way. He lived with his wife Mary Caroline next door to the Bordens at 96 Second Street.

He and his wife had an Irish maid, Mary Doolan. The maid conversed over the common fence with Bridget Sullivan, the Borden maid, on the morning of the murders before she knew her employers were dead. While she was talking to the Kellys' maid, Bridget was washing the outside windows on the orders of Abby Borden.

Michael Kelly was born in Ireland and arrived in Fall River in 1870. He graduated from Holy Cross College in Worcester, Massachusetts in 1879 and received a medical degree from Bellevue Hospital Medical College in 1885. He was known as a specialist in the diseases of children. Kelly was appointed city physician in Fall River in 1890 by Mayor John W. Coughlin, himself a doctor.

Kelly married Mary Caroline Cantwell of Providence, Rhode Island, in 1891. Eventually returning to Holy Cross College to complete his education, he received an Masters of Arts in 1896. He was interested in Irish politics, especially the "home rule" movement, and entertained Irish politicians in his home if they happened to be in the area. Kelly died in Fall River at the age of sixty.

Kennedy, ??

Kennedy, a conductor on the Fall River trolley line, received a brief mention in the *New Bedford Evening Standard* of August 6, 1892. He confirmed the alibi of John Vinnicum Morse that Morse had been riding on a trolley far away from the Borden house when the killings occurred.

Morse said he was on a trolley and in the car with him were six priests. Conductor Kennedy, in a passing trolley, remembered seeing the six priests. Morse could not have known of them unless he was at the scene at the right time (see William Whittaker).

Kenyon, Henry W.

Henry W. Kenyon was a plumber's helper in New Bedford when he appeared for jury duty on the first day of the Borden trial. He stated that he was related to one of the lawyers connected with the case and was excused.

Kerouack, Philip [?] (c.1880-?)

Kerouack was a young boy of about 12 years of age. He lived with his family on Central Street in Fall River. He said that as he walked past 92 Second Street on the morning of the murders, he saw a man jump over the Borden back fence into the Chagnon yard. The boy went home and told this to his father, who then went to City Marshal Rufus B. Hilliard.

Hilliard later interviewed the boy. Young Kerouack's description of the man was similar to that given by Joseph Lemay, who saw a man crying and moaning on a road four miles from the Borden house about twelve days after the crimes occurred (see Joseph Lemay). The following year, the Kerouack family relocated to Providence, Rhode Island.

Kieran, Thomas

Thomas Kieran was an engineer who worked for the City of Fall River. He was called upon by the Commonwealth of Massachusetts to draw surveys and plans of Fall River showing the general area around 92 Second Street, the site of the Borden murders. He also drew detailed blueprints of the Borden home with measurements of every conceivable relationship between points that had relevance to the killings.

Kieran's plans and blueprints were entered into evidence at the Borden trial. Illustrations based upon his measurements and drawings are the basis of most of the sketches found in books about the Borden case to this day. They were also entered into evidence at the trial.

Kieran was also called as a witness for the prosecution and was the first person questioned when testimony began on June 6, 1893. In answering prosecutor William H. Moody's questions, Kieran gave detailed information of such facts as the measurements of the Borden property, the size and locations of all of the rooms and the spatial relationship between the house, the barn and neighboring homes. At that point court adjourned for the day so the jury could travel to Fall River and view the murder house firsthand.

When the trial reconvened on the following day, Kieran was asked by prosecutor Hosea M. Knowlton if a murderer could have hidden unobserved in a closet in the front of the house after killing Abby and remain undetected for approximately one and one-half hours, while awaiting the return of Andrew Borden from downtown. Kieran said that he tested this theory and believed a person could remain unobserved in a closet if he was quiet and did not attract attention.

That same day, Kieran made at least one statement that took the prosecution by surprise. Given the dimensions of the guest room, Prosecutor William Moody asked, was it possible for Lizzie Borden to go up the front stairs and pass the guest room that contained Abby Borden's mutilated body and not see it, especially if Abby was lying in plain sight?

Kieran stated that he had tested for that very situation by placing an assistant on the same spot and in the same position where Abby had fallen. Kieran then walked up the stairs. He noted that he could not see his assistant even when he knew where he was in the room.

That meant, as defense attorney Andrew Jennings later pointed out, that Lizzie could have traveled up and down the stairs without realizing Abby was dead in the guest room, just as she had stated at her inquest. There was only a single angle where one could see a body between the bed and the north wall from the stairs. Only by stopping on the stairs where one's line of sight was level with the guestroom floor could one see a body from outside of the room. In the hallway and from Lizzie's bedroom, Kieran concluded, nothing could be observed.

In general, and especially because Kieran was a witness for the prosecution, Kieran's testimony helped Lizzie. He said that she could have travelled up and down the stairs that day and not noticed Abby's body, especially if she were not looking for it. Kieran had also stated, as mentioned above, that it was possible for a murderer to remain hidden in the first floor closet undetected while awaiting Andrew Borden's return.

Thomas Kieran was born to Owen and Ann Kieran and became a civil engineer. He lived in Fall River between 1884 and 1899. He then moved to New York City, where he was last recorded as residing in 1917.

Kilroy, Frank H. (1872-1912)

Frank H. Kilroy was in D.R. Smith's drug store and claimed to have observed Lizzie Borden's attempt to purchase prussic acid there on Wednesday, August 3, 1892, the day before the murders. His name was on a handwritten list of witnesses composed by prosecutor Hosea M. Knowlton. Kilroy testified at the preliminary hearing but was not allowed to take the stand at the final trial because the court ruled that all statements related to prussic acid were inadmissible as evidence (see Eli Bence).

Kilroy was a medical student and a customer in Smith's drug store. When Lizzie entered the establishment, Kilroy was talking to drug clerk Eli Bence. Kilroy claimed that he knew Lizzie by sight and heard her ask for the prussic acid. He also remembered Bence denying her request. Another drug clerk at Smith's store, Frederick B. Hart, also observed the incident.

Frank Kilroy was born in Fall River to John and Julia (Morrow) Kilroy. A medical student at Harvard in 1892, he moved to Boston in 1897 and returned to his hometown two years later. He was employed as a drug clerk and died in Fall River in 1912.

King, George F.

George King, of Easton, Massachusetts, was called to New Bedford for jury duty at the Borden trial. He stated on the stand that he could not find the defendant guilty under any circumstances and was excused.

King, Martin L.

Martin King, a resident of North Attleboro, Massachusetts, was part of the grand jury that found cause to put Lizzie Borden on trial for the murders of her father and stepmother.

King, Philip

Philip King was a hack driver. He drove the three presiding justices in the Borden trial, Albert Mason, Caleb Blodgett and Justin Dewey, along with Sheriff Andrew R. Wright, to the courthouse in New Bedford for the opening day of the trial, June 5, 1893.

King, Thomas

Thomas King was a friend of Fall River police officer William Medley. The *Fall River City Directory* for 1892 listed two Thomas Kings.

Medley's friend was either a weaver or a lamplighter. On August 4, the day of the Borden killings, the policeman accompanied King to the North Police Station in Fall River. Medley mentioned King during his trial testimony to pinpoint the time he first heard about the murders. Medley said he was walking home from the North Police Station and had gone about fifty yards when a janitor at the station called to him at 11:25 A.M. and said that there was a telephone call. Medley then went directly from the North Police Station to City Marshal Hilliard's office, where he was ordered to go to 92 Second Street.

Kingsley, Mrs. Horace A.

Mrs. Horace A. Kingsley confirmed to Fall River authorities that John Vinnicum Morse was visiting his niece on Pine Street at the time the Bordens were murdered and could not have been the killer. She lived at 82 Pine Street on the first floor of the building where the Emerys, who Morse had gone to visit, also lived. Kingsley said she saw Morse come to the house in the late morning of August 4, 1892. Although not exactly certain of the time, she was sure it was after 11:00 A.M. because she was preparing her dinner when she saw Morse.

Kirby, Albert C.

A.C. Kirby was a deputy sheriff in Taunton. On Saturday, June 10, 1893 Kirby, along with deputies John W. Nickerson and George H. Arnold took the jury members for a ride as a relief from being in the jury room or the Parker House, the local hotel where they were put up for the duration of the trial. According to an article in the *New Bedford Evening Standard* of June 12, 1893, Kirby drove the jury around the Point Road and planned to take them to a religious service presided over by the Reverend M.C. Julien the next day if the jurors were able to agree that Julien's efforts were acceptable.

Kirby, Aruba P. (Tripp) (1828-1912)

Aruba P. Kirby was a witness for the defense. She said she saw no one attempting to sneak away from the Borden property during the time of the murders. She was on District Attorney Hosea M. Knowlton's handwritten list of witnesses under the heading, "As to not seeing prisoner escape."

Kirby lived with her husband on Third Street next to the Chagnon house. She had an clear view of the Borden back yard from her kitchen. Kirby testified at the trial on June 14 that she was in her kitchen all morning and occasionally peered out of her window, never seeing anyone. Her kitchen window was in the front of her house facing across Third Street towards the Chagnon house and the Borden back yard. A portion of the passageway leading to the Bordens' rear fence could be seen from the Kirby kitchen.

Aruba Kirby, the wife of defense witness Uriah Kirby, was born in Westport, Massachusetts. She arrived in Fall River in 1859 where her husband made his reputation as a skilled liveryman. Kirby died in Fall River at the age of eighty-four.

Kirby, Uriah

Uriah Kirby, a foreman for a local company, saw a stranger asleep on the front porch of Charles N. Gifford's house on Third Street. Kirby was with Gifford at the time. Gifford was the next door neighbor of the Chagnon family. Kirby and Gifford woke the sleeping man and sent him on his way at about 11:00 P.M. on Wednesday, August 3, the night before the murders. The defense used this as proof there were strangers in the area who could have committed the crime.

Kirby was called as a witness to corroborate the testimony of Charles N. Gifford. Some Borden historians believe that the sleeping man was not the murderer, but a local alcoholic known as "Mike the Soldier" (see Michael Graham).

Kirschbaum, William G.

William G. Kirschbaum reported on the Borden trial for the *New Bedford Evening Standard*.

Knight, Charles W.

Charles W. Knight was listed in the *New Bedford City Directory* of 1892 as being the manager of the *New Bedford Evening Journal*. He was called to the courthouse for jury duty in the Borden case. Knight stated that he was against capital punishment and excused.

Knowlton, Hosea Morrill (1847-1902)

Hosea Morrill Knowlton was the district attorney for the Southern District of Massachusetts and as such led the prosecution team at the trial of Lizzie Borden for the murders of her father and stepmother in June 1893. He was assigned the case by Massachusetts Attorney General Albert E. Pillsbury, and four months after the trial he succeeded Pillsbury as Attorney General of Massachusetts.

Knowlton was part of the group that met at the Mellen House, a Fall River hotel, on the Saturday after the murders to decide what action to take in order to calm the public, which had demanded that a suspect be arrested as soon as possible. The decision was to send Mayor

Hosea M. Knowlton c.1892-1895.

John Coughlin and City Marshal Rufus B. Hilliard to the Borden house to offer police protection.

During this gathering at 92 Second Street, Coughlin told Lizzie Borden that she was a suspect in the murders. This had important ramifications for the trial almost a year later. Her incriminating inquest testimony was ruled inadmissible by the justices at the trial because of Coughlin's statement to Lizzie. The other members of the group who met at the Mellen House included Mayor Coughlin, Marshal Hilliard and County Medical Examiner William Dolan.

From the time he was assigned to the Borden case, Knowlton believed he would never be able to obtain a conviction from a jury and was unenthusiastic in his role as prosecutor. He felt, as did many others then and since, that Pillsbury assigned him to the trial because the attorney general knew it could not be won and did not want a defeat in such an important case to blemish his record. Most Borden historians feel, however, that the district attorney did a credible job and performed to the best of his ability in spite of the odds against him.

Knowlton personally questioned the witnesses at the preliminary hearing, held between August 25 and September 1, 1892. During this hearing, the district attorney read Lizzie's inquest testimony to presiding Judge Josiah C. Blaisdell from Annie White's stenographic notes taken earlier that month. These statements represent the only formal remarks Lizzie ever made concerning the murders.

The district attorney also presented the evidence to the grand jury, which met between November 7 and 21. Knowlton, in a highly unusual move, invited defense counsel Andrew Jennings to present his case before the same grand jury. Jennings refused. On December 2, 1892, the grand jury returned three indictments against Lizzie Borden: one for the murder of Andrew, one for the murder of Abby, and a third for the murder of both. Although Attorney General Pillsbury was expected to prosecute her, he assigned that task to Knowlton after the grand jury decision. He also ordered Knowlton to bring Essex County district attorney William H. Moody — a particularly competent lawyer and friend of future president of the United States Theodore Roosevelt — on board the prosecution team.

At times during the trial, Knowlton seemed lackluster and resigned that the outcome would not be in his favor. He admitted in court that he himself had never seen the handleless hatchet. When the justices ruled that all evidence pertaining to the purchase of prussic acid was inadmissible, he took everyone by surprise by ending the argument for the prosecution. Many believed his closing argument was weak and that he did not explain the case against Lizzie Borden as well as William Moody had presented it to the jury in his opening statement.

Prior to Emma Borden's appearance on the witness stand, Moody conducted most of the prosecution. With Emma on the stand, however, Knowlton assumed a larger role. During the trial he questioned, among others, Thomas Kieran, Bridget Sullivan, Mrs. Caroline Kelly and Dr. Edward S. Wood. He also cross-examined Charles Gardner, Emma Borden and Hyman Lubinsky, the latter harshly and persistently, "almost viciously," in the words of Borden historian Robert Sullivan. He drew out the fact from Emma Borden that she had hired Pinkerton detective O.M. Hanscom. Knowlton also drove her hard on the fight she was said to have had with Lizzie in the Taunton jail cell. He emphasized that Emma's version of the dress burning incident the Sunday after the murders was suspect, and he brought out the story of the anger Lizzie felt towards Andrew and Abby as a result of a gift Andrew made to Abby's sister of the house on Fourth Street (see Jane E.B. (Negus) Gray).

Knowlton bolstered what he thought was a strong case against Lizzie Borden with testimony from Dr. Edward Wood, pharmacist Charles H. Lawton, fur dealer Henry H. Tillson and chemist Nathaniel Hathaway concerning her attempt to buy prussic acid. He also planned to call as a prosecution witness druggist Eli Bence, the clerk who refused to sell the acid to Lizzie. When the court ruled against the admission of this evidence on June 15, 1893, Knowlton rested his case.

In his summary, Knowlton stressed the utter brutality of the crimes and Lizzie's hatred for Abby. He also reminded the jury of several crucial points. Neither the sick friend nor her note to Abby had ever been located. Lizzie and Abby were alone in the house when the latter was killed. It was possible for Lizzie to hide bloodstains on her body and dress. The dress worn on the morning of the murders was not the dress she turned over to the Fall River police. She suspiciously burned a dress in her kitchen stove the Sunday after the killings. The handleless hatchet was freshly broken and coated with ashes to hide the fact it was the murder weapon. Witnesses who were near the front and rear of the Borden property never saw any stranger enter or leave the house during the times the murders occurred. Many writers about the crime consider Knowlton's explanation of this last point the strongest and most convincing part of his summary.

Knowlton was short of stature and stocky. He had about him what Robert Sullivan called "an air of impatience" and impressed contemporaries with his exuberance. He was born in Durham, Maine and moved to New Bedford when he was 19 years old after living in several towns because his father Isaac Case Knowlton had been a travelling minister. He graduated from Tufts University and read law at the New Bedford offices of Edwin L. Barney. He then attended Harvard Law School. After being admitted to the bar in 1870, Knowlton began his own practice in partnership with Barney, which lasted for seven years.

He began public service when appointed registrar of bankruptcy for the First District in Massachusetts, an office he held until it was abolished in 1878. Knowlton was also a member of the New Bedford school committee, 1874–1877, a city solicitor, a representative in the state legislature and a state senator, all between 1877 and 1879. Knowlton was named district attorney for the Southern District of Massachusetts, a position he held until January 1, 1894, when he resigned to become the attorney general for the Commonwealth of Massachusetts. He was re-elected to that office a total of five times.

Knowlton also had numerous business interests. He served on the boards of several companies, including that of the Edison Electric Light Company of New Bedford and the Citizens' National Bank of New Bedford. He was a trustee of Tufts and a member of the Universalist Society. Even though he lost his most famous trial, he was well respected and garnered praise from many in public and private life. Hosea Morrill Knowlton died at his summer home in Marion, Massachusetts.

L

Lamphier, Charles

Charles Lamphier of North Attleboro, Massachusetts, was present as a prospective juror at the Borden trial. He was not questioned and was not picked for the jury.

Lane, Dwight F.

Dwight Lane was summoned to appear at the beginning of the Borden trial as a possible juror. He claimed to be indifferent to the case and although Lizzie Borden approved of Lane as a juror, the prosecution challenged him. He did not sit on the jury.

Lavalle, Fred

Fred Lavalle and Thomas J.L. Brown worked near the Borden home at the Fall River Ice Company, according to an interview given to policeman William H. Medley on September 25, 1892. Neither saw any strangers at the time of the murders (see Thomas Joseph Lee Brown).

Lawton, Charles Henry

Charles Henry Lawton was a pharmacist from New Bedford. He, along with analytical chemist Nathaniel Hathaway and fur dealer Henry Tillson, testified for the prosecution on June 15, 1893 on the danger and uses of prussic acid. After the three gave their statements the court declared all testimony relating to the purchase of prussic acid inadmissible as evidence since neither Abby nor Andrew Borden died as a result of that chemical. Soon after the court's decision the prosecution rested its case.

Lawton had been a resident of New Bedford for forty years by June 1893, according to the *New Bedford Evening Standard*. He had been a druggist for two decades. Lawton testified that prussic acid was available only through a doctor's prescription, clearly implying it was not used as a fur cleaner, as Lizzie had claimed. All other questions directed at Lawton by the prosecution were met with objections by defense attorney George Dextrer Robinson. Robinson's protests were sustained by the court; Lawton was not allowed to answer these questions.

Lawton, Frederick E.

As he was questioned by the lawyers as a possible juror in the Borden trial, Frederick E. Lawton hesitated in giving his answers about opinions he might have formed regarding the murders. He was subsequently excused.

Leach, Harry J.

Harry J. Leach was a carpenter from New Bedford. He stated as a potential juror at the Borden trial that he had no opinion about the guilt or innocence of the defendant but that he was against capital punishment. He was excused and did not serve on the jury.

Learned, William T.

William T. Learned was a respected physician who practiced in Fall River. He was vice president of the Fall River Medical Society in 1890 and president of that organization the following year.

Learned was present at the first autopsies of Abby and Andrew Borden They took place at 3:00 P.M. the day of the murders on the dining room table at 92 Second Street. With him were Doctors William A. Dolan the leader of the autopsy team, Fall River mayor William

Coughlin, Albert C. Dedrick, John H. Leary, Thomas Gunning, Emmanuel C. Dutra, Anson C. Peckham, Seabury W. Bowen and J.Q.A. Tourtellot.

Learned's statement at the preliminary hearing had to do with his detailed description of Abby's body before it was taken to the dining room for the autopsy. He included in his testimony the observation that in death, her arms were on her body rather than over her head. This showed that Abby was probably taken by surprise and had no time to defend herself with her arms before being struck by the murder weapon.

Leary, John Hurley (1863-1901)

Dr. John Hurley Leary was a member of the first autopsy team (see William T. Learned above). Leary was born in Fall River to Jeremiah and Julia (Hurley) Leary. After receiving his education in the Fall River public school system, he attended Holy Cross College in Worcester, Massachusetts, and earned a B.A. from Boston College. He then attended Harvard Medical School and received a Doctor of Medicine degree from Bellevue Medical College in New York City.

He practiced medicine in Newport, Rhode Island, before returning to Fall River in 1888. There Leary was appointed city physician, a position he held for several years and in which capacity he served as a witness at the first Borden autopsy. He died a patient at Butler Hospital in Providence, Rhode Island.

Leary, Kate

Kate Leary was summoned to New Bedford as a witness but was not called upon to testify. Her name appears on District Attorney Hosea M. Knowlton's handwritten list of witnesses as to not seeing strangers in the area during the time the murders occurred.

Leary was possibly the servant girl of Margaret L. (Wallace) Crapo, who was also on Knowlton's list under the same heading. Mrs. Crapo lived at 39 Third Street. She also was not called upon to testify, perhaps because her house was located too far north of the Borden home to convince a jury her observations were relevant.

Leavitt, George K.

George K. Leavitt owned a home in Newmarket, New Hampshire. He sold it on November 9, 1915 to Mary Connor for $2,500. The house became the residence of Mary Connor, her sister Annie and a third woman whose identity was a mystery to the local citizenry when the women moved into the house the following year. The third woman turned out to be Emma Borden, who probably put up the money to purchase the house and preserve her privacy (see Annie Connor and Mary Connor).

Leduc, Peter

Occasionally listed by his French name Pierre, Leduc was Andrew Jackson Borden's barber. In reporting Borden's movements in the hours before he was murdered, the *Fall River Daily Globe* stated that Borden visited Leduc's barber shop that fatal Thursday morning, probably after he left the National Union Bank, and cashier John Thomas Burrill, for his daily shave.

Lee, Abraham (1866-?)

Abraham Lee was a hack driver by profession and worked for the New Bedford firm of Kirby and Hicks. He drove Lizzie Borden and Deputy Sheriff A.C. Kirby to the courthouse on June 5, 1893, the first day of the trial. He apparently did his job well and was hired to drive the defendant to court every day until a verdict was reached.

Leighton, Helen (1867-1950)

Helen Leighton was a librarian and also the founder and president of the Animal Rescue League, an organization that Lizzie supported for much of her life. She was also one of Miss Borden's few close friends towards the end of Lizzie's life. After Borden died, Leighton said that Lizzie was extremely unhappy with the way her life had turned out after the murders, and Leighton questioned the wisdom of Lizzie choosing to remain in Fall River after the trial. Leighton said Lizzie had about a dozen friends who were devoted to her and that Lizzie was never really alone. In her talks about Lizzie Borden, Leighton always portrayed her in a sympathetic light.

Lizzie, unlike her father Andrew, left a will when she died. In it she gave a large amount of cash and valuable stock she owned in the Stevens Manufacturing Company, worth about $30,000 in total, to Leighton's Fall River Animal Rescue League. This was the largest single bequest Lizzie gave. To Helen and Lizzie's cousin Grace Howe, wife of the future presidential adviser Louis Howe, Lizzie gave much of her jewelry, some books, furniture, china and her half of the A.J. Borden Building (Emma owned the other half). Twenty-nine other people also received gifts from Lizzie.

Lemay, Joseph, Jr.

Joseph Lemay was a farmer who lived on Wilson Road in Fall River. He cultivated fifty-six acres in the area known as "Steep Brook." Lemay was prepared to be a witness for the defense and claimed to have seen a man he believed was the true murderer of the Bordens.

Lemay was French-Canadian and did not speak English. He made his statement through Fall River police officer George Gendron, who acted as Lemay's interpreter. Lemay stated that he had talked to a stranger who claimed to know about the murders. He encountered this man about four miles from the Borden home twelve days after the killings took place. Defense lawyer Andrew Jennings said that Lemay told him the stranger had blood on him and carried a hatchet. This testimony would help the defense prove that there were other people in the area who could have committed the crimes.

Prosecutor Hosea M. Knowlton objected to the statements of Lemay on the grounds that his information was not relevant to the murders. The court agreed with Knowlton's objections and Lemay was not al-

Joseph Lemay, the Frenchman.

lowed to testify before the court, although his remarks were written into the official court records.

Lenehan, John

John Lenehan was a Fall River policeman who lived at 221 Second Street, a few blocks south of the Borden residence. He was one of the officers who followed John Vinnicum Morse, at the time one of the suspects in the Borden murders, around town. The other officer was either John J. Devine or John Minnehan (see John J. Devine and John Minnehan).

According to the *Fall River Herald*, Lenehan shadowed Morse by day and Devine followed him at night (The *Fall River Globe* reported that it was Minnehan, rather than Devine, who trailed Morse). Apparently nothing of interest occurred while Lenehan was on duty. He was not mentioned again in connection with the Borden murder case. Newspapers and some Borden authors have spelled his last name "Linnehan," which could indeed be the correct spelling.

Leonard, Augustus B.

Augustus B. Leonard was the clerk of the Second District Court of Bristol County. His jurisdiction included Fall River, Freetown, Somerset and Swansea. Leonard was also a justice of the peace. He was on duty when Lizzie Borden, through her attorney Andrew Jennings, asked that Judge Josiah C. Blaisdell recuse himself from presiding at the preliminary hearing because he had also been the judge at the Borden inquest.

At the preliminary hearing, Judge Blaisdell asked Lizzie what her plea would be. Jennings answered for her, "Not guilty." The judge said Lizzie must answer for herself, and she repeated the plea in a weak and quiet voice. Clerk Leonard, for the record, wanted to make sure he had heard her correctly and so asked her to repeat her plea. Lizzie did, in a steadier and stronger voice.

Augustus Leonard is remembered as a dignified gentleman with a long beard who, as one of his responsibilities, administered to witnesses the oath to swear to tell the truth.

Leonard, Augustus D.

Augustus D. Leonard of Mansfield, Massachusetts, was summoned as a possible juror for the Borden trial. He was not questioned and did not serve on the jury.

Leonard, James

James Leonard was the carriage driver for physician Seabury Bowen, the Borden family's doctor who lived directly across the street from the two murder victims. Leonard told police officer Albert E. Chase on August 24, 1892 that when he arrived at the Bowen house with the doctor, Mrs. Bowen rushed out her front door and told him that "something terrible" had happened at the Borden home. This occurred at 11:05 A.M. according to Leonard.

Leonard, Marcus

Marcus Leonard was a Fall River police officer who along with fellow policeman Philip Harrington travelled to New Bedford, Massachusetts, to search for clues in the Borden murder case. They went into the New Bedford Savings Bank and arrested a Portuguese man who was in the process of withdrawing all the money from his account. They brought the man to the police station in Fall River but soon released him because he gave a "satisfactory account of himself."

Lewis, James A.

James A. Lewis of Fairhaven was a hostler. He was in the New Bedford courtroom as a possible juror in the Borden case. He was not questioned and did not serve on the jury.

Libby, Maurice

Maurice Libby, a hairdresser in Fall River, turned a bloodstained apron over to the police on August 17, 1892, thirteen days after the Bordens were murdered. It yielded no clues to the mystery.

Lincoln, Alcott

Lincoln, a resident of Raynham, Massachusetts, served on the grand jury that heard the evidence against Lizzie Borden in November and December 1892 and decided that she should stand trial for murder.

Lincoln, Harrison T.

Harrison T. Lincoln of Norton, Massachusetts, was a prospective juror in the trial. He was present in the courtroom on June 5, 1893 but was neither questioned nor picked for the jury.

Lincoln, Lloyd S.

Lloyd S. Lincoln was, like Harrison T. Lincoln, from Norton and probably related to him. When questioned for the Borden jury, Lincoln said that he was against capital punishment and had already formed an opinion. Lloyd Lincoln was excused and went home.

Lincoln, (Stephen) Russell

Russell Lincoln was a deputy sheriff in Raynham, Massachusetts. Along with Taunton deputy sheriff A.C. Kirby and Mansfield Deputy Sheriff Alson W. Cobb, he was in charge of the west door of the New Bedford courthouse. His duty was to admit into the courthouse only those who had official business with the court on June 5, 1893. With such a large number of potential jurors waiting to be formally questioned, there was hardly room for anyone else.

Lindsey, Mrs. William

Mrs. Lindsey was the wife of the president of Globe Yarn Mills, a firm in which Andrew Borden had an economic interest. She was also called a "close" friend of Lizzie Borden by the *Fall River Herald* and made statements to the press that in her opinion, Lizzie was innocent of the murders of her father and stepmother. She was quoted in the *Herald* at the time of the preliminary hearing, which took place August 25–September 1, 1892.

Linnehan, John

See Lenehan, John.

Lipman, Max de

Max de Lipman was a sketch artist from New York who gained admittance to the trial as a spectator on June 13, 1893. He was forcefully removed from the courtroom that day on orders from Bristol County Sheriff Andrew Robeson Wright. Lipman later told the *New Bedford Evening Standard* that he was considering legal action against the sheriff for assault. Nothing more came of the incident; de Lipman probably thought the better of a formal charge and hearing.

Livermore, Mary Ashton Rice (1820-1905)

Mary A. Livermore and was a popular author of books and magazine articles. She was also a close friend of Sarah Borden, the first wife of Andrew and the mother of Lizzie. Mary Livermore received permission to interview Lizzie as she awaited trial in the Taunton jail after her preliminary hearing. She reported that Lizzie was feeling well and was not at all depressed. Livermore gave the details of her interview to fellow writer Amy Robsart, who wrote the story for newspaper publication.

Mary A. Livermore was born to Timothy and Zebiah Vose Glover (Ashton) Rice in Boston and was educated first in New York and then

Mrs. Livermore consoles Lizzie after adjournment of the court.

at Miss Martha Whiting's Female Seminary in Charlestown, Massachusetts. She graduated from Miss Whiting's in 1836 and taught there for two years. She then relocated to Virginia where she was employed as a tutor.

She was repulsed by the southern institution of slavery and soon moved back up north to Duxbury, Massachusetts, and married David Parker Livermore, a minister, in 1845. She traveled with her husband to various Universalist churches in New England, including Fall River. She later relocated to Chicago and became a noted writer and lecturer during the Civil War, speaking out against slavery and for women's suffrage.

Livermore returned to Boston in 1869 as editor of the magazine *Women's Journal*. She also authored a popular book on the Civil War in 1888. Readers purchased 60,000 copies of her autobiography, published in 1897, making it a best seller. Livermore retired from the lecture circuit in 1895 and died in Melrose, Massachusetts, at the age of eighty-five.

Loomis, W.H.

W.H. Loomis was a staff artist for the *Providence Journal*. He sketched the highlights of the trial for the *Journal* while reporter John J. Rosenfeld wrote the stories.

Lorrigan, Patrick F.

Patrick F. Lorrigan was summoned to testify at the Borden trial but was not called to the stand. No other information can be found concerning Lorrigan, and no one knows what his testimony would have covered.

Loud, Hulda B.

Ms. Loud, editor of the *Rockland* (Massachusetts) *Independent,* covered the Borden trial for her newspaper. She was one of the few female reporters present at the New Bedford courthouse.

Lovell, Henry S.

New Bedford resident Henry S. Lovell was on the grand jury that found Lizzie Borden "probably guilty" and therefore fit to stand trial for the murders of Andrew and Abby Borden.

Lubinsky, Hyman (1874-1923)

Hyman Lubinsky, a Russian immigrant, drove an ice cream wagon in Fall River. He testified that he saw a woman leave the Borden barn and enter the house by the side, or north, door. He also stated that he knew the Borden maid Bridget Sullivan and the woman he saw was not Bridget.

Lubinsky picked up his horse and wagon at Gardner's livery stable on the south end of Second Street, far from the Borden home, a few minutes past 11:00 A.M. on the day of the murders. He said at the trial that he left Gardner's between 11:05 and 11:10 A.M. and passed 92 Second Street at a trot minutes later. As he was passing the Borden residence, he saw a female figure leave the barn and enter the house by

Hyman Lubinsky

the side door. He actually said she went to the back of the house, but that entrance led only to the basement.

The ice cream vendor stated that the woman he saw was wearing a dark dress. He looked at the woman when she was only a few feet from the kitchen entrance, but was still confident enough to say that he was sure the woman was not Bridget. His testimony confirmed Lizzie Borden's inquest statement that she was in the barn at the time the murder of her father took place. However, it is possible that the woman he saw near the Borden barn was neither Lizzie nor Bridget but a thirty-five year-old passer-by, Mrs. Ellen T. Eagan (see Ellen T. Eagan).

Lubinsky also claimed he had told this very story to Fall River policeman Michael Mullaly on August 6, two days after the murders, but Mullaly apparently ignored him. Defense lawyers Andrew J. Jennings and Arthur S. Phillips sought Lubinsky out and had him testify.

He was cross-examined by Hosea Knowlton, who treated him roughly. The ice cream peddler spoke Yiddish and Russian well but apparently understood little English. Possibly in order to discredit him, Knowlton showed no patience with Lubinsky's difficulty in understanding English and spoke quite rapidly. Lubinsky, in a fit of frustration on the stand, at one point begged Knowlton, "Please. I don't know what you say. You go too fast." A reporter for the *New York Sun* wrote of the cross-examination, "Never did a lawyer try harder to confuse a witness...He walked up and down between the witness and his desk, prodding him with rapid questions. He was nervous, agitated and scolding in his tone." Yet Lubinsky stood by his statements.

When Officer Michael Mullaly took the stand he was asked about his conversation with Lubinsky. Mullaly stated that he wrote down the peddler's story exactly as he told it and that, according to his notes, Lubinsky claimed he saw the woman at 10:30 A.M. However, Andrew Borden did not arrive home for another ten minutes. Although Mullaly's account seemed to weaken Lubinsky's testimony somewhat, defense lawyer George Dexter Robinson still used it in his summation to bolster the defense argument that Lizzie was telling the truth about her visit to the barn.

Writer Victoria Lincoln had another explanation for the sighting of the woman near the barn. In *A Private Disgrace*, Lincoln theorized that

Lizzie did go to the barn after killing Andrew to hide the hatchet and wash herself. When she tried to sneak out of the barn she saw that she had been spotted by Lubinsky in his wagon and had to say she was in the loft. Lincoln noted that besides tools and axes, the barn had running water.

Hyman Lubinsky was born in Russia to Jacob and Bessie (Sinderhoff) Lubinsky. By 1892 he was living in Fall River and employed by Charles A. and Agnes Wilkerson, Confectioners, with their store located at 42 N. Main Street. He was a packer in Fall River at the time of his death.

Lynch, George

George Lynch was a prospective juror for the Borden trial. He was from Somerset, Massachusetts, and said during questioning that he was prejudiced. Lynch was then excused from jury duty.

M

MacKenzie John M.

John M. MacKenzie was a physician who practiced in Fall River at the time of the Borden murders. He was mentioned briefly in an article that appeared in the *Fall River Daily Herald* on August 8, 1892 as being present at a meeting at the Mellen House, a Fall River hotel. Also present were Massachusetts Attorney General Albert E. Pillsbury, District Attorney Hosea M. Knowlton, Dr. William A. Dolan and Dr. Edward S. Wood. There was no mention of why MacKenzie was at the meeting. MacKenzie became president of the Fall River Medical Society in 1896.

Macomber, Henry B.

Henry B. Macomber, a clerk from Taunton, was summoned to jury duty in the Borden trial. He was not questioned and did not serve on the jury.

Macomber, Leonard K.

Leonard K. Macomber of Dartmouth, Massachusetts, served on the grand jury that indicted Lizzie Borden for murder on December 2, 1892.

Macomber, Mary C.

Mary C. Macomber of Westport, Massachusetts, was listed as a potential witness on District Attorney Hosea M. Knowlton's handwritten list. She was near 92 Second Street on the morning of the Borden murders. She was standing near Louis Hall's livery stables and saw Adelaide Churchill on Second Street following the discovery of Andrew Borden's hacked body. Macomber was not called to testify at the trial.

Macrae, Annie Campbell (c.1871-?)

Annie Macrae was Lizzie Borden's physician during her last years. She publically announced the death of Miss Borden on June 2, 1927, the day after she passed away.

"Maggie"

"Maggie" was the name sometimes used to refer to Bridget Sullivan, the Bordens' maid. Since many maids in Fall River were Irish, it was common to call them "Maggie." Also, the Bordens had a maid whose name actually was Maggie before Bridget Sullivan came to work for them.

Maguire, Edwin J.

Boston Sunday Post reporter Edwin J. Maguire attempted to interview Lizzie Borden at Maplecroft in 1913. He approached the house on French Street and knocked on the door. When no one answered, he left the house and called Lizzie on the telephone. When Maguire requested an interview, Lizzie told him that there was nothing to say and when Maguire persisted, she hung up on the reporter.

The enterprising Maguire then learned that Lizzie's sister Emma was residing with Alice Lydia Buck, the daughter of the late Rev. Edwin A. Buck, a supporter of Lizzie during her ordeal. Rev. Buck had died in 1903. The Buck's home on Rock Street bordered the Central Congregational Church. Emma happened to be at home when Maguire called and consented to an interview. This was the first public statement either sister had made about the murders since Lizzie's acquittal in June 1893. Emma told Maguire that her sister felt Rev. Buck was her best friend. It was Buck, Emma said, who advised her to move out of Maplecroft when life with Lizzie became unbearable for her. Emma refused to tell Maguire why she felt living there was so difficult, but said Lizzie agreed to pay Emma rent for her half of the house.

Emma told the reporter that the net worth of Andrew's estate was approximately $250,000, less than most people believed the value of the sisters' inheritance to be, although still a fortune by 1892 standards. By the time both sisters died in 1927, the estate was valued at close to half a million dollars.

In answer to a question posed by Maguire, Emma said she always believed that Lizzie did not commit the crime and believed that still. When asked how her faith in Lizzie survived so many years and conflicts at Maplecroft, Emma stated that Lizzie always maintained her innocence to Emma and that no murder weapon was ever found. She also insisted that there was no hiding place in the house that the police could have overlooked if the weapon had been hidden there. Emma also recalled that she had promised their late mother Sarah that she would always care for her younger sister, and she did.

Mahaney, Peter

Peter Mahaney was named in the *Boston Globe*'s sensational article of October 10, 1892 known ever after as the "Trickey-McHenry Affair" (see Edwin D. McHenry and Henry G. Trickey). Mahaney was one of the potential witnesses against Lizzie Borden named in that article.

He reportedly lived at 103 Pleasant Street in Fall River and was employed as a timekeeper at the Troy Mill in that city. Mahaney supposedly was standing in front of the Borden home with a Mrs. Gustave Ronald at about 9:30 A.M. on the morning the Bordens were killed. He just happened to look up at the guest room window of 92 Second Street after hearing what the *Globe* described as "a terrible cry or groan." He saw someone framed in the open guest room window wearing a rubber hood over his or her head. Since no outsider was in the house at the time, according to statements made by Lizzie and Bridget Sullivan, it could only have been Lizzie herself.

Most likely, neither Mrs. Ronald nor Peter Mahaney really existed and fictitious statements were part of the hoax which helped turn public sympathy towards Lizzie and caused the *Globe* to issue an embarrassing retraction and apology in its next day's edition.

Maher, John Joseph

John Maher was known around Fall River as a drunk. He was a supposed witness to the murders of the Bordens and said that for a reward he could name the culprit.

Maher told the Fall River police on August 5, the day after the Bordens died, that he was drunk on the New Boston Road on the afternoon of the crimes and could locate the murderer within fifteen minutes. He said that a small boy saw a man with a dark moustache leave the Borden residence at about the time of the killings and go in a northerly direction towards Pleasant Street.

Instead of receiving a reward Maher was arrested for public drunkenness, mainly because he seemed to know a lot about the murders and was therefore a possible suspect. He was quickly released when the police realized he knew nothing more about the killings and was never again considered a witness or a suspect.

Mahoney, Benjamin F.

Benjamin F. Mahoney was a Fall River policeman who testified for the prosecution on the sixth day of Lizzie Borden's trial, June 10, 1893. His most important statements concerned the dress Lizzie said she had been wearing on the morning of the murders.

Mahoney said that he arrived at the Borden home with Officer Francis L. Edson at about 3:45 P.M. on Thursday, August 4, 1892, the day the Bordens died. He said he tried to enter the house but could not.

Mahoney also testified that he took a dress belonging to Lizzie from Dr. Edward S. Wood, a chemist at Harvard, on May 30, 1893 under instructions from District Attorney Hosea M. Knowlton. He described the blue dress and then said he returned the dress to Wood. In the time

Officer Mahoney.

he had it in his possession, Mahoney said, no one else had access to the dress and it never left his sight.

Mahr, Henry

Henry Mahr, who also went under the alias of John Wood, was an early suspect in the Borden killings. He had lived in Fall River in 1890 and boarded at the home of Mrs. Ella Cross at 17 John Street. He worked for three months in 1890 at Marshall's hat factory.

Mahr left Fall River for New York City to visit a brother who was a theatrical agent. From New York, he wrote to friends informing them of his plans to sail for London, England. Mrs. Cross claimed that she had letters and telegrams from Mahr in England, proving he was not in Fall River when the Bordens were murdered.

Maier, John A.

John A. Maier was a professional safe operator in Boston. He travelled to Fall River on August 12, 1892 to open Andrew Jackson Borden's combination safe at 92 Second Street. He opened the safe at about 11:00 A.M. after working at the task for eight hours. In the safe was a large amount of cash and some papers. No clues or leads as to who killed the Bordens were discovered in Andrew's safe.

Manchester, Bertha M. (1871-1893)

Bertha Manchester was the victim in a murder chillingly similar to the hacking deaths of Andrew and Abby Borden almost ten months earlier. She was found dead behind the stove in the kitchen of her Fall River farmhouse on May 31, 1893. Lizzie Borden was in the jail at Taunton at the time awaiting her trial for the murders of her father and stepmother and therefore could not have killed the Manchester woman.

No one today can gauge the effect the Manchester killing may have had on potential jurors. Most of them had probably heard about the murder since it occurred before the selection of the jury. However, the sequestered jurors did not know that while the trial was going on a suspect later convicted of the crimes had been arrested.

Bertha Manchester was the daughter of Stephen "Old Steve" Manchester. He was highly unpopular in Fall River and most of its citizens knew him as mean, cruel and possessed of such a repulsive personality that two wives had deserted him. He was also said to be hard and unsympathetic to the hired help, most of whom were farm laborers. His daughter Bertha managed the farm and was, according to local gossip, as muscular as a man and as flinty as her father.

The parallels to the Borden killings made many believe that a crazed murderer was still on the loose in the Fall River area. Both Bertha and the Bordens were hacked to death with a hatchet. The time of both crimes was in the morning and all victims died from head trauma. All of Fall River, and, indeed, those who were following the Borden case all over the world, heard about the Manchester slaying.

The Fall River police eventually arrested an ex-laborer who had recently been fired by "Old Steve," Manuel José Correira, who had come to the United States from the Azores Islands eight months prior to the Manchester killing. He was, therefore, not in the country when Andrew and Abby died. The Borden jury, however, did not learn of Correira's arrest until after Lizzie was acquitted (see Manuel José Correira and Stephen Manchester).

Manchester, George

George Manchester, a mason in Newton, Rhode Island, told his brother Gideon in Fall River that he had been hired to transport a strange man to Newport, Massachusetts, and that this man had knowledge of the Borden killings. Manchester's description of the stranger was similar to that of Dr. Benjaman Handy's "wild-eyed man" (see Dr. Benjamin Handy). Neither stranger was ever found.

George Manchester told Gideon that he drove the man from Fall River at about noon on August 4, 1892, the day of the murders. He described the strange man as being 5'4" tall with a pale, almost white complexion, dark hair, dark eyes, a moustache and dark clothing. This story appeared in the August 13, 1892 edition of the *New Bedford Evening Standard*. Some saw Manchester's statement as proof that strangers who could have committed the murders abounded in Fall River on the day of the crime.

Manchester, Gideon

Gideon Manchester, the drawmaster at the Stone Bridge, said he saw a stranger on the day of the Borden murders like the fellow Dr. Benjamin Handy described. Manchester stated that his brother George was hired to drive the weirdly acting man to Newport, Massachusetts and that the stranger told George of the murders. This claim appeared in the same *New Bedford Evening Standard* article as the statement of George Manchester (see George Manchester).

Manchester, John Henry

There was a rumor that brothers Gideon and George Manchester were involved in an incident concerning transporting a stranger out of the Fall River area shortly after the Bordens were murdered. Gideon Manchester said that he knew nothing about it and that his brother

George had been dead for the past four years. S.R. Paquin said that the driver was neither of the Manchester brothers, but was instead John Henry Manchester of Porthsmouth, Rhode Island. Nothing from this story resulted in leads useful in the Borden case (see S.R. Paquin, George Manchester, Gideon Manchester and George H. Kelly).

Manchester, Stephen C.

Stephen Manchester was the father of murder victim Bertha Manchester, the unfortunate target of a hatchet-wielding killer on May 31, 1893. In his youth, Manchester was a mate on the whaling ships *Caravan* and *Polar Star*. He eventually settled on a farm in the Fall River area.

Manchester, known as "Old Steve" to most, had the reputation as a hard and cruel man, a miser who had two wives leave him over the years. He also treated his hired farm laborers poorly. One of those was Manuel José Correira, an immigrant from the Azores who was fired by "Old Steve" without getting his final pay. Correira returned to the farm house on May 31 intending to get his money from Manchester, but the owner of the farm was out delivering milk. Steve's daughter Bertha, who helped her father run the farm, was at home. Correira, frustrated at missing Steve, fought with twenty-two year-old Bertha and after a furious struggle with the work-hardened farm girl, killed her (see Bertha Manchester and Manuel José Correira).

Manley, Delia Summers (Manchester) (1850-1919)

Delia S. Manley testified at both the preliminary hearing and the Borden trial. She lived at 206 Second Street, about two blocks south of the Borden home, and said she and her sister-in-law Sarah B. Hart saw a strange man by the Bordens' north front gate the day of the murders.

Manley, walking up Second Street with Hart to catch a street car on Main Street, stopped on the sidewalk by the Borden house to have a word with Hart's nephew Ezra P.B. Manley who was riding on the street in a carriage. Manley and Hart noticed an elderly man whom she did not recognize leaning on the Borden's front gate. At the trial Manley could not remember what the man looked like or how he was dressed. She was sure the man was not Andrew Borden, whom she knew by sight.

Delia S. Manley was born in Tiverton, Rhode Island to William and Rhoda Manchester. She married Seabury T. Manley in 1869. She was the sister-in-law of Sarah B. Hart, the aunt by marriage to Alice Manley Russell and the sister-in-law of Alice Russell's mother (see Alice M. Russell).

Manley was a Christian Scientist who took instruction from Mary Baker Eddy, the founder of that religious movement. She began to teach Christian Science in Fall River in 1883 after graduating from the Massachusetts Metaphysical College in Boston.

Delia Manley became a widow in 1904 but continued to reside in Fall River until 1919 when she relocated to Warwick, Rhode Island. She died there at the home of her daughter at the age of sixty-nine.

Manley, Ezra P.B.

Ezra Manley was the nephew of Sarah B. Hart. It was he who was riding down Second Street near the Borden house on the morning of the murders and stopped to talk with his Aunt Sarah and Delia S. Manley and show them some water lilies he had in his carriage. While conversing, the two women noticed a stranger lounging at the front gate post of the Borden house (see Sarah B. Hart and Delia S. Manley). It is this carriage that Borden author Frank Spiering may have been describing in his book *Lizzie* when he wrote that Emma Borden had driven into Fall River from Fairhaven, killed her father and stepmother and raced back to Fairhaven. His proof was accounts of a carriage near the Borden house at the time of the murders.

Manning, John J.

John J. Manning was a reporter for the Associated Press. He testified at the Borden trial as to his movements around the property, house and barn of 92 Second Street on the day of the Borden murders.

Manning arrived at the Borden residence at 11:25 A.M., before Officer William Medley got there. Charles Sawyer, the painter whom Officer George A. Allen assigned to guard the side door, did not allow Manning in the house but he gained entrance when invited in by policeman Patrick Doherty.

Manning was in the house for about ten minutes. He saw Alice Russell and Adelaide Churchill fanning Lizzie Borden in the kitchen and then viewed the bodies of Andrew and Abby Borden. At the trial, Manning remembered being surprised that there was not more blood on the victims.

He then left the house and inspected the Borden yard seeking clues. He walked along the south border of the property where it abutted the Kelly house along the flower garden. He followed along the Kelly fence and saw a pile of lumber near the rear of the Borden property.

Manning proceeded along the property line to the barn and saw two or three people there. He recognized Alfred Clarkson but did not see Thomas Barlow or Everett Brown, the two boys who claimed they made footprints in the loft before Medley inspected it and said he saw no disturbances in the dust (see Thomas Barlow and Everett Brown).

After he left the barn Manning saw another reporter, Walter Stevens of the *Fall River Daily News*. Manning testified at the trial that he and Stevens went to the cellar door to see if there were footprints leading out from the cellar into the yard. They saw no footprints and when Stevens attempted to open the cellar door he found it locked from the inside. The defense, in calling Manning to the stand, wanted to demonstrate to the jury that a lot of people were milling about the Borden property after the murders and could have destroyed evidence of the real killer by wandering over the property and obliterating footprints and other clues in the barn and in the yard.

Manning was also questioned about the story in the *Fall River Daily Globe* that concerned an argument between Lizzie Borden and her sister Emma while Lizzie was in a Taunton jail cell awaiting trial. Mrs. Hannah Reagan, the jail matron, stated that she witnessed the argument and described the details. If true, this event would have put Lizzie in an extremely poor light (see Hannah Reagan). Manning testified that he knew of the *Globe* story and had asked Reagan whether or not the tale was true. Manning said that Reagan answered, "There was nothing to it." In cross-examination by Knowlton however, Manning admitted that Reagan might have answered that all she knew of the incident she would tell at the trial.

Marshall, Mrs. John

Mrs. John Marshall lived in Pawtucket, Rhode Island. She claimed that she was in Fall River on the day of the murders and while driving down Second Street saw what appeared to be a messy man come out of the front door of the Borden home. She also saw something on Third Street.

Marshall made this statement for the first time on September 3, 1892. When asked why she waited so long to come forward, Mrs. Marshall replied that she hated the idea of testifying at trial, but since events had progressed as far as they had (the preliminary hearing had recently ended), she decided to tell her son to inform Borden lawyer Andrew Jennings that she would be available to testify.

City Marshall Rufus B. Hilliard sent Officer William Medley to Pawtucket to interview Mrs. Marshall, but he was turned away at her door by her husband John. Mrs. Marshall was never called to testify at the Borden trial (see Mrs. Robert Marshall).

Marshall, Mrs. Robert

Mrs. Robert Marshall was interviewed at a Fall River hotel, the Mellen House, by police officer William H. Medley and Assistant City Marshall John Fleet on September 8, 1892. She was in the company of Mrs. John Marshall, her mother-in-law. Mrs. Robert Marshall disagreed with the statement Mrs. John Marshall made to the effect that a man parked his horse and buggy on Third Street near the rear of the Borden homestead by the Chagnon residence at the time the murders took place (see Mrs. John Marshall and M. Marthe Chagnon).

Martel, Hypolyte

Hypolyte Martel was a clerk in the drug store of Philias Martel on Pleasant Street in Fall River. Since he and Philias both boarded at 26 Flint Street, they were most likely related and probably brothers.

Hypolyte Martel said that on Monday, August 1, 1892 he was approached at work by a woman who wanted to purchase prussic acid. Philias Martel was out of the store at the time and Hypolyte told the woman he could not sell the prussic acid to her. The woman left the store but returned about twenty minutes later. He once again refused her because Philias had not yet come back. Hypolyte described the woman as about twenty-six years old and weighing around 150 pounds. He stated to the police that he did not recognize her when she entered the store and did not know her. He was not asked to testify at the trial.

Martel, Philias

Philias Martel was a druggist at the drug store on Pleasant Street where Hypolyte Martel, probably his brother, was a clerk. Lizzie possibly attempted to buy prussic acid there on Monday, August 1, three days before the Bordens were murdered (see Hypolyte Martel).

Martin, Edward H.

Edward H. Martin reported on the happenings at the Borden trial for the *New Bedford Evening Standard*.

Martin, William R.

William R. Martin testified before the grand jury on November 17, 1892. He was summoned to appear at the trial in New Bedford by the prosecution but was not called as a witness. Martin claimed that Lizzie had entered his drug store in New Bedford and tried to purchase prussic acid (see Edward E. Wright).

William Martin was first listed as being a resident of Fall River in the 1891 *City Directory*. He was employed as a clerk for William A. Bennett, a pharmacist on N. Main Street. Martin moved to New Bedford in 1892 and worked there as a clerk for Charles H. Church until 1894.

Mason, Albert C. (1836-1905)

Albert C. Mason was the chief justice of the superior court of Massachusetts. As such, he was the most important sitting judge at the trial of Lizzie Borden. Being the chief justice, he was empowered to choose the three-judge panel that would preside at the murder trial. He selected Associate Justice Justin Dewey, Associate Justice Caleb Blodgett and for the third judge, he chose himself.

The most important decisions during the trial involved the admissibility of evidence. These decisions probably marked the turning points of the case. In the name of the court, Mason disallowed evidence in several instances that were crucial to the prosecution's argument against the defendant.

Albert Mason, c.1890.

On June 8, 1893 the prosecution recalled Bridget Sullivan, the Borden maid, to the stand and began asking her about a robbery in the Borden house about a year before the murders. She was also asked about a break-in at the barn on the property four months before the Bordens died. The prosecution wanted to introduce to the jury the idea that Lizzie had planned both events as reprisals against Abby. Mason, in the name of the court, said that the incidents had happened too far in the past to be relevant to the murders of the victims.

In possibly the most important evidentiary ruling of the court, on June 12 Justice Mason announced that, due to legal technicalities, the statements Lizzie Borden made at the inquest could not be used against her at the trial (see John William Coughlin). The contradictory statements Lizzie made at the inquest would have greatly embarrassed her and quite possibly could have convinced the jury of her guilt.

Anna H. Borden was called to the stand to describe a trip to Europe she took with her cousin Lizzie in 1890. On the voyage home Lizzie confided to Anna how much she disliked her stepmother Abby (see Anna H. Borden). The court on June 14 said that discussion happened too far in the past to have importance in the murders, even though the prosecution wanted to show a pattern of hatred by Lizzie for Abby that went back at least several years.

The next day, June 15, the court ruled inadmissible the testimony of Mark P. Chase and that of Joseph Lemay the day after. These decisions were minor blows to the defense, which wanted to prove strangers had been near the Borden property at the time of the murders. They were two insignificant setbacks compared to what the prosecution had suffered earlier that day (see Mark P. Chase and Joseph Lemay).

The prosecution wanted to link Lizzie Borden with an attempt to buy prussic acid the day before the murders. District Attorney Hosea M. Knowlton was prepared to present to the jury Eli Bence, the druggist who planned to testify that Lizzie had tried to purchase the poison the day before the murders. He also planned to put on the stand others who saw Lizzie in the store and experts on prussic acid to testify it had no use whatsoever as a household chemical. The court, with Justice Mason announcing, said that since the Bordens were not killed by acid poisoning the evidence was inadmissible. The prosecution was so upset at the ruling that it ended its case at that point.

Contemporary legal experts and modern students of the trial have criticized most of these decisions. The rulings were almost always to the advantage of the defense and many said then — and agree now — that they severely weakened the case of the prosecution. No one will ever know whether or not Lizzie would have been found guilty had the excluded testimony been allowed. The procedural peculiarities add much to the fascination so many people today hold for the Borden murder case.

Justice Mason was portly and of medium height. He had a beard and thinning white hair at the time of the trial. In 1857 he married Lydia F. Whiting of Plymouth, Massachusetts and had three daughters who were approximately the age of Lizzie Borden. He served on a select judiciary committee of the Massachusetts legislature during his term in the state's House of Representatives. Also serving on the committee was state senator George Dexter Robinson, who would later become Lizzie Borden's most important attorney.

Albert C. Mason was born in Middleborough, Massachusetts, and, after a public school education, worked for a manufacturing firm in Plymouth, Massachusetts. He then began to study law and was admitted to the bar in 1860. He practiced for two years, then joined the United States Army to fight in the Civil War.

Mason left the Army in 1865, and while working as a lawyer he again became interested in politics. He was elected to the Massachusetts House of Representatives in 1873 and again the next year. He continued to practice the law and opened an office in Boston in 1874 in partnerships with Charles H. Drew, Arthur Lord and Benjamin R. Curtis.

Mason was appointed an associate justice of the superior court in 1882 and chief justice in 1890. He died in Brookline, Massachusetts, at the age of sixty-nine.

Mason, William

Leonard Rebello, in his book *Lizzie Borden Past and Present*, writes that William Mason was Lizzie Borden's personal physician during the last years of her life. David Kent, in *The Lizzie Borden Sourcebook*, reprints a newspaper article that reports the announcement of Lizzie's death was made on June 2, 1927 by Annie Campbell Macrae, whom the article describes as "her physician" (see Annie Campbell Macrae).

Mather, James (1860-1921)

James Mather was a carpenter in Fall River. He testified at the preliminary hearing and at the final trial concerning the downtown movements of Andrew J. Borden on the morning he was killed. He and several others were called to document Borden's travels before Andrew returned home for the last time.

Mather was an assistant to carpenter Joseph Shortsleeves. They saw Andrew Borden downtown between 9:30 A.M. and 10:45 A.M. Borden had just rented a space in the Borden Building to hatmaker Jonathan Clegg, who wanted some renovations done before moving into the store. Borden hired Mather and Shortsleeves to do the repair work.

Mather and Shortsleeves were lowering a front window to meet Clegg's specifications when Borden walked into the store and began talking with Shortsleeves. Mather saw Andrew inspect a broken lock on the floor, put it down to review work being done on the second floor, come back downstairs, pick up the broken lock and leave the store with the lock in his pocket.

James Mather was born in Scotland and immigrated to the United States. He was employed in Fall River as a carpenter and later in the city's textile mills. He died in Fall River at age sixty-one.

Mather, Joseph

Joseph Mather, a Taunton, Massachusetts, policeman, was stationed at the front door of the courthouse in New Bedford on June 13, 1893. He kept a crowd of approximately one hundred persons from entering the building and also kept them orderly.

Matherson, Thomas A.

Thomas Matherson stated to police officers Philip Harrington and Patrick Doherty on August 8, 1892 that he heard Charles Baldwin say he knew who killed the Bordens. Matherson lived at 12 Brownell Street in Fall River. His lead bore an interview with Baldwin, but resulted in no new clues (see Charles Baldwin).

Maude, John

See John Vinnicum Morse, who was called John Maude in at least one early *Fall River Daily Herald* newspaper article.

May, Henry L.

Although it was considered unusual, Henry May covered the Borden trial for two different Boston newspapers, the *Record* and the *Advertiser*. It was rare for a reporter to represent two papers from the same city.

Mayall, Joseph

Joseph Mayall was a Fall River police officer. He, along with officers James Dyson, George Ferguson, Patrick Doherty, and Philip Harrington, was assigned to guard the Borden residence until 1:00 P.M. on the day of the murders. The officers were all relieved by policemen Patrick Doherty, Philip Harrington (who both remained on the scene), John McCarthy, Joseph Hyde, and Michael Reagan.

Mayberry, George L.

George Mayberry was the mayor of Waltham, Massachusetts, at the time of the Borden murders. Andrew Jackson Jennings, Lizzie Borden's lawyer, telegraphed Mayberry to seek his help in locating Samuel Robinsky, who claimed in a letter to Emma Borden to have knowledge of the murders of her father and stepmother. Although Robinsky claimed to live in Waltham, he was never located or heard from again (see Samuel Robinsky, Emma Borden, J. Ryder and Lawrence Cain).

McAdams, Thomas

Fall River policeman Thomas McAdams and fellow officer Fred E. Davis met Lizzie Borden at the entrance of the Central Police Station and escorted her to the room of jail matron Hannah Reagan. At the time, Lizzie was a prisoner at the Taunton jail and was in Fall River for her preliminary hearing, scheduled for August 25. After being arraigned on August 22, Lizzie was returned to Taunton.

McBay, ??

New Bedford policeman McBay, along with fellow officer John Talford blocked a crowd of curious onlookers as Lizzie Borden arrived at the Taunton courthouse after her arraignment in superior court which was sitting in New Bedford on May 8, 1893.

McCaffrey, ??

Mrs. McCaffrey was the wife of Inspector McCaffrey of Fall River. The *Fall River Daily Herald* observed that she resembled Lizzie Borden. Mrs. McCaffrey was in Corneau and Latourneau's drug store on Pleasant Street in Fall River on Monday, August 1, 1892.

Clerk Hypolyte Martel and druggist Philias Martel told a *Herald* reporter that a woman resembling Lizzie Borden entered their store. She did not request prussic acid. It was later established that she was Mrs. McCaffrey rather than Lizzie and that she was on what the *Herald* described as a "crusade against the drug stores." She was, perhaps, the woman some people claimed was Lizzie Borden's double, and therefore did things and went places that Lizzie's accusers believed Miss Borden did or went. There was never any talk, however, that it was Lizzie's double who committed the murders.

McCarthy, John

John McCarthy was a Fall River policeman. He was among the group of officers who relieved policemen James Dyson, George Ferguson and Joseph Mayall, who had been guarding the Borden premises since 11:00 A.M. the day of the murder. The other officers with McCarthy were Patrick Doherty, Joseph Hyde, and Michael Reagan, all of whom remained on guard until 11:00 P.M. that evening.

McCarthy, John F.

John F. McCarthy was a hairdresser from Taunton. He was present for jury selection in the Borden trial but was not questioned or selected. According to the *Taunton City Directory*, McCarthy had expanded his business interests by 1902 and owned a bowling alley.

McDonald, Patrick

Patrick McDonald was a laborer who worked in the stone yard owned by John Crowe. The stone yard was on Third Street, almost directly in back of the Borden home. Prosecution witness Joseph Desrosier said on the stand that McDonald went into the Borden yard the morning of the murders and stole some pears off the trees in the Borden back yard. The prosecution wanted the jury to understand that the workers would be able to see anyone enter or leave the Borden property via the back yard (see John Crowe).

When cross-examined by defense attorney George Dexter Robinson, however, Desrosier said he saw McDonald go into the yard for the pears but did not actually see him with pears on his person. Thus Robinson attempted to counter Desrosier's testimony by showing McDonald went into the Borden yard and did things that were unobserved by Desrosier and, possibly, by the other laborers. If McDonald could have been about the yard unobserved, so could have a hatchet-wielding stranger.

McGowan, Patrick (1859-1938)

Patrick McGowan was summoned to the New Bedford courthouse to testify to comings and goings in the Borden back yard on the morning of the Borden murders. He testified on June 14, 1893.

McGowan worked in the stone yard of John Crowe with Joseph Desrosier, John Dinnie and Patrick McDonald. He was in a position to observe the Borden back yard between 10:08 and 10:28 A.M. on the morning of the murders. He saw no one enter or leave the Borden property during that time. It was he who Mrs. Nathan Chase said she saw steal pears in the Borden back yard. It turned out that Mrs. Chase was incorrect. Patrick McDonald stole the pears.

Patrick McGowan was born in Ireland to Patrick and Mary McGowan. He emigrated to the United States and by 1889 was employed in John Crowe's stone yard as a mason's laborer. He married Mary A. Doyle of Fall River. Many years later, after working as a farmer, he formed P. McGowan and Sons, Sand and Gravel. McGowan died in Fall River at the age of seventy-nine.

McGuirk, Kate Swan

Mrs. McGuirk was the wife of former Fall River reporter Arthur J. McGuirk and a journalist in her own right who had moved away from Fall River years before the murders. She published an interview with Lizzie Borden in the *New York Recorder* on September 20, 1892.

The interview was supposedly given while Lizzie was in the Taunton jail. According to author David Kent in *Forty Whacks: New Evidence in the Life and Legend of Lizzie Borden* (1992), Lizzie granted Mrs. McGuirk the interview because the two women had previously worked together in the Fall River Fruit and Flower Mission providing food for the poor on hoildays. Mrs. McGuirk grew up in Fall River as a child.

The interview was strongly sympathetic to Lizzie, in contrast to the articles in the *Fall River Globe*. Mary Livermore, a friend of Lizzie's late mother Sarah (Morse) Borden, also claimed to have interviewed Lizzie exclusively. Kent seems to believe that the McGuirk-Borden interview really took place. However, another noted Borden chronicler, Edwin H. Porter, wrote in the first book about the murders, *The Fall River Tragedy* (1893), that the interview was a "magnificent fake." Porter, however, was also a reporter for the *Fall River Globe* and a foe of Lizzie who believed in her guilt.

Detective Edwin D. McHenry.

McHenry, Edwin D.

Edwin D. McHenry was a private detective from Providence, Rhode Island, who was hired by the Fall River police to find information pointing to Lizzie Borden as the killer of her father and stepmother. He was also a principle in the infamous Trickey-McHenry hoax that almost ruined the reputation of Lizzie Borden and greatly embarrassed the twenty year-old and widely-respected New England newspaper, the *Boston Globe*.

On the day after the Borden murders, August 5, 1892, Fall River Mayor John W. Coughlin and City Marshal Rufus B. Hilliard hired McHenry to both hunt for clues implicating Lizzie in the murders and keep a watchful eye on Pinkerton detective O.M. Hanscom. Hanscom was hired by Borden and her lawyer Andrew Jennings to make his own investigation of the killings independent of the local authorities.

McHenry was present on Monday, August 8 when Jennings, Hanscom and police officers Francis L. Edson, Dennis Desmond, Patrick Connors, William H. Medley and Martin Quigley searched the Borden house for clues. When McHenry caught Hanscom attempting to overhear a private conversation about the case between Marshal Hilliard and police officer George F. Seaver at a rear window of the Hilliard home, McHenry chased Hanscom away.

But by far, the event for which scholars of the Borden case best remember McHenry is the hoax he perpetrated against Lizzie Borden with the unwitting aid of newspaper reporter Henry G. Trickey. McHenry and Trickey were acquainted with each other and had worked together on other murder cases in the past. McHenry had sold information to Trickey for a *Boston Globe* exclusive.

Some time in early October 1892, McHenry contacted Trickey and told him that he possessed the names of twenty-five witnesses Marshal Hilliard said would testify against Lizzie Borden at her trial. The detective also said these witnesses represented the Commonwealth's entire case against Miss Borden. McHenry offered to sell the names and description of their testimony for $1,000. This would be a major scoop for the *Boston Globe* and its ace crime reporter Trickey.

Trickey immediately gave McHenry all the cash he had on him at the time, $30, and rushed back to Boston via train to get the rest of the money from the newspaper. He soon returned to Fall River and gave McHenry another $400.

McHenry asked Trickey not to publish his article until the detective could leave Fall River before the police realized McHenry had betrayed them. Trickey was afraid McHenry wanted more time so he could sell the same information to the *Globe*'s rivals. Trickey then rushed back to Boston and convinced the *Globe* editor to run the story on the front page with no verification of McHenry's "facts." The *Globe*, in a quick and uncharacteristically unprofessional decision, decided to print the story in full.

The sensational scoop appeared in the Monday, October 10, 1892, edition of the *Globe*. Named as witnesses were John H. Murphy, Mrs. Gustave Ronald, Peter Mahaney, Augustus Gunning, Mr. and Mrs. Fred Chace and their daughter Abigail, G. Romaine Pittson and Mr. and Mrs. George J. Sisson.

Among the stories they supposedly would recount before a jury were that Lizzie was seen through the guestroom window wearing a rubber hood, that screams of terror were heard coming from that very room and that Lizzie was pregnant and her father threatened to throw her out of the house unless Lizzie divulged the perpetrator of the foul deed. Also added to the *Globe* story for good measure were claims that Lizzie bribed Borden maid Bridget Sullivan to remain silent about the killings and that she had physically assaulted her sister Emma while at the Taunton jail.

The day the *Boston Globe* circulated through most of New England, Inspector Philip Harrington and Andrew Jennings both denied the veracity of the story. A belated check of the facts in the Globe article showed that the "witnesses" could not be located and probably did not exist. Most of the addresses linked to their names were either totally fabricated or were vacant lots. Lizzie's physician Dr. Seabury Bowen issued a statement declaring that Lizzie was not pregnant.

McHenry countered by saying the names and addresses were fictitious to protect the privacy of the real witnesses "for obvious reasons" but even the *Globe*, which had defended the story as good journalism, was beginning to have doubts. It finally printed a retraction and strong apology in its October 11, 1892 evening edition.

Trickey was indicted for "interference with the proper administration of justice" by the same grand jury that indicted Lizzie Borden in November, 1892. He later fled to Canada and was killed there attempting to board a moving train. McHenry's reputation as a private detective was severely damaged and he moved his office from Providence to New York City, and then to Buffalo, New York.

If anyone benefitted from this example of "yellow journalism" it was Lizzie Borden. Two of New England's most influential newspapers, the *Boston Globe* and the *Boston Herald*, became Lizzie's staunch supporters. Public opinion also turned sympathetic towards Lizzie; the reading population now saw her as a victim of vicious rumors and a vindictive press.

Edwin D. McHenry was living in Providence, Rhode Island by 1889. He was the general manager of the Rhode Island Detective Bureau Company, which he founded in 1886. In 1891 McHenry renamed the enterprise McHenry and Company. The firm was dissolved in 1892 because of the Lizzie Borden story and that year McHenry and his wife Nellie relocated to New York City.

In February, 1894 Nellie successfully sued her husband for divorce on grounds of adultery. McHenry relocated to Buffalo, New York and by 1895 was in partnership with Frank H. McDonald in what they called the International Detective Agency. They were, however, only in business for one year. In 1897 McHenry changed the name of the agency to McHenry's Detective Bureau, and then to McHenry's Street Secret Service in 1899.

He was last known living in Buffalo in 1899 and there is no information of his activities after that date. According to author David Kent, McHenry occasionally wrote strange letters to Fall River City Marshal Rufus B. Hilliard and Massachusetts Attorney General Albert E. Pillsbury asking to be paid for services rendered during the Lizzie Borden investigation (see heading entries in this book for all names mentioned above as well as Mary J. Wilson, Minnie C. Wilson, Eliza J. Bell, Frank Burroughs, Hannah Fish and George F. Revere).

McKeon, Thomas

Thomas McKeon, of Taunton, was a moulder who appeared for jury duty at the Borden trial. He was not questioned by counsel and was not picked for the trial.

McNally, J.F.

As a reporter for the *Boston Herald*, J.F. McNally was present in New Bedford for the Borden trial in June 1892.

McReady, E.W.

E.W. McReady attended the Borden trial in New Bedford, Massachusetts, as a reporter for the *Boston Post*.

Medbury, Charles E.

Charles Medbury of Rehoboth, Massachusetts, served on the grand jury that indicted Lizzie Borden for the murders of her father and step-mother.

Medley, William H. (1853-1917)

William H. Medley was a Fall River policeman who was involved in many aspects of the Borden murder case. He testified at the final trial as a witness for the prosecution concerning his actions on the day of the killings. Medley was a patrolman at the time of the Borden deaths but had been promoted to the rank of Inspector by the time he testified at the trial of Lizzie Borden on June 10, 1893.

Medley was one of the first policemen to arrive at 92 Second Street the day the Bordens died, along with officers Charles Wilson and Philip Harrington. When they arrived they found that they had been preceded by fellow police officers Frank Wixon, Michael Mullaly and John Devine. Medley participated in the first search of the Borden house that day.

When he heard that Lizzie had told Assistant City Marshal John Fleet in her bedroom interview that she had gone to the loft in the the barn before she discovered the body of her father on the sitting room couch, Medley rushed to the barn and inspected the loft floor for footprints.

At the trial Medley testified that he found the loft insufferably hot and that it was almost impossible to breathe up there. He inspected the floor of the loft and found no footprints in the thick dust where Lizzie said she had been looking for weights to make fishing sinkers. He also went down into the cellar that day with Borden maid Bridget Sullivan, Assistant Marshal Fleet and Officer Patrick Doherty and took three hatchets out of a box (see Patrick Doherty).

The following Monday, August 8, Medley was involved in another search at the Borden home for clues to the murders. This time police officers Francis L. Edson, Dennis Desmond, Patrick Connors and Martin Quigley, Borden family lawyer Andrew J. Jennings and Pinkerton detective O.M. Hanscom were with him.

On the witness stand at the trial, Medley said that it was he who had discovered the handleless hatchet. He also said that he showed it to Officer Desmond, wrapped it in brown paper on Desmond's advice and brought it to the police station. Desmond, the next witness, agreed with most of what Medley said, but stated that he, Desmond, wrapped the hatchet in newspaper. These conflicting statements weakened the testimony of both men and made the police force seem less than professional.

When the defense had its turn at the trial, it successfully weakened Medley's testimony concerning his inspection of the barn. If the jury believed Medley's version of the condition of the loft, it would have appeared that Lizzie lied when she told Fleet that she was up in the barn. She would have told that lie to hide the fact that she was in the house murdering her sleeping father.

The defense produced witnesses Everett Brown, Thomas C. Barlow, Walter P. Stevens and Alfred Clarkson, all of whom said they were in the loft before Medley and had made footprints in the dust. If the jury believed them, Medley was either lying on the stand or incredibly incompetent.

William H. Medley was born in England and worked as a child in the city of Lancashire's textile mills. He immigrated to the United States in 1876 and settled in Fall River where he worked as a spinner in local textile mills. He was active in the mule spinners' union and contributed to the Fall River union periodical *The Labor Standard*.

Medley joined the police force in 1880 as a foot patrolman, was appointed Inspector by 1893, made Assistant City Marshal in 1910 and succeeded John Fleet as City Marshal in 1915. He lived in Fall River with his wife Mary and was active in numerous fraternal organizations. William H. Medley was killed in an automobile accident in 1917 in Fall River.

Metcalf, Stephen O.

Stephen Metcalf was a reporter for the *Providence Journal*. He claimed that he was present as a witness at the Tilden-Thurber art gallery in 1897 when Lizzie Borden signed a confession admitting to having killed Andrew and Abby Borden five years earlier. She supposedly did this so that she would not be arrested for shoplifting. Also present as witnesses were gallery owners Henry Tilden and William Thurber, employee Morris House and detective Patrick H. Parker.

It was in February 1897 when Tilden met with Metcalf and concocted the idea of forcing Lizzie to confess and avoid embarrassing publicity in the form of an article in the *Journal*. Metcalf agreed to go along. His presence was needed to convince Lizzie Borden that a story would indeed appear in this major New England newspaper about her shoplifting.

Many Borden historians believe the incident never happened and that the paper signed by Lizzie was a forgery. Writer Edwin D. Radin in *Lizzie Borden, The Untold Story* (1961) devoted more space to the shoplifting incident than any other writer. He related the history of the document purported to be Lizzie's confession and concluded that it was forged (see Henry Tilden, William Thurber and Morris House).

Michaud, Joseph (1876-?)

Young Joseph Michaud, sixteen years of age, lived at 83 Jencks Street in Fall River. His father was Louis Michaud, a laborer. Interviewed by police officer Joseph M. Heap on August 14, 1892, Michaud claimed that he, along with four other people, saw a man offer a sum of money to Romauld St. Amant for a ride to New Bedford (see Joseph M. Heap, Jean St. Laurant, Exentive St. Amant, Romauld St. Amant, Francios Charrete and Alexander Côté).

"Mike the Soldier"

See Graham, Michael.

Millea, Patrick F.

Patrick F. Millea worked at 54 Spring Street. The 1892 *Fall River City Directory* listed his occupation as "provisions." Clerk John J. Eagan, who was on Second Street at the time of the murders and gave a statement to the police, worked for Millea as a clerk (see John J. Eagan).

Miller, Ellen Bennett (1890-1980)

Ellen B. Miller was Lizzie's housekeeper at Maplecroft. In her will, Lizzie left Miller the sum of $3,000.

Miller, Esther

On the afternoon and evening of the day the Bordens were murdered, maid Bridget Sullivan made four trips from the Borden home. The fourth of those trips was across the street to 93 Second Street, the home of Esther Miller and her husband Southard Harrison Miller. The Millers shared the property with their daughter Phoebe Bowen and her husband Dr. Seabury W. Bowen, who lived at 91 Second Street. Bridget Sullivan was a friend of the Millers' maid and stayed with her in the Miller home the night of the murders.

Miller, Southard Harrison (1811-1895)

Southard Miller was a longtime friend of Andrew Borden. His son-in-law, Dr. Seabury W. Bowen who lived on the same lot in another house at 91 Second Street, was the family physician of the Bordens and their maid was friends with the Borden maid, Bridget Sullivan. Miller's son Frank Miller, a noted artist, also lived at 93 Second Street with his parents.

Miller was interviewed by the *Fall River Herald* the day after the murders. He told the *Herald* that he knew of no motive for the double murders and said there were no family arguments as far as he knew that would result in these crimes. Miller also stated that he was acquainted with Lizzie Borden's uncle John Vinnicum Morse for about a year and found nothing in Morse to dislike. Southard Miller further remarked to the newspaper's reporter that he considered both Lizzie and Emma Borden to be fine, upstanding ladies who would never act in an inappropriate manner.

Miller was also interviewed for the "sanity survey" that Moulton Batchelder conducted for District Attorney Hosea M. Knowlton. He remarked to Batchelder that he believed the Morse family was on the peculiar side but not insane (see Moulton Batchelder).

Southard Harrison Miller was born in Middleborough, Massachusetts, and arrived in Fall River in 1827 at the age of sixteen. He learned carpentry and became a contractor in partnership with James Ford. After the partnership dissolved he ran his own business successfully for several years.

Miller was the Fire Chief of Fall River from 1860-1869 and ran unsuccessfully for mayor in 1868. He served almost four decades as director of the Massasoit National Bank and retired in 1893 due to his age. He spent the rest of his life in retirement in Fall River and died there at the age of eighty-four. When asked his reaction to the murders after Bridget Sullivan informed him of the death of his friend Andrew, Miller told Moulton Batchelder, "I did not want anything to do with (the murders) and I did not go near the house."

Milliken, George H.

George H. Milliken, listed as a "manager" in the *New Bedford City Directory*. He was called for jury duty in the Borden case and presented a medical certificate to the court stating that he was unfit to serve on the jury. Milliken was excused and allowed to leave the courthouse.

Mills, William J.

William J. Mills was a New Bedford grocer who was called to serve on the Borden jury. During questioning, Mills stated that he was indifferent about the case. He was challenged by the prosecution and did not serve on the jury.

Milne, John C. (1824-?)

John C. Milne was the editor of the *Fall River Daily News*. He and Frank L. Almy posted $500 bail for John Vinnicum Morse to guarantee that Morse would appear as a witness at the preliminary hearing of Lizzie Borden.

Milne was born in Millfield, Scotland, on May 18, 1824. He moved to Nova Scotia and was trained in the printing trade as a compositor. By 1845 Milne was a resident of Fall River and that year started the *Fall River Weekly News* with partner Frank L. Almy. Milne sat for five terms on the Fall River City Council and served in the Massachusetts state legislature from 1884–1888. He married Abby A. Gifford of Fall River in 1849 and had nine children.

Minnehan, John (1845-1893)

John Minnehan was a Fall River policeman who lived at 88 Mulberry Street. He was involved in the first search of 92 Second Street and stood guard duty on the Borden property the night of the killings. He also possibly saved John Vinnicum Morse from being beaten or killed by a mob the day after the murders and searched the nearby woods for clues as a result of a statement by a witness who later testified at Lizzie Borden's trial. John Minnehan himself might have been called as a witness, but on February 8, 1893, four months before the trial began, he died of pneumonia at his home.

Minnehan was with Assistant Marshal City John Fleet and Officer Charles H. Wilson when they searched Lizzie Borden's bedroom on the afternoon of the double murders, according to Fleet's trial testimony. After Lizzie let the policemen into her bedroom the officers looked in drawers and a closet while Marshal Fleet questioned Lizzie.

After they completed searching her bedroom without discovering any evidence, the three policemen went into the bedroom of Andrew and Abby, then to the guestroom. Finding nothing, they searched the attic room of Borden maid Bridget Sullivan and another room on the west side of the attic. Still empty-handed, they all went to the cellar where others were searching for clues and were there when the handleless hatchet was discovered by John Fleet. After leaving the cellar, Minnehan was possibly put on guard duty around the Borden property until at least 9:00 P.M. that evening.

The next day, Friday, August 6, Minnehan once again guarded the Borden house, this time at the rear door. He saw John Vinnicum Morse trying to leave the house unnoticed at around 8:00 P.M. and followed him. A crowd of people who recognized Morse gathered at the post office. He picked up his mail and returned home, oblivious to the fact that the crowd, now estimated at between 400 and 1,000 people, were following him.

An hour later Morse emerged from the house, walked down Main Street and boarded the Bowenville trolley, Minnehan still behind him. Morse, with Minnehan continuing to keep his eye on him, went to Turner Street, stayed at a home there for a short visit and then returned to the Borden residence.

One writer, Arnold Brown, speculated that Morse went to visit Hiram Harrington, the husband of Andrew Borden's sister whom Lizzie and Emma Borden loathed (see Hiram Harrington). David Kent in *Forty Whacks* (1992) describes Morse's sojourn but does not mention a trip to Turner Street. He does say, however, that Minnehan hustled him back into the 92 Street house to escape a possible lynching (some writers credit Officer John Devine with saving Morse from this mob).

Weeks later Joseph Lemay, who became a witness for the defense, said that he saw a suspicious man in the woods near the Chace Mill. On Saturday, August 13, Minnehan and fellow policeman Philip Harrington searched the woods for signs of this stranger but found nothing. This was the last record of Minnehan's involvement in the Borden case other than reference to him made by other policemen who were witnesses at the trial of Lizzie Borden.

Moody, William Henry (1853-1917)

William Moody, district attorney for the Eastern District of Massachusetts and friend of future president of the United States Theodore Roosevelt, was on the prosecution team at the trial of Lizzie Borden. As such, he delivered the prosecution's opening statement and questioned and cross-examined many of the witnesses. He was the youngest of the prosecution lawyers and the Borden trial was the first murder case of his career.

William H. Moody, c.1890.

Many contemporary observers were favorably impressed with the quality of his opening remarks. Moody showed he knew the facts of the case and that he had prepared himself well for the trial. His comments lasted about two hours and clearly outlined the path the prosecution was prepared to follow.

During his presentation a dramatic event occurred. Whether he did this inadvertently or on purpose, the effect was electrifying. While talking about Lizzie's dress, which he held in his hand at the time, Moody threw it on the prosecutors' table. On the table at the time was an open handbag covered with tissue paper. When the dress Moody was holding landed on the paper near the bag, it blew away the tissue paper to reveal the white skulls of Andrew and Abby Borden. Upon seeing the craniums, Lizzie fainted.

Moody was considered the most competent member of the prosecution. Although he shared the chore of questioning witnesses with District Attorney Hosea M. Knowlton, William Moody was seen as being strong in his questioning and cross-examination of witnesses and in his arguments about the admissibility of evidence the defense wanted omitted. That the court ruled against him in many cases takes nothing away from his reputation as a skillful tactician.

Moody's first witness was engineer Thomas Kieran, a solid witness for the prosecution. Moody started off badly when he let Kieran testify that it was possible to stand on the second floor landing of the house and not see the body of Abby Borden in the nearby guestroom.

He questioned Dr. Seabury Bowen as to whether the dress Lizzie turned over to the authorities was the one she wore on the morning of the murders. He also questioned Adelaide Churchill and Alice Russell about the dress. He asked Assistant City Marshal John Fleet about the handleless hatchet, police Officer Frank H. Wixon about the condition of the Borden bodies and policeman Philip Harrington about the roll of burning paper smoldering in the kitchen stove.

Moody also asked Dr. Edward S. Wood, a Harvard chemist, about prussic acid. He argued, in vain as it turned out, that the jury should be able to hear evidence concerning the attempt of the defendent to buy the poison the day before the murders. The court ruled that evidence inadmissible.

When the prosecution finished its case, Moody successfully argued that defense witness Joseph Lemay's story of a stranger he had seen twelve days after the murders was not relevant to the trial. Lemay's testimony was written into the official court record but excluded from being heard by the jury.

Moody was also active in the cross-examination of defense witnesses. He called City Marshal Rufus B. Hilliard to counter the testimony of Hannah Reagan, Officer Michael Mullaly to nullify that of ice cream peddler Hyman Lubinsky and stenographer Annie White to read testimony showing contradictions in the statements of Alfred Clarkson and his presence in the Borden loft.

William Henry Moody was born in Newbury, Massachusetts. He attended public schools in Salem and Danvers, Massachusetts, and the Phillips Academy before entering Harvard where he graduated in 1876, third in his class. While there, Moody befriended fellow student Theodore Roosevelt. He continued his studies at Harvard Law School and at the law offices of Richard Henry Dana, who wrote the classic novel *Two Years Before the Mast*.

Moody was admitted to the bar in 1878 and became active in civic affairs in Haverill, Massachusetts, where he opened up a law office with Edwin N. Hill. Moody served on the Haverill school board, was city solicitor for the year 1888-1889 and then won election as district attorney of Essex County, a post he held from 1889-1895. It was as district attorney that Massachusetts attorney general Albert E. Pillsbury appointed Moody to assist Hosea M. Knowlton in the Lizzie Borden trial.

Moody knew defense attorney George Dexter Robinson professionally before the Borden case went to trial. In 1892, the year the Bordens were killed, Moody and Robinson had worked together successfully representing the city of Haverill, Massachusetts in an eminent domain case in which the city acquired a privately-owned water company. A large fee was paid by the city and Moody and Robinson split $22,000.

After the Borden trial ended, Moody continued to serve as district attorney until 1895, when he was elected to the United States House of Representatives. He was re-elected in 1896, 1898 and 1900. When Theodore Roosevelt became president of the United States in 1901, he nominated Moody to succeed John D. Long as Secretary of the Navy. During his tenure in Washington, D.C. Moody, a bachelor, frequently escorted Roosevelt's oldest child Alice to social affairs.

Moody received honors in the form of Doctor of Law degrees from Amherst and Tufts Universities and was appointed attorney general of the United States by his friend Roosevelt in 1904. He remained in that office until he was appointed to the United States Supreme Court in 1906. Moody retired from the nation's highest court in 1909 due to poor health and returned to Haverill, Massachusetts, where he died that same year. In 1918, the United States Navy named newly constructed destroyer #227 after him in recognition of accomplishments while Secretary of the Navy.

Morrill, Jonathan E.

Jonathan E. Morrill was the superintendent of Oak Grove Cemetery in Fall River where the bodies of Andrew and Abby Borden were laid to rest. After the August 6 funeral the bodies were put in a burial vault until an extensive autopsy could be performed. Even though Borden family members and friends believed the bodies were buried immediately after the services, in fact they were not interred until August 17, 1892 at 8:00 A.M. No one was present for the actual burial of the Bordens except Superintendent Morrill and the gravediggers.

Morse, A. Alan

A. Alan Morse of Fall River was questioned about the Borden murders on August 6, 1892, two days after the killings. Morse was employed by the firm of Covell and Osborn and had an alibi that police officers Philip Harrington and Patrick Doherty were able to confirm. The police quickly lost interest in Morse as a suspect.

Morse, Anna E.

Anna E. Morse, sometimes called "Annie," was the niece of John Vinnicum Morse. She was visiting at the home of Mr. and Mrs. Daniel Emery of 4 Weybosset Street in Fall River, Massachusetts on the day that Andrew and Abby Borden were murdered.

Anna was the daughter of first cousins Mary Louisa Morrison and Joseph L. Morse, Sr. Mary Morse died by 1892 and so, most likely, had Joseph. Anna had been living at the home of her uncle, William Bradford Morse, in Excelsior, Minnesota and it was from there that Anna had travelled to Fall River to visit the Emerys. Daniel Emery was a cousin not only of John Vinnicum Morse but also of William Bradford Morse and both of Annie's parents. Accompanying Anna to Fall River was a nephew of John Vinnicum Morse, probably Anna's brother, Joseph, Jr. Although Anna was at the Emery home to receive John Vinnicum Morse on the morning of August 4, 1892, Joseph had gone out and did not see him that morning.

Morse, John Vinnicum (1833-1912)

John Vinnicum Morse was the eldest brother of Sarah Morse Borden, the first wife of Andrew Jackson Borden and thus the blood uncle

John Vinnicum Morse.

of Lizzie and Emma Borden. Another of Morse's sisters married Joseph Morse, a second cousin, and his brother William, aged sixty-five in 1892, lived with his family in Excelsior, Minnesota.

Morse was an early suspect in the murders of Abby and Andrew Borden. He was soon cleared of the crime after he proved he was away from Second Street when the murders occurred. Morse, or "Uncle John" as he is frequently called in many of the books and articles about the case, was a witness at both the preliminary hearing and the final trial. Morse's testimony concerned his knowledge as a family member of events in the lives of the Bordens.

John Vinnicum Morse was born in Somerset, Massachusetts, to Anthony and Rhody (Morrison) Morse. As a youth, Morse worked for the meat business of Charles and Isaac Davis in Westport, Massachusetts. This was the same Isaac Davis in whose house he lived at the time of the murders. Morse then entered the furniture business with his brother-in-law Andrew J. Borden. When that venture proved unsuccessful Morse moved to Illinois in 1865 and worked as a farmer and a butcher before relocating to Iowa in 1879, where he had a successful horse trading business.

Morse travelled east every summer to visit the Fall River-New Bedford area. He was a familiar annual visitor there and was remembered as a man who kept a boat in New Bedford and loved fishing. Morse never married and, while out west in Illinois and Iowa, enjoyed a local reputation as an honest, if hard, businessman. After the trial that resulted in Lizzie's acquittal, Morse left the Fall River area never to return. Little is known about Morse's life after the trial except that he died in Hastings, Iowa on March 1, 1912 at the age of seventy-nine.

After his business success in Iowa, Morse moved back to Bristol County, Massachusetts, about 1891 and lived with the family of Isaac Davis on S. Mill Road in South Dartmouth (see Isaac C. Davis and William Davis).

Morse was reportedly at the Borden house when a robbery occurred there four months before the double murders. Only possessions belonging to Abby Borden were taken. Many historians of the murder believe Lizzie stole Abby's watch and jewelry as a token of the resentment she felt for her stepmother.

Morse arrived unannounced at 92 Second Street on Wednesday, August 3, the day before the killings, at about 1:30 P.M. Abby put him up in the second floor guestroom, the same room where her mutilated body was found less than twenty-four hours later. John and Andrew Borden were best friends and Borden frequently asked "Uncle John" for business advice, which was possibly why Morse was at the Borden home that day.

Morse ate dinner with the Bordens that Wednesday evening, then left the house alone and returned about 8:30 P.M. He and Andrew talked downstairs until almost 10:00 P.M., then went to bed. Morse awoke at 6:00 A.M. the following morning, ate breakfast and then left the house at approximately 7:00 A.M. to visit a niece and nephew from Minnesota who were visiting the nephew's mother and father, Mr. and Mrs. Daniel Emery. Upon leaving the Borden house Morse said he would return around noon.

The Emery house was at 4 Weybosset Street, about one and one-quarter miles from the Borden home. Annie (Morse) Emery, whom Morse had gone to see, was the daughter of Morse's brother William.

Morse stated that he was at the Emery house when the murders took place. He was able to detail the whole of his trip to Weybosset Street, including streetcar numbers. After the police interviewed Mrs. Emery, Morse was cleared as a suspect in the Bordens' murdrers.

When Morse returned to Second Street, he later testified, he did not realize anything was amiss at the house. He professed not to notice the large crowd outside of the Borden home and said he talked to no one, not even Charles Sawyer, the painter whom Officer George A. Allen had deputized to guard the rear door of the residence. Morse said he pushed his way through the crowd and went to the back yard where he picked several pears, leaned against the barn and ate his snack. He stated he ate only one piece of fruit. Witnesses said he ate three. Only then, Morse testified, did he enter the house.

According to his statement before the jury, he stayed only about three minutes. He viewed the dead bodies of Andrew and Abby and then exited the residence. Morse returned to the house later that evening and slept in the guestroom on the night of the murders. He remained there with the Borden sisters until at least Sunday, August 7.

It was from the Borden home on Friday, the day after the murders, that Morse walked to the post office and was threatened by a crowd who believed him to be the murderer. Luckily, policeman John Minnehan had been following him and hurried Morse into the house, preventing possible injury to the seemingly oblivious guest (see John Minnehan).

Morse was also present at 92 Second Street when the Borden funeral took place on Saturday, August 6, and was still there that evening when Fall River Mayor John W. Coughlinn and City Marshal Rufus B. Hilliard visited the Bordens and informed Lizzie that she was the major suspect in the killings (see John William Coughlin).

Morse's name came up soon again. The *Boston Globe* printed an extraordinary story in its October 10, 1892 edition. Known as the "Trickey-McHenry Affair," the story was a total hoax, complete with phony names and false accusations. Among the latter was that Lizzie Borden had been pregnant at the time of the murders and Andrew Borden found out that the father was none other than Lizzie's Uncle John.

The story was so fanciful that it fell apart almost the minute it was released and the next day the *Globe* printed a full retraction and apology. John Morse was one of many who said the story was false and he even threatened to sue the *Globe* although neither he nor anyone else mentioned in the article ever did (see Edwin D. McHenry and Henry G. Trickey).

After the trial Morse left Massachusetts for Iowa and never returned, although he supported Lizzie Borden throughout her ordeal. In his obituary in the *Fall River Evening News* of March 1, 1912, a story appeared that Morse used to tell about the murder. It seems that the day before the Bordens died, Morse went to a fortune teller who would not tell Morse what she had learned. When Morse asked the woman why, she answered that he would not want to know. Morse reflected that he would have given $50 to know what the fortune teller refused to say that day.

Morse, Joseph G.

Joseph G. Morse, a machinist in Fairhaven, Massachusetts, was a member of the grand jury that decided Lizzie Borden must stand trial for the murders of Andrew and Abby Borden.

Morton, James Madison, Sr.

James M. Morton was the law partner of Borden family attorney Andrew Jackson Jennings from 1876-1890. That year, Morton was appointed to the supreme judicial court of Massachusetts. When the Borden trial began Jennings could not ask the now Judge Morton for aid, and so Jennings worked with a young law associate, Arthur S. Phillips, instead.

Mosher, Augustus M.

Augustus M. Mosher was summoned to New Bedford for the Borden trial from his home in Westport, Massachusetts. When questioned for possible service on the jury, Mosher said that he had already formed an opinion and would not agree with a verdict of "guilty." He was excused and did not serve at the Borden trial.

Mullaly, Michael (1848-1908)

Michael Mullaly was a Fall River policeman who participated in several aspects of the Borden murder case. He was one of the first officers at the scene after the murders were reported, and he participated in searching the premises the day of the murder. He also was involved with the discovery and controversy concerning the handleless hatchet and with Hyman Lubinsky, one of the trial witnesses for the defense. Mullaly himself testified at the preliminary hearing and the final trial.

After policeman George A. Allen, the first officer to arrive at the scene of the murders, returned to report to police headquarters, Mullaly, along with fellow officers Frank Wixon, Patrick Doherty and John Devine, entered the Borden house at 11:37 A.M. They were followed within minutes by fellow policemen Assistant City Marshal John Fleet, William Medley, Charles Wilson and Philip Harrington.

Officer Michael Mullaly, c.1892.

Mullaly asked Lizzie Borden some questions about how she first discovered her father's body. He then took part in the first search of the Borden residence with Doherty. He saw the attic room of Borden maid Bridget Sullivan, then aided in the search of the second floor. When nothing was discovered he followed Bridget Sullivan down into the cellar.

In the cellar Mullaly, who was looking for hatchets that possibly could be the murder weapon, saw a hatchet near some washtubs. This was at first an exciting find, for the hatchet had gray or white hairs on it. Perhaps they belonged to Andrew or Abby Borden. When an analysis on this hatchet was later performed, however, the hair turned out to be from a cow and was, therefore, a dead end.

In the fruit cellar Bridget took a box from a chimney that also held some hatchets, including one with only the head; the handle was broken off with just a small piece of wood left in the eye of the head. Mullaly gave this to Fleet which, along with the hatchet that had the hairs, was sent to Dr. Edward S. Wood at Harvard Medical School for analysis.

At the trial, Mullaly told defense lawyer George Dexter Robinson in cross-examination that he had seen the broken handle in the same box as the hatchet head. This admission took everyone by surprise because the prosecution believed the handle, covered with the Bordens' blood, had been burned in the kitchen stove. On the stand Fleet, who took possession of all of the hatchets and sent them to Dr. Wood at Harvard, said that he never saw the handle in the box.

If the handle existed, of course, it would have proven Lizzie Borden did not try to destroy evidence that might convict her. Robinson demanded that prosecutor Knowlton turn over the handle to the defense. Knowlton, as surprised as anyone in the courtroom, said not only did he not have it, but that he never even knew of its existence. This was important because with the handle, it could have been proven either that the handleless hatchet was or was not the murder weapon. Since it was missing, however, each side could argue effectively about the the broken hatchet and confuse the jury. That is exactly what happened.

After coming up from the cellar, Mullaly again spoke to Lizzie Borden. This time he asked her about strangers near the Borden home and then, since no record describes anything else he did at the Borden home, he probably left.

Mullaly was also involved in the testimony of Hyman Lubinsky, the ice cream vendor who said he saw a woman, definitely not Bridget Sullivan, leaving the barn at about the time of the murders. Lubinsky stated that two days after the Bordens died he told Officer Mullaly that he had seen this woman, but Mullaly ignored his story. This would have verified Lizzie's answer as to where she had been when Andrew was being killed. It was brought out later, however, that Mullaly did write down Lubinsky's remarks and that his notes said Lubinsky saw a woman leave the barn at about 10:30 A.M. Since Andrew did not return home until at least 10:40, Lubinsky's observations were of no value (see Hyman Lubinsky).

Michael Mullaly was born in East Taunton, Massachusetts, and was employed as a longshoreman. He applied for a position with the Fall River Police Department and was put on night patrol in 1877. Because of his experience as a longshoreman, Mullaly was usually put on duty near the waterfront. He was eventually put on day patrol and over the years was active in the Police Beneficial Association of Fall River. He died unexpectedly in that city in 1908.

Munroe, Willard D.

Willard D. Munroe from Rehoboth was one of the younger potential jurors summoned to appear at Lizzie Borden's trial. He was questioned and challenged by the prosecution and did not serve on the Borden jury .

Murphy, Edward M.

Edward M. Murphy was a clerk from New Bedford. He was ordered to appear for jury duty at the Borden trial but was neither questioned nor picked for the jury.

Murphy, John H.

John H. Murphy was named as a witness who would testify against Lizzie Borden in the *Boston Globe* article of October 10, 1892 known as the "Trickey-McHenry Affair." The article was a total hoax and the *Globe* had to issue a retraction and apology the next day.

According to the story, Murphy, of Bedford Street in Fall River, was standing on the sidewalk near 92 Second Street and saw Lizzie Borden open the second floor guestroom window at the time Abby Borden's dead body would have been lying near it. Lizzie "must have been standing over the mutilated remains of her stepmother" to open the window, Murphy was quoted as saying.

Most likely, not only was Murphy not standing near the Borden house on the morning of the murders, but in all probability John H. Murphy never existed at all (see Edwin D. McHenry and Henry G. Trickey).

Murphy, W.E.

W.E. Murphy was a reporter for the *Fall River Daily Herald* and wrote about the trial of Lizzie Borden for that newspaper.

N

Newhall, Charles V.

Charles V. Newhall was a "drummer" or travelling salesman from Worcester, Massachusetts. He hired Charles M. Gardner, owner of the stables where ice cream vendor and defense witness Hyman Lubinsky started out on his rounds the morning the Bordens were killed. Newhall paid Gardner to drive him to appointments he had with customers in the Fall River area and then get him to the railroad station by 11:50 A.M. to catch a train for New Bedford (see Hyman Lubinsky).

Newhall, as a witness for the defense at the Borden trial, supported the statements of Gardner and Lubinsky as to the time each left the stables. Lubinsky said he left between 11:05 and 11:10 A.M., and Gardner stated he departed about ten minutes later. That would put Lubinsky by the Borden home at the time he said he saw a woman leave the barn. Newhall also substantiated Gardner's claim that as he passed 92 Second Street, he heard people shouting that something terrible had happened in the house. The prosecution wanted Gardner to say he and Lubinsky left earlier than they claimed they had departed, which would have discredited Lizzie's alibi that she had been in the barn when Andrew was killed.

Gardner said he was sure of the time he left the stables because he kept track of the hour since he wanted to change a $100 bill at the bank and get an order at a harness shop before picking up Newhall and going to the train station. Newhall backed up the testimony of both Lubinsky and Gardner on the witness stand.

Newton, John Crompton (1854-1893)

Known as a local eccentric, Newton was at one time a hostler and later a janitor in Fall River. In 1893, he committed suicide by leaping from the Cunard steamship *Campania*. His obituary in the *Fall River Daily Globe* called him an important person in the Borden murders although his identity and involvement had been kept "a profound secret."

At the time Borden and his wife were murdered, Newton worked as a janitor at the B.M.C. Durfee Safe Deposit and Trust Company, where Andrew Borden was supposed to have kept his money. Newton claimed David Sewell Brigham, an ex-Fall River City Marshal who died in 1893 and had a connection to the Durfee Safe Deposit and Trust Company, killed the Bordens.

Newton's wife, Margaret Ann Brewer Newton, believed that he was murdered aboard the *Campania* because of what he knew about the Borden crimes. This lead was never followed up by the Fall River police (see David Sewell Brigham).

Nicholson, Robert (1843-1908)

Robert Nicholson was interviewed by Fall River policemen Patrick Doherty and Philip Harrington on September 25, 1892 and his name appeared on District Attorney Hosea Morrill Knowlton's handwritten list under the heading, "As to not seeing prisoner escape." He had told the two officers that he saw nothing out of the ordinary near 92 Second Street the morning the Bordens were murdered. Nicholson was summoned to the Borden trial as a witness but was not called to the stand.

Robert Nicholson was born in Dundee, Scotland, to Mitchell and Matilda (Keith) Nicholson. He worked as a mason, a trade he learned from his father. Nicholson emigrated to the United States in 1874, eventually settled in Fall River and was employed in the construction business.

Nicholson later became a contractor. He married Alice Crammond and had at least one son who joined his contracting firm in 1895. The main office of his business was located at 147 Second Street. Nicholson was active in several civic organizations at the time of his death.

Nickerson, John Wesley (1818-?)

John W. Nickerson was a deputy sheriff in New Bedford, Massachusetts, at the time of the Borden trial. He had a list of reporters who were allowed to enter the courtroom and view the trial of Lizzie Borden, and he assigned seats to those who entered. Nickerson was also one of the deputies, along with George H. Arnold, Alfred B. Holmes and E. Carlisle Brown, who accompanied the jurors from New Bedford to 92 Second Street in Fall River on the second day of the trial so that the jurors could view firsthand the scene of the murders. This was done at the request of prosecuting attorney Hosea M. Knowlton.

John Wesley Nickerson was born in Plymouth, Massachusetts, on May 5, 1818. He arrived in New Bedford in 1837 and worked as a grocery clerk in a dry goods store. He later bought several ships and sailed to Brazil, Africa and the Cape Verde Islands to purchase goods for sale in the United States.

Deputy Nickerson.

Nickerson sold his ships and applied for a position as a deputy sheriff in Bristol County, Massachusetts, in 1858. He was Chief of Police in New Bedford at one time under Mayors G.H. Dunbar and Abram H. Howland. Nickerson was the father of eight children, only three of whom were living by 1897.

Niles, William B.

William B. Niles worked at a restaurant in Fall River. City Marshal Rufus B. Hilliard ordered Niles to go into the Borden back yard on the afternoon of August 8, 1892 and dig up a pile of bloody clothes and towels which had been used on murder victims Andrew and Abby Borden along with several pieces of their skulls. Two days earlier, John Vinnicum Morse had paid David R. Keefe three dollars to bury the gruesome objects (see David R. Keefe).

Norlander, C.

Norlander was mentioned in one of the many crank letters concerning the Borden murders that City Marshal Rufus B. Hilliard received shortly after the press reported the news of the killings throughout the nation. Norlander supposedly was a Swedish newspaperman who lived on Third Avenue in New York City. This was one of many "leads" that were ignored by the Fall River authorities as ruminations of the mentally unstable.

Normand, Jean Napoleon

Jean Napoleon Normand was the clerk of Dr. W. Jean Baptiste Chagnon. It was Normand who hired Lucie Collett to watch the Chagnon home on Third Street while the Chagnon family was out on the day the Bordens were murdered. This put Collett in a strategic position to view the comings and goings of anyone who attempted to cross the Borden back yard onto Third Street. As a result, Lucie Collett was called to testify at the trial of Lizzie Borden. Collett and Normand later married (see Lucie Collett).

Nottingham, Ellen R.

Ellen R. Nottingham put her signature on a will written by Lizzie Borden on January 30, 1927. She was office manager for the law firm of the two other two witnesses, Carl A. Terry and Charles L. Baker.

Nye, George F.

George F. Nye of New Bedford was summoned to jury duty in the Borden trial. He was listed in the *New Bedford City Directory* as having no job. He was probably retired. Nye was not questioned or picked to serve on the Borden jury.

O

O'Donnell, Patrick

Patrick O'Donnell, a Fall River resident, served on the grand jury that indicted Lizzie Borden for murder on December 2, 1892. Several Patrick O'Donnells are listed in the *Fall River City Directory* of 1892. The O'Donnell who served on the grand jury was by occupation either a common laborer, an operative teamster or an employee of the Merchants' Mill.

Oesting, F. William

F. William Oesting was a real estate agent from New Bedford. He was summoned to the courthouse for possible duty on the Borden jury. While being questioned, Oesting stated that he was biased and could not render a fair judgement. He was excused and did not serve on the jury.

O'Leary, Florence

Mrs. Daniel O"Leary lived at 63 Fifth Street in Fall River and occasionally worked for the Bordens. The Fall River police interviewed her on August 21, 1892 at the suggestion of Mrs. Rescome Case. Mrs. O'Leary had no information that the police found useful.

O'Leary, James, Jr.

James O'Leary, Jr. was a jeweler from New Bedford. He appeared for jury duty in the Borden trial. When questioned, he stated that he was against capital punishment. Since Lizzie Borden could have been sentenced to death if found guilty, O'Leary said he could not agree to such a verdict. O'Leary was excused.

O'Neil, Nance (1874-1965)

Nance O'Neil, who was born Gertrude Lamson in Oakland, California, was a stage actress who became one of the few close friends of Lizzie Borden after the Borden trial ended. Borden's friendship with O'Neil may have been the reason Emma Borden left Maplecroft, the home she shared with her sister, in 1905.

By all accounts, Nance O'Neil was a tall and dazzling beauty. She had light hair, mesmerizing blue eyes and a cool, controlled persona. Her photographs show delicate features combined with a look of strong will and determination.

O'Neil first performed on stage in *Trilby* at the Alcazar Theater in San Francisco on October 16, 1893. Instead of using her given name, she first appeared on the stage as Nance O'Neil. She had chosen her

Nance O'Neil, c.1890.

new name to honor eighteenth-century British thespian Nance Old-
field and Irish actress Eliza O'Neil. Nance O'Neil was a hit in her first
dramatic endeavor, although she shocked the opening night audience
for daring to play one scene in her bare feet.

O'Neil enjoyed success again in 1896 when she impressed critics in
New York City with her performance in *True to Life*. She toured the
United States and then the world performing in Australia, South
Africa, New Zealand, Egypt and, especially, in London. There, she
played the lead in both *Magda* and *Elizabeth, Queen of England* during
the 1902 season.

Lizzie Borden first saw O'Neil perform as the Shakespearian character Lady Macbeth at the Colonial Theater in Boston on February 23,
1904. O'Neil was by then a successful actress, but deep in debt. Lizzie
gave O'Neil gifts and money to get out of debt and the two women
began seeing each other socially. Lizzie traveled to Boston, New York
and Washington, D.C. to see her favorite actress and encouraged
O'Neil and other show people to come Maplecroft for parties when
O'Neil performed in Boston or Providence, Rhode Island.

Emma Borden made no secret of her loathing for Nance O'Neil.
One night at Maplecroft in 1905, Lizzie hosted a large party for
O'Neil, and Emma left the house forever, never to see her sister again.
In 1909, when famed Broadway producer David Belasco offered
O'Neil the lead in his new play *The Lily*, Nance took it, along with Be-
lasco's offer to be her sole manager.

At about that time Nance O'Neil also terminated her association
with Lizzie Borden. No one knows why. Frank Spiering, in *Lizzie*
(1984), speculated that O'Neil may have believed that associating with
such a controversial character would damage her still-developing stage
career. Another possibility was that Belasco, her new manager, promised
to keep her busy on Broadway, and she would be hard-pressed to travel
to New England or anywhere else outside of New York City. Whatever the reason, O'Neil's relationship with Lizzie Borden came to an
end.

While appearing in numerous hit plays during the next twenty years,
O'Neil attempted to duplicate her stage successes on the silver screen.
Her first movie role was in *Kreutzer Sonata* in 1915. Her thirty-second

(and last) film appearance was in *The Titfield Thunderbolt* in 1953. Most of her film performances were second- or third-rate efforts that won her few accolades. At the age of sixty, Nance O'Neil retired and lived alone on West 55th Street in New York City. She moved into the Actor's Fund Home in Englewood, New Jersey at age eighty-eight and died there on February 7, 1965.

Some contemporaries who knew of Lizzie's friendship with Nance O'Neil believed that it went deeper than mutual admiration. Modern writers still speculate openly about a sexual affair between the two, a lesbian relationship that may have resulted in, among other things, the split between Lizzie and Emma and the final bar to Lizzie ever being accepted by Fall River high society. At least two writers mentioned the possibility of physical intimacy between Lizzie Borden and Nance O'Neil, but neither committed firmly as to whether or not there really was a sexual bond between them. There is no direct proof either way, and one is left with many opinions but no facts to support them.

Osborne, James Munroe (1822–?)

James Munroe Osborne was one of the six pallbearers for Andrew Jackson Borden at the August 6, 1892 double funeral of murder victims Borden and his wife Abby. Osborne was a successful Fall River businessman and president of the Merchants' Manufacturing Company by April 1893. The other pallbearers for Andrew Jackson Borden when the bodies arrived at Oak Grove Cemetery, were Richard C. Borden, Abraham G. Hart, George W. Dean, Jerome C. Borden and Andrew Borden. All three Bordens at the funeral were relatives of the deceased.

James W. Osborne was born in Tiverton, Rhode Island, on August 27, 1822. He moved to Fall River in 1845 and married Mary B. Chace, the daughter of Nathan and Elizabeth (Buffinton) Chace in 1847. Osborne worked as a machinist as a young adult in Fall River until he purchased a blacksmith shop with his brother Weaver Osborne in 1855. He helped build the Union Mill and was a director of the Merchants' Mill and the Stafford Mill as well as president of several local companies by the mid-1890s.

P

Paige, Nomus

Nomus Paige was the official doctor at the Taunton jail. He treated prisoner Lizzie Borden when on May 15, 1893 she fell ill. The *New Bedford Evening Standard* reported that Lizzie had tonsillitis and had caught a cold on May 8, 1893, the day she was arraigned. Dr. Paige said that Lizzie's illness was of "a bronchial nature." The next day, according to the article, Lizzie began suffering from chills and spent most of the week recovering at the home of jail keeper Josiah A. Hunt.

Palmer, Benjamin R.

Palmer reported on the proceedings of the Borden trial for the *New Bedford Evening Journal*.

Palmer, Lyman

Lyman Palmer, a machinist from Taunton, was questioned at the Borden trial as to his fitness to serve on the jury. Palmer said that he was prejudiced and capable of bias in the Borden case and that his opinions would prevent him from making a fair judgement. He was excused from having to serve on the Borden jury.

Paquin, S.R.

S.R. Paquin of Bliss Fourcorners was interviewed to confirm the story of a stranger asking Gideon or George Manchester for a ride to Newport, Rhode Island, the day of the Borden killings. Paquin told the interviewing police officers that it was not George or Gideon Manchester who was involved with the stranger, but John Henry Manchester of Portsmouth, Rhode Island. Paquin further added that John Henry Manchester did indeed drive a young stranger to Newport on August 5, the day after the Bordens were murdered, but the man was simply looking for work and only mentioned the Borden murders in a passing comment. This turned out to be another dead-end lead for the Fall River police (see George Manchester, Gideon Manchester and John Henry Manchester).

Parker, Frederick

Frederick Parker of New Bedford was in the business of "water repair," according to the *New Bedford City Directory*. He was called to serve on the jury which was to judge the guilt or innocence of Lizzie Borden and under questioning said he had no personal interest at all in the case. He also stated that he was against capital punishment. Since if Lizzie Borden was found guilty she could have been sentenced to death, Parker was excused from jury duty.

Parker, John C.

John Parker was a detective from New Bedford. The *Fall River Globe* reported on August 18, 1892 that Parker and fellow New Bedford inspector Frank Hathaway were researching the theory that the Borden murders occurred over a real estate dispute. Whether or not the *Globe* realized it at the time, the dispute was probably over Andrew Borden giving to his wife's younger half-sister shares in a house on Fourth Street in Fall River (see Sarah Bertha (Gray) Whitehead).

Parker and Hathaway frequently travelled between 92 Second Street where the victims and the accused lived and the South Dartmouth home of Isaac C. Davis where Lizzie Borden's uncle John Vinnicum Morse resided. Although both Parker and Hathaway were working on behalf of the Fall River authorities their conclusions, weak at best, were not deemed important enough to be of help to the prosecution at the Borden trial.

Parker and Hathaway also investigated a trip Emma Borden made to Dartmouth and John V. Morse's trips to Fall River in the months preceding the murders. The two inspectors worked on the Borden case for two weeks but were never called to testify at Lizzie Borden's trial.

Parker, Patrick H.

Patrick H. Parker was a detective with the Providence, Rhode Island, police department. He was involved in eliciting Lizzie Borden's 1897 supposed confession to the murders in Fall River.

Almost four years after she had been acquitted of killing Andrew and Abby Borden, Lizzie was accused of shoplifting two paintings on porcelain from an art gallery in Providence owned by William G. Thurber and Henry Tilden. To avoid prosecution for the crime and embarrassing stories in the New England press, Lizzie Borden was forced to sign a document that was really a confession to committing the murders of Andrew and Abby Borden four years earlier. Those present when Lizzie allegedly signed the confession were Parker, Thurber, Tilden, store employee Morris House and newspaper reporter Stephen Metcalf. Some Borden historians believed that the paper was a forgery and that the signing never took place (see William G. Thurber, Henry Tilden, Morris House and Stephen Metcalf).

Detective Parker, when informed that it was the infamous Lizzie Borden who stole the items, travelled to Fall River and confronted Lizzie at Maplecroft. Miss Borden hotly denied pilfering the stolen goods and claimed that she in fact purchased the items in question. After Parker returned to Providence, Henry Tilden swore out a warrant for Lizzie Borden's arrest. Lizzie reportedly travelled to Providence to avoid a public spectacle and there in the art gallery typed out her confession.

When at first she refused to sign it, a story about the shoplifting incident appeared in the February 16, 1897 edition of the *Providence Journal*. Parker once more visited Lizzie in Fall River the day the article appeared in the *Journal* and had another arrest warrant in his possession. Lizzie again travelled back to Providence and this time signed the confession.

Respected author Edward D. Radin, in his 1961 book on the Borden murder case *Lizzie Borden: The Untold Story*, devotes eleven pages to the typed confession and calls it a hoax. His argument seems convincing. Many, however, continue to delight in any story, true or not, that enhances the allure of the unsolved mystery for modern historians and armchair detectives.

Pasel, Francis A.

Francis A. Pasel was a New Bedford florist and gardener. He was called for jury duty in the Borden murder case and admitted that he was biased. Pasel was excused and did not serve on the Borden trial jury.

Patty, George A.

See Pettey, George Ambrose.

Pearce, Harry C.

Although not listed in the *Fall River City Directory* until 1894, Pearce was on District Attorney Hosea M. Knowlton's handwritten list of witnesses to be called to testify at Lizzie Borden's trial under the heading "As to escape," a reference to those who were in a position to see anyone leaving the Borden house at the time of the double murders but did not. Although summoned to the trial as a witness, Pearce was never called upon to testify.

Pearce was the son of Nathaniel A. and Mary (Davis) Pearce. He was listed in the 1894 *Directory* as being a teamster. He boarded with his family at 25 Third Street, Fall River. Years later, Pearce was employed at the Fall River Iron Works Company. He eventually relocated to Chicago, Illinois, and by 1923 was a resident of Montreal, Canada.

Pease, James H.

James H. Pease was listed as a "city sealer of weights and measures" in the *New Bedford City Directory*. Pease was present on the first day of the Borden trial to be questioned and, perhaps, picked for the jury. Pease, however, was neither questioned on the stand nor picked to be on the jury for, most likely, the required number of jurors had been chosen before Pease took the stand.

Pease, Walter

Walter Pease, a young man from East Freetown, stated that he was against capital punishment during questioning for jury duty in the Borden trial. He was excused and did not serve as a member of the jury.

Pease, Zephaniah W.

Zeph Pease was a reporter for the *New Bedford Mercury*, a morning newspaper. Pease wrote an article in the *Mercury* which claimed that Massachusetts Attorney General Albert E. Pillsbury believed Lizzie was insane. Pease's story included a quote from District Attorney Hosea M. Knowlton to a *New Bedford Evening Standard* reporter that Pillsbury's theory of Lizzie Borden's insanity was totally wrong and "as far off from the truth as any other reports which have been published." Knowlton called the quote and the *Evening Standard's* story "all bosh."

An article in the December 2, 1892 issue of the *Mercury* stated that Knowlton claimed he had never criticized Pillsbury's theory of Lizzie's insanity. The *Evening Standard* stood by its original claim that Pillsbury believed Lizzie to be insane and that Knowlton did criticize the Attorney General. The *Evening Standard* also cited reports that several citizens had been interviewed as to the possibility of insanity in the Borden family. These people also claimed that the interviewer said he was sent to conduct his survey by District Attorney Knowlton.

In all probability, the story referred to the "sanity survey" conducted by Moulton Batchelder at the request of Hosea M. Knowlton. In all, Batchelder interviewed at least twelve people on the possibility of insanity in the Borden and Morse families. The information that Batchelder collected and gave to Knowlton was of such poor quality that Knowlton decided none of it would help solve the Borden murder case. In the papers of Hosea M. Knowlton, published by the Fall River Historical Society in 1994, is a letter from Attorney General Pillsbury dated November 28, 1892 that states, "I return Batchelder's report, which seems to contain nothing" (see Moulton Batchelder).

Peckham, Annie F.

Annie F. Peckham's name was on a summons issued by District Attorney Hosea M. Knowlton to appear as a witness at the trial of Lizzie Borden. The summons was undated but was issued about May 29, 1893. Among the twenty-two other names on that summons were those of policemen Michael Mullaly, Dennis Desmond, Frank L. Edson, Patrick Connors and Joseph Hyde along with Adelaide Churchill's hired man Thomas Boulds and Frank H. Kilroy, who claimed he witnessed Lizzie Borden's attempt to buy prussic acid at D.R. Smith's drug store.

Peckham was never called by the prosecution to testify at the trial and nothing more is known about her life or identity. Also unknown is the subject matter she would have covered had she been called to the witness stand.

Peckham, Anson C. (1855-?)

Dr. Anson C. Peckham was a member of the first autopsy team that performed the examinations on the bodies of Andrew and Abby Borden on the dining room table of the Borden home at 3:00 P.M. on the day of the murders. The other members of the team were Drs. William A. Dolan, John W. Coughlin, Albert C. Dedrick, John H.Leary, Thomas Gunning, Emmanuel C. Dutra, John Quincy Adams Tourtellot and Seabury Bowen.

Peckham, a physician and a surgeon, was born in Somerset, Massachusetts on September 3, 1855. His family moved to Fall River in 1858. He attended Dartmouth College and received a medical degree in 1877. Peckham began his practice in Fall River that same year and was one of the original staff members of Fall River Hospital. The doctor was the first secretary of the Fall River Medical Society in 1889 and later became its president.

Peckham, Charles H. (1830-?)

Charles H. Peckham was an early suspect in the Borden murders because on August 18, 1892 he confessed to the crime at the Fall River police station. He was released the following day after he retracted his statements and was allowed to return home to Westport, Massachusetts, under the care of his wife.

Peckham turned himself in to the police at about 10:30 A.M. two weeks after the murders occurred and made a confession to Assistant City Marshal John Fleet. He said he had murdered the Bordens and leapt over a barbed wire fence in the Borden back yard.

He told Fleet that the clothes he wore to the police station were the clothes he had on when he killed the Bordens. His attire showed no traces of blood. Peckham explained that away by saying the Bordens' blood had "stagnated" as a result of poison they had taken before being killed. Peckham was searched and arrested while his story was checked out by Fleet.

While being held in custody, Peckham asked the local authorities to hang him immediately. Fleet found out that he worked on a farm in South Westport owned by Edmund Davis and had a reputation for being an "eccentric." The day after Peckham confessed, he changed his story and said he really had nothing to do with the deaths of Andrew and Abby Borden. He was released the next day.

Peckham was born in Middletown, Vermont. He was sixty-two years old when the Bordens were murdered, had a thin, gray beard, weighed about 150 pounds and was 5'6" tall. He was married to a woman born in England and had several children. When Peckham's wife found out where her husband was and what he had confessed, she sent a neighbor to retrieve him. Peckham was released into her custody and returned home.

Peirce, J. Henry

Harry Peirce of Fall River was called before the grand jury. The *New Bedford Evening Standard* stated that he was questioned about an aspect of the discovery of the bodies. The newspaper printed no other information about his testimony. The *Fall River City Directory* of 1894 listed him as a wholesale wood dealer who resided at 50 Prospect Street.

Peltier, Joseph

Peltier was French-Canadian and lived in Taunton. He was a citizen of Bristol County and, as such, was summoned to appear for jury duty in the Borden trial. He claimed that he did not speak English well enough to serve on the jury and was excused.

Percy, Mrs. J.H.

Mrs. Percy was a reporter for the *New York Herald* and was in Fall River to cover the Borden murders. She was present at the August 12, 1892 preliminary hearing and also at the Fall River jail when prison matron Hannah Reagan said that a newspaper story concerning an argument between Lizzie Borden and her sister Emma was a lie and that the fight never happened.

Percy did not testify at the Borden trial because she was travelling in Europe at the time, but her presence at the jail matron's incident was mentioned at the trial in the testimony of another witness, reporter John R. Caldwell. Caldwell claimed to witness an exchange between Reagan and City Marshal Rufus B. Hilliard in which Hilliard refused to allow Reagan to sign a letter stating that the argument between the two sisters never took place.

After realizing that a reporter was listening to his refusal to let Reagan sign the document, the city marshal ordered Caldwell out of his office and went to the guard room. Percy was also in that room. There the two reporters, according to Caldwell's trial testimony, overheard

Reagan say that a *Fall River Daily Globe* newspaper story of the argument between the Borden sisters was a lie.

On the witness stand, Reagan insisted that the argument did occur, that she did not say anything to the contrary and never planned to sign a paper offered to her by attorney Jennings. She also said under oath that City Marshal Hilliard never told her she could not sign Jennings' statement.

Perron, Adelard (1859-1933)

Adelard Perron was a member of the Fall River police force. He was French-Canadian and fluent in that language. He acted as the interpreter for prosecution witness Joseph Desrosiers, a stone cutter in the Crowe stone yard on Third Street in back of the Borden yard (see Joseph Desrosiers).

Adelard Perron was born in Canada to Francis X. and Luce (LeBoeuf) Perron. He first became a Fall River policeman in 1885 and was promoted to the rank of lieutenant in 1893. He retired from the police force in 1916 and died in Foxborough, Massachusetts, in 1933.

Pettey, George Ambrose (1839-1906)

George Ambrose Pettey appeared under the heading "Miscellaneous" on District Attorney Hosea M. Knowlton's handwritten list of witnesses to appear at the Borden trial. He was also asked questions by Moulton Batchelder, who was taking a "sanity survey" for Knowlton (see Moulton Batchelder). He testified at the trial on June 10, 1893 as to what he saw when admitted to the Borden home after the murders were discovered.

Pettey had lived on the upper floor of 92 Second Street before Andrew Borden purchased the property in 1871 (at that time, the address was 66 Second Street). He was near his former residence on the day of the murders and was allowed to enter the Borden home shortly after the bodies were inspected by the local authorities.

Pettey testified that he passed 92 Second Street at about 10:00 A.M. and saw Borden maid Bridget Sullivan washing the outside windows.

After the murders were discovered, Pettey stayed around the house until invited inside by Dr. Seabury Bowen at about 11:00 A.M. He viewed Andrew in the sitting room and remembered fresh blood on the body. He then saw Abby's corpse and stated at the trial that her blood was matted and drying.

When interviewed by Moulton Batchelder for the "sanity survey," Pettey said that he knew of no insanity in the Morse family but that "Lizzie is known to be ugly." In Batchelder's notes, included in the papers of Hosea Knowlton, Batchelder referred to Pettey as "Geo A. Patty."

George A. Pettey was born in Tiverton, Rhode Island, to Jireh Bennett and Sarah (Church) Pettey. He labored on a whaling vessel as a young man and quit to work in Fall River. He was employed as a farmer and married Lydia G. Manchester in 1860. He worked in his father's firm, Wade and Pettey, Grocers, as a clerk for ten years beginning in 1869. The store was located on Second Street, south of the Borden home. Years later, Pettey worked as a bookkeeper at the Tiverton Dye Works in his native Rhode Island. He died in Fall River at age 67.

Phillips, Arthur Sherman (1865-1941)

Arthur S. Phillips was listed in the 1892 *Fall River City Directory* as a law student during the previous year. He acted as the legal assistant to Lizzie Borden's family lawyer Andrew Jackson Jennings.

Phillips replaced Jennings' long-time law partner James M. Morton who had been appointed to the Massachusetts Supreme Judicial Court in 1890. Phillips played no part in the actual trial. His contribution was investigating the alleged facts that the defense wanted to use on Lizzie's behalf and helping prepare Jennings for presentation of the evidence before the jury.

When Emma Borden legally filed to be the executor of the estate of Andrew Borden, her application, because of Massachusetts law, had to run in a local daily newspaper for three straight weeks. Twenty-nine days after the murders of Andrew and Abby Borden, she gained full control of Andrew's property. The one page legal document which granted her control of Andrew's estate was officially witnessed and signed by Arthur S. Phillips. The estate was estimated to be worth $500,000.

Defense witness Hyman Lubinsky stated at the trial in New Bedford that before the preliminary hearing in Fall River he told Phillips his story of seeing a woman on the Borden property walk from the barn to the side door of the house. Lubinsky was not called as a defense witness at the preliminary hearing or before the grand jury. Phillips also attempted to interview Eli Bence at D.R. Smith's drug store about Lizzie Borden's alleged attempt to purchase ten cents worth of prussic acid without a doctor's prescription, but Bence refused to talk to Phillips about the incident.

For the remainder of his life after Lizzie's acquittal, Phillips believed that she was innocent. He wrote a well-respected book, *History of Fall River*, which was published privately in three volumes in 1944 and 1946. In this work, Phillips claimed that Lizzie's attempt to buy the prussic acid was for an innocent reason and was not in any way connected to the murders of her father and stepmother.

Phillips is remembered today as weeping uncontrollably as Jennings gave his closing summation at the preliminary hearing in August 1892. By the time he died in 1941, Phillips was one of the last survivors of the drama that unfolded in Fall River, Massachusetts, in 1892.

Pickering, Frederick A. (1849-1906)

Frederick A. Pickering's name appeared on Hosea M. Knowlton's handwritten list of potential witnesses under the heading "As to escape." This probably referred to people in a position at the time of the murders to view the killer leaving the Borden home if the killer was not a resident of the house. The witnesses on Knowlton's list said they saw no one leave the house. Pickering was not called as a witness by the prosecution during the Borden trial.

Frederick A. Pickering was born in Fall River to Thomas J. and Jemima (Cornell) Pickering. He was considered a pioneer in the field of electrical engineering and was employed by the Fall River Electric Light Company for many years. He later accepted a job with a New

York firm and helped establish electric plants across the United States. He died in Fall River at the age of fifty-seven.

Piece, Curtis I.

A reporter from the *Fall River Daily News* told policeman William H. Medley that Curtis Piece of Westport, Massachusetts was "an old lover" of Lizzie Borden. Piece later told Medley that he first met Miss Borden at the home of Augusta D. Tripp in Westport in 1882. Piece said that at that time he was a travelling minister. Mrs. Tripp told Medley that Lizzie did not like Piece at all and Medley concluded that there never was a relationship between Piece and Lizzie Borden. Medley also felt that, contrary to Piece's claim, he had never been inside the Borden home and did not know anyone who lived at 92 Second Street (see Augusta D. Tripp, Carrie Poole and Mrs. Poole).

Pierce, A.

Pierce reported on the Borden trial for the *New York World*.

Pillsbury, Albert Enoch (1849-1930)

Albert Enoch Pillsbury was the attorney general of the Commonwealth of Massachusetts. As such, he was the person who should have led the prosecution team in the Borden trial since the attorney general usually prosecuted all murder cases that could result in a death sentence. Pillsbury realized, however, that prosecuting Lizzie Borden was unpopular with the public and might ruin his reputation if he won the case. However, if he lost the case, he would look incompetent in the eyes of that same public.

Pillsbury therefore, citing health concerns, declined to prosecute the case and announced that he would begin an extended vacation in Florida beginning in June 1893, the time that the trial was scheduled to begin in New Bedford. Pillsbury gave the unenviable task of prosecuting Lizzie Borden to the district attorney for the Southern District of Massachusetts, Hosea Morrill Knowlton. He also ordered the district attorney for the Eastern District of Massachusetts, William H. Moody, to assist him.

Albert E. Pillsbury was born in Milford, New Hampshire. He was educated in the Milford public school system before attending college preparatory academies in New Ipswich, New Hampshire, and Groton, Massachusetts. He attended Harvard College but did not attain a degree from that institution until he was given an honorary M.A. in 1890. Instead of completing his degree, Pillsbury moved to Sterling, Illinois and taught school while studying law with an uncle, John Dinsmoor.

Pillsbury was admitted to the Illinois bar in 1869 and to the Massachusetts bar one year later. He moved to Boston and opened a practice there. Active in community affairs, Pillsbury was vice president and later president of the Mercantile Library Association of Boston. He was also a member of the corporation of the Franklin Savings Bank and a director of the United States Trust & Safe Deposit Company.

Pillsbury was also active in politics. He was elected to the Massachusetts House of Representatives in 1876, 1877 and 1879 and represented the Sixth District of Suffolk County in the Massachusetts senate in 1884, 1885 and 1886. He was Massachusetts attorney general for the period 1891-1893, and in that position he became involved, albeit reluctantly, in the Borden murder trial.

After the trial and the apparent recovery of his health Pillsbury became known for his successful work as a prosecutor, most notably in the Trefethen murder case. He later became a professor of constitutional law at Boston University (1896-1908) and wrote *Daniel Webster, The Orator* (1903). He received an honorary Doctor of Laws degree in 1913 from Howard University in Washington, D.C. and died in West Newton, Massachusetts, in 1930.

Piper, David M.

David M. Piper was a janitor at the Taunton courthouse. He received a brief mention in the June 13, 1893 edition of the *New Bedford Evening Standard* for keeping the offices of the reporters, telegraphers and type writers covering or working on the Borden trial clean.

Pittson, G. Romaine

Pittson was named in the Trickey-McHenry article that appeared in the *Boston Globe* on October 10, 1892 which later turned out to be a hoax (see Henry G. Trickey and Edwin D. McHenry).

Pittson was described as a witness for the prosecution who would state on the stand at Lizzie Borden's trial that Lizzie's father Andrew had discussed with him Lizzie's supposed pregnancy a few days before the murders. Pittson, like many of the other "witnesses" described in the article, most likely never existed and was wholly a product of the imagination of detective Edwin D. McHenry.

Poole, Bert

Bert Poole was a staff artist for the *Boston Globe*. He accompanied *Globe* reporter John W. Carberry and fellow staff artist L.F. Grant to New Bedford to cover the trial of Lizzie Borden.

Poole, Carrie M.

Lizzie Borden travelled to 20 Madison Street in New Bedford, Massachusetts on July 21, 1892 to visit with her friend, a Mrs. Poole, and her daughter Carrie. Emma Borden accompanied her sister to New Bedford, where Lizzie and Emma split up. Lizzie stayed in New Bedford and later went to Westport with the Pooles to visit another of Mrs. Poole's daughters, Mrs. Augusta D. Tripp, while Emma continued on to Fairhaven. Emma Borden was in Fairhaven when she received the message that her father and stepmother had been murdered. The *New Bedford City Directory* listed the occupation of Carrie Poole as "clerk" (see Mrs. Poole and Augusta D. Tripp).

The name "Miss Carrie Poole" was also on a list of possible witnesses for the prosecution, and the word "mad" was penciled in on the back of of the page containing the names. Also on the roll was the inscription "Michael [?]," a possible reference to Michael Graham, also known as "Mike the Soldier" (see Michael Graham). Neither Poole nor Graham were called to the stand as witnesses at the Borden trial.

Poole, Mrs. ??

Mrs. Poole, a friend of Lizzie Borden, lived at 20 Madison Street in New Bedford with one of her daughters, Carrie M. Poole. Lizzie stayed at the Poole home after Emma dropped her off in New Bedford on the way to Fairhaven. Later that week, Lizzie, Carrie and Mrs. Poole travelled to Westport, Massachusetts, to visit another daughter of Mrs. Poole, Mrs. Augusta D. Tripp (see Carrie M. Poole, Augusta D. Tripp and Emma Borden).

Porter, Charles Burnham (1840-1909)

Dr. George Gay, Albert E. Pillsbury's personal physician, recommended to the attorney general that he designate Dr. Charles B. Porter as a medical expert for in the Borden murder. Though Porter was well-respected in the field of medicine, Pillsbury did not use him as an advisor. Gay had also recommended Dr. Henry Harris Aubrey Beach as a medical expert. Pillsbury did not make use of Beach's services either.

Porter was born in Rutland, Vermont. He received his B.A. from Harvard University in 1862 and an M.A. from the same institution the following year. He earned a Doctor of Medicine degree from Harvard Medical School in 1865 and taught there for seven years as assistant demonstrator of anatomy. In 1875 Porter became instructor of surgery and advanced up the academic ladder, becoming assistant professor of surgery in 1882 and professor of clinical surgery in 1887. He also had a medical practice in Boston and was associated with Massachusetts General Hospital.

Porter, Edwin H. (1864-1904)

Edwin H. Porter was a reporter for the *Fall River Globe* who closely followed the Borden case to its conclusion. He always felt that Lizzie Borden had killed her father and stepmother and wrote the first book about the murders, *The Fall River Tragedy: A History of the Borden Murders*, in 1893. It is a rare volume today and considered a collectable not only by Borden aficionados but by book collectors the world over.

Porter was involved in the story of an argument between the Borden sisters in the Fall River room of jail matron Hannah Reagan. When Fall River City Marshal Rufus B. Hilliard ordered Reagan not to sign a written statement to the effect that no argument ever took place between Lizzie and Emma Borden, a shouting match occurred between Borden lawyer Andrew Jackson Jennings (who wrote the statement for Reagan to sign) and Porter.

On the witness stand at the trial, Reagan said that she had told Porter the story of the squabble between the two sisters and he reported it in the *Fall River Globe*. Porter stressed the importance of the argument in his book on the murders, perhaps because he played a part in the release of that story.

In *The Fall River Tragedy*, Porter also clarified the Trickey-McHenry hoax and why the respectable *Boston Globe* printed the story before fully checking out all of the facts. Porter wrote that *Globe* reporter Henry G. Trickey feared that detective Edwin D. McHenry, the source of the false information, was trying to sell the sensational article to *Globe* arch-rival the *Boston Herald* and wanted to make sure that his paper was the first to break the story.

Edwin Porter was born in Glasgow, Kentucky, to Columbus and Margaret (Davis) Porter. He was employed as a teacher, then learned typesetting as a trade. He travelled to New England and was employed for a time by the *Providence Telegram*. From there he went to Fall River as city editor of the *Fall River Tribune*.

When the *Tribune* folded, he got a job on the *Fall River Globe*. There, Porter's main focus became crime and police work. Besides being a reporter for the *Globe*, Porter also was a correspondent covering the Fall River area for the *Boston Herald*, the *Boston Globe's* main competitor. Porter married Winnie Leonard of Fall River in 1891 and died in that city in 1904.

Potter, Arthur E. (1879-?)

Arthur Potter, a young man of fifteen, was the son of C.C. Potter, a clerk in the Fall River water works office. He lived at 36 Third Street in Fall River.

The Associated Press reported across the nation that on June 14, 1893 young Potter found a rusted hatchet on the roof of a barn in the yard of John Crowe, who owned property in back of the Borden rear yard. He discovered the hatchet while looking for a lost ball.

The elder Potter felt that the find was important enough to go to the police. He also wanted to tell Borden attorney Andrew Jennings about the hatchet but said that he could not locate Jennings.

The AP reported that C.C. Potter still had the hatchet in his possession at the time the story was printed and that Potter described the hatchet as ordinary-looking with a hammer head. He said that the blade was covered with rust and appeared "weather-beaten." When the rust was cleaned, Potter said that there was still gilt on the blade. This meant that when the hatchet had been discarded, it was still fairly new, since gilt wears off a blade quickly when used.

There were reports of gilt in the wounds of the Bordens, meaning that a new hatchet was used to kill them. Some speculated that the hatchet found by Arthur Potter was the actual murder weapon. It was possible that Potter's discovery could have been the tool used to kill the Bordens if the handleless hatchet produced at the trial was not, since the Potter hatchet could have lain on the Crowe roof for ten months before being found.

The Potter hatchet, unfortunately, disappeared and has been lost to history. No one can know for sure if Potter's hatchet had any connection to the murders of Andrew and Abby Borden. For the most detailed study of the hatchet found by Arthur Potter, see *Lizzie Borden and the Mysterious Axe* by Robert Flynn (1992).

Potter, George (1839-1909)

George Potter was the first of the twelve jurors chosen to sit in judgment of Lizzie Borden for the murders of her father Andrew and her stepmother Abby. Potter owned a large farm on a river road 12 miles from New Bedford, where the trial was held. He lived in Westport, Massachusetts, with his wife Emma.

Potter was described by the *New Bedford Evening Standard* as "level headed" and "true as steel." He died in Westport in 1909.

Pratt, Henry N.

Henry N. Pratt was an ice cream manufacturer from Taunton, Massachusetts. He was called to New Bedford as a possible juror in the Borden trial. Pratt was not questioned, however, and did not serve on the jury.

Prescott, Albert S. or Charles D.

Dr. Prescott was a New Bedford doctor and the courtroom physician during the Borden trial. When juror Louis D. Hodges fainted during the gruesome testimony given by Dr. William A. Dolan concerning the hatchet wounds to the bodies, District Attorney Hosea M. Knowlton called for Dr. Prescott to give assistance. Prescott was not in the courtroom at the time and the jury took a short recess. Hodges recovered and the questioning of Dr. Dolan resumed.

Newspaper accounts of the incident do not give Dr. Prescott's first name. There are, however, two Prescotts who were physicians listed in the *New Bedford City Directory* for the year 1892: Albert S. Prescott and Charles D. Prescott. The doctor who was absent from the courtroom when he was needed is most likely one of the two Prescotts here mentioned.

Q

Quigg, Lemuel Ely

L.E. Quigg covered the Borden trial for the *New York Tribune*. He wrote an average of 10,000 words per day about the trial.

Quigley, Martin

Martin Quigley was a Fall River police officer. He participated in the search of the Borden house on Monday, August 8, 1892. Others participating in the search that day along with Quigley were Officers Francis Edson, Dennis Desmond, Patrick Connors, William Medley, Borden lawyer Andrew Jennings and Pinkerton detective O.M. Hanscom.

R

Ralph, Julia (1853–1903)

Julien Ralph was a reporter for the *New York Sun*. He covered the trial of Lizzie Borden and wrote many interesting stories about the case and its cast of colorful characters.

Ralph was born in New York City on May 27, 1853. He left school at the age of thirteen and later became interested in journalism. Ralph apprenticed at several different newspapers and later wrote books and magazine articles. He died in New York City on May 20, 1903 and is buried in New Jersey.

Randall, E. William

E. William Randall of Easton, Massachusetts served as a member of the grand jury that indicted Lizzie Borden for the murders of August 4, 1892.

Ratcliffe, John

John Ratcliffe was a weaver from New Bedford. He was summoned to jury duty in the Borden trial but was neither questioned nor selected for the jury.

Raymond, Mary A.

Mary A. Raymond was the seamstress who made the Bedford cord dress that Lizzie Borden burned in her kitchen stove the Sunday after her father and stepmother were murdered. She was called to the trial as a witness for the defense.

Raymond testified on June 16, 1893 that she made a Bedford cord dress for Lizzie Borden during a three-week stay at the Borden home at 92 Second Street in Fall River. Raymond said that the Bedford cord was one of several dresses she sewed for Lizzie and Abby Borden in May 1892. Raymond described the cord dress as being light blue with a dark figure in the cloth pattern, long and trimmed with a white ruffle. She added that when Bedford cord fades, the color takes on a drab appearance.

Mrs. Raymond also stated that at the time she was finishing the dress, the Borden home was being painted. Lizzie wore the dress during this period, and according to Raymond it became stained with paint almost immediately. This testimony was used by George Dexter Robinson of the defense as proof that Lizzie burned the dress because it had become unwearable, not because she had it on during the murder of the Bordens.

The act of burning the dress was, in the opinion of Lizzie and her lawyers, an innocent, if a badly timed act, not an attempt to destroy evidence of her own guilt. The testimony of Mary A. Raymond was used to support that claim.

Read, Benjamin

Benjamin Read said he was present when Andrew Borden mentioned that he was having family problems. This occurred when Borden visited one of his mills and had a conversation with its treasurer. This happened, according to Read, on August 2, 1892, two days before Borden and his wife Abby were murdered.

Read reported this conversation to a Fall River detective and said he remembered the conversation because it was so out of character for Borden to discuss his personal life with a business associate. He also requested that his name be kept out of the investigation of the double homicide. Writer Victoria Lincoln wrote in her book *A Private Disgrace* (1967) that the prosecution did not think that the incident was important enough to summon Read into court as a witness for the prosecution.

Reagan, Hannah B. (Howe) (1848-1924)

Hannah B. Reagan was one of two female police officers in Fall River and matron at the Fall River jail. After Lizzie Borden's inquest on August 9-11, 1892 and arraignment on August 12, she was kept in the Taunton jail. On August 22, Lizzie was brought back to Fall River for the preliminary hearing, which was held between August 25 and September 1, 1892. During that time Lizzie lived at the jail in Fall River.

Because the Fall River facility had no accommodations for females Lizzie Borden spent her time in the room of Matron Reagan at the Central Police Station rather than in a typical jail cell. It was there that a controversial incident occurred that might have reflected poorly on the accused, but instead remains shrouded in mystery to this day.

Hannah Reagan, police matron, c.1892.

Emma Borden visited her sister at Mrs. Reagan's quarters at 8:40 A.M. on August 24, 1892. According to the story believed by many, and doubted by just as many, Emma was admitted to Reagan's room to visit with Lizzie. Reagan retreated to a toilet area about four feet away to give them some privacy and could hear all of the conversation between the two sisters.

Reagan later said that she heard the sisters arguing in loud voices and that Lizzie stated, "Emma, you have gave (sic) me away, haven't you?" Emma retorted that she had not and Lizzie once again said that she had. Lizzie then lay upon her cot and turned her face to the wall, away from her sister, and the two did not speak again during that visit even though Emma remained in the room until sometime after 11:00 A.M.

Within minutes, the local press heard of the argument because Reagan told the story to *Fall River Globe* reporter Edwin Porter and the story made that newspaper's next edition. Soon after the press heard of the story, Reagan denied that the incident ever happened. Months later on the witness stand, Reagan denied that she ever said the story was untrue.

Within a short time Andrew Jennings, Lizzie Borden's attorney, drew up a statement for Reagan to sign that stated the incident between the sisters never happened and the story in the *Globe* and other newspapers was a lie and totally produced from Porter's imagination. The Reverend Edwin A. Buck presented the statement to Reagan and asked her to sign

The jail matron, according to the defense version, wanted to sign it. Reagan first went to the office of her superior, City Marshal Rufus B. Hilliard, who refused to let Reagan affix her signature to the document, telling her, "If you sign that paper, it will be against my express orders" or, in another version, that if she signed the statement, "... you do it in direct violation of my orders." The jail matron never signed the paper.

Those who believe Lizzie innocent are also convinced Reagan was threatened with the loss of her job if she signed the paper because Hilliard felt that Lizzie was the killer and wanted her to receive bad publicity. Such publicity would increase the chance of a guilty verdict at her trial. Others, who believe that she did indeed kill her father and stepmother, thought that Reagan did witness a real argument and was pressured to affirm the story at Lizzie's trial. The heated discussion between the two sisters, if it did take place, could be interpreted by a jury as an admission of the defendant's guilt.

Did Hannah Reagan hear a verbal spat between the Borden sisters in her room at the Central Police Station? On the witness stand at Lizzie's trial, Reagan described the fight between the two women and strongly stated that the event did occur. She further said that she told the story to Porter and never called the *Globe* story a lie.

When asked why she did not sign Jennings' statement, Reagan said she never intended to sign it and also denied that Hilliard ordered her refuse to put her name on it. When Emma Borden was put on the witness stand she, to the surprise of almost no one, denied Reagan's answers and said she had never had words with her sister about giving her away.

Although the jail matron's testimony strongly supported the argument that the Bordens did trade words over Emma having "gave" Lizzie away, the defense produced witnesses who swore on the stand that Reagan's statement was untrue. Seven witnesses were called by the defense on June 16 to counter Reagan's statements.

Associated Press reporter John J. Manning said that he talked to Reagan after the story was released by the press and that Reagan told him the fight between the sisters never happened. "There was nothing to it," Manning quoted Reagan as telling him, although he admitted under cross-examination that she might have said that she would say nothing more about the story until called as a witness at the trial.

Boston Globe reporter Thomas F. Hickey testified that Reagan told him there was no truth to the Porter story, as did Lizzie's friend Mary Anna Holmes. Holmes' husband Charles claimed that he heard Marshal Hilliard tell Reagan not to sign Jennings' statement and that the matron said the statement was true, meaning the quarrel never took place.

New York Herald reporter John R. Caldwell and Borden friend Mary E. Brigham also stated on the stand that Reagan called the story of the argument a lie and she would have signed the statement of Jennings if Hilliard would have allowed her to do so. Hilliard himself, as a witness for the defense, admitted he told Reagan to refuse to sign the paper.

Who was telling the truth? Was there an argument? Did Reagan want to sign lawyer Jennings' statement? Should one believe the only witness who was present during the visitation or the seven others who said Reagan changed her story, which would have cast doubt on Lizzie Borden's innocence if the spat had really occurred? And, would it have affected the ultimate outcome of the trial?

We will probably never know the answers to most of these questions, but the possibilities have entranced students of the Borden case for over a hundred years. Also, in spite of the fact that Reagan said on the witness stand that the argument did occur, Lizzie Borden was acquitted. If the truth were known then, the trial's outcome would most likely have been the same.

Reagan was born Hannah B. Howe in Ireland to Henry and Catherine (McCarthy) Howe. She immigrated to the United States and married Quinlan M. Reagan, a stonecutter in Fall River. She was the first matron of the Fall River City Police Station and served in that capacity from 1888 until 1909 when she resigned. Reagan was active in several church societies and died in Fall River at the age of seventy-six.

Reagan, Michael

Michael Reagan was a policeman in Fall River. He, along with fellow officers Patrick Doherty, Philip Harrington, Joseph Hyde, and John McCarthy, relieved policemen James Dyson, George Ferguson, and Joseph Mayall at 1:00 P.M. at 92 Second Street on August 4, 1892. Dyson, Ferguson, and Mayall were standing guard at the Borden house the day of the murders and were relieved by the others, who stayed late into the evening on the Borden property.

Reed, William

William Reed and his wife were the first people to hire Bridget Sullivan as a maid when Sullivan arrived in Fall River about 1888. After she left the Reed's employ, Sullivan got a job performing the same tasks for the family of Clinton Remington, then for the Bordens.

Remington, Clinton Van Santvoort (1839-1920)

After Bridget Sullivan left the employ of the William Reed family, she was hired by cotton broker Clinton Remington in 1888. She stayed with the Remington family until November, 1889 when she became the maid of Andrew and Abby Borden.

Remington worked for the firm of Remington and Devol. The *Fall River City Directory* of 1894 listed his business as dealing in cotton, cotton cloth and yarn. He lived at 89 High Street.

Remington, Louise 0. (1869-1950)

Louise Remington was one of a group of five female friends who had planned to meet Lizzie Borden in Marion, Massachusetts for a brief vacation. The murders of Lizzie's father and stepmother prevented Lizzie from leaving Fall River. The four other friends were Anna C. Holmes, Elizabeth M. Johnson, Isabel J. Frazer and Mary L. Holmes.

Remington, Sarah Wheaton (1851-?)

Sarah Remington was one of the few friends Lizzie Borden kept after her acquittal. Shortly after the jury found her "not guilty" of the murders of her father and stepmother, Lizzie, seeking privacy, stayed in Remington's isolated cabin in a forested area near Newport, Massachusetts. Borden stayed there for several weeks and gave Remington a set of sterling silver pie forks as a token of thanks for the use of her secluded cabin.

Renwick, James C.

James C. Renwick was an undertaker at James E. Winward's, the undertaking establishment of Fall River's upper crust. He prepared the bodies of Andrew and Abby Borden for the funerals that took place on Saturday, August 6, 1892. Although Winward and not Renwick attended the funeral, Renwick was called at the Borden trial as a witness for the defense. He was asked if Andrew Borden was wearing a high school ring on his finger while Renwick was preparing his body for burial. Lizzie was supposed to have given him the ring years before as a token of her love for him. Renwick answered that he did not remember whether or not there was a ring on Borden's finger.

Revere, George F.

George F. Revere was mentioned in the sensational article that appeared in the *Boston Globe* on October 10, 1892 known as the "Trickey-McHenry Affair," a hoax that greatly embarrassed the newspaper (see Edwin D. McHenry and Henry G. Trickey). Revere was described as living in Somerset, Massachusetts, and promised to be an important witness against Lizzie Borden at her trial. He probably never existed. Neither did almost all of the others mentioned in the article written by Trickey.

Rhodes, John

John Rhodes was a Fall River law enforcement officer, a "district officer" in the words of reporter Edwin H. Porter. He was present at the inquest of Lizzie Borden. Others who were at the inquest, held at the police station on August 9-11, 1892 were Judge Josiah C. Blaisdell, District Attorney Hosea Morrill Knowlton, Dr. William A. Dolan, official stenographer Annie M. White, City Marshal Rufus B. Hilliard, Massachusetts State Patrolman George Seaver and, in Porter's words, "a couple of police officers," presumably from Fall River.

Richards, Charles Isaac (1829-1910)

Charles I. Richards was appointed foreman of the jury that acquitted Lizzie Borden of complicity in the murders of her father and stepmother, Andrew and Abby Borden. Notes that Knowlton made by hand indicated that he believed Richards would be a fair juror. He wrote next to Richards' name, "...he would be a [?] straight Kind (sic) of man no matter what Anyone (sic) said to him."

Richards was born to Henry and Fanny (Holmes) Richards in North Attleboro, Massachusetts, and employed in the real estate business. At the time of the Borden trial, Richards was also one of Fall River's assessors. His photograph in Porter's book and a staff artist's drawing of him in the *New Bedford Evening Standard* of June 17, 1893 showed him to be a distinguished gentleman with flowing white hair and a long white moustache and side-whiskers.

Richards was extremely excited when asked what the final verdict of the jury was. After the jury returned from its deliberation on June 20, 1893, before clerk of courts Simeon Borden could finish asking his formal question, "What say you, Mr. Foreman?" Richards blurted out "Not Guilty."

Richardson, M.T.

M.T. Richardson claimed to be the publisher of a journal called *Boots and Shoes Weekly*. He wrote a crank letter to City Marshal Rufus B. Hilliard soon after the Borden murders declaring that he could tell if Lizzie Borden killed her father and stepmother if only he could get a clear photograph of Lizzie's head. Hilliard did not take Richardson up on his offer.

Richardson, Maurice Howe (1851-1912)

Maurice Howe Richardson was a noted physician, surgeon, professor and later chairman of the American Medical Association. He served at the Borden trial as a medical expert for the defense and in that capacity examined the skulls of Andrew and Abby Borden. He was not called to testify at the trial.

Richardson was born in Athol, Massachusetts, and moved to Fitchburg at age eleven. He received his early education there and graduated from Harvard University in 1873. He taught high school in Salem, Massachusetts and studied medicine with Dr. Edward B. Peirson. Later, Richardson attended Harvard Medical School and received his Doctor of Medicine degree in 1877. That year he established a private practice in Boston.

He became surgical officer at Massachusetts General Hospital and re-signed to become a demonstrator of anatomy at Harvard in 1882. Richardson remained at that post for five years. He was then given the honor of being named assistant professor of anatomy. He was also a visiting surgeon at this time at Massachusetts General Hospital and a consultant to other hospitals in the Boston area. Richardson became an assistant professor of clinical surgery in 1895 and a full professor in 1905.

Active in the medical profession, Richardson was not only chief exec-utive of the American Medical Association but a charter member of the International Surgery Society and a frequent contributor to medical jour-nals. He became president of the American Surgery Association in 1902.

Riley, John (1849-1906)

John Riley was a Fall River policeman who was at the Borden home on the day of the murders. He was present at the preliminary hearing on August 31, 1892 and summoned to testify at the trial in New Bedford. Riley appeared at the trial but was not called to the stand as a witness.

On the afternoon of August 4, 1892, Riley and fellow police officers Philip Harrington, Patrick Connors, Patrick Doherty and Assistant City Marshal John Fleet searched the Borden barn for clues to the murders. There, they found no new leads in the Borden homicides.

Ritchie, Norman William

Norman Ritchie was a staff artist on the *Boston Post*. He accompa-nied female reporter Amy Rosbart to New Bedford to cover the Bor-den trial.

Robinsky, Samuel

Samuel Robinsky wrote a letter to Emma Borden dated August 17, 1892. In somewhat broken English, Robinsky described himself as a Jewish peddler who had seen a man covered with blood on August 4, 1892, the day Andrew and Abby Borden were murdered.

Robinsky said that the man was sitting on the side of a road near New Bedford and was of medium height, weighed about 135 pounds, had dark brown hair, reddish whiskers and wore a gray suit and a derby hat. Robinsky wrote that he believed this man might have been the murderer of the Bordens.

Robinsky went on in the letter to explain why he did not come forward earlier with this information. He said that he had no legal license to sell and was afraid he might be arrested by the authorities.

According to the heading on the letter, Robinsky mailed his information from Waltham, Massachusetts. Lizzie Borden's lawyer Andrew J. Jennings attempted to locate Robinsky, but was unable to find him. Jennings went so far as to contact Waltham mayor George L. Mayberry for information on Robinsky and even requested that the Boston police look for him.

All of these attempts failed, for the peddler disappeared into history and no one connected with the Borden case ever heard from him again. It was possible that the letter was simply another of the many crank messages that those connected with the murders received during the course of the investigation (see Emma Borden, George L. Mayberry, Lawrence Cain and J. Ryder).

Robinson, Edson M.

Edson Robinson was one of the pallbearers who accompanied the casket of Lizzie Borden to the family grave in Oak Grove Cemetery after her death on June 1, 1927. The other three men who carried Lizzie to her final resting place on Saturday, June 4 were Fred Coggshall, Norman Hall and Ernest Terry. Robinson, from Swansea, was Lizzie's cousin.

Robinson, George Dexter (1834-1896)

George Dexter Robinson headed Lizzie Borden's defense team. Although not known as a brilliant courtroom lawyer, Robinson's influence might have made the difference between a "guilty" verdict for Lizzie and the decision that the jury actually reached.

George Dexter Robinson.

Robinson was an ex-governor of the Commonwealth of Massachusetts. As such he carried more prestige into the trial than any other person in the courtroom. He had a strong, commanding personality but lacked the air of dominance and superiority that repelled many people. Thus the jurors retained a positive image of Governor Robinson throughout the trial.

He also knew or recommended to office the judges at the Borden trial. They were familiar with Robinson and either respected him or felt they owed him a debt for achieving the pinnacle of any legal career—a judicial appointment. In court Robinson sported a neatly trimmed mustache and always dressed in a high-style which added to his impressively large physique.

Usually, lawyers from eastern Massachusetts did not try cases in the western part of the commonwealth, and vice-versa. Robinson, from the eastern Massachusetts town of Chicopee was an exception. He was an ex-governor and therefore known to the people of western Massachusetts and Bristol County. He was also familiar with prosecutor William H. Moody. Both had represented the city of Haverill in October 1892 in an eminent domain case in which the city won the right to take over a private water company. Robinson, Moody and a third lawyer shared a $22,000 fee for that victory.

Robinson had also served on the judiciary committee in the state legislature with then-senator Albert Mason of Plymouth County. By 1893, Mason was chief justice of the superior court and presiding judge at the trial of Lizzie Borden. As governor, Robinson appointed Justin Dewey to the superior court for life. Robinson was not as experienced a lawyer as were his co-defense attorneys Moody and Andrew Jennings. He began studying the law relatively late in life, when in his thirties. Yet, his influence and presence was well worth the $25,000 fee he received from Lizzie Borden after the jury found her "not guilty."

Robinson did play an important role in the trial. He cross-examined prosecution witnesses Bridget Sullivan and Adelaide Churchill about the dress Lizzie wore and later burned. Neither saw any blood on the body, hair or clothes of the accused. He also cross-examined them regarding both Lizzie's presence in the barn while her father was being attacked and the note Lizzie claimed her stepmother Abby received on the morning she died. He cross-examined Officers Patrick Doherty and Michael Mullaly concerning Lizzie's dress and their search of the Borden home, and he questioned Lizzie's Uncle John Vinnicum Morse about the breakfast he and the Bordens consumed that fatal morning.

Although defense attorneys Jennings and Moody interrogated most of the defense witnesses, Robinson was involved in the direct examination of many of them. He questioned Hyman Lubinsky about the woman he saw leave the Borden barn at the time Andrew was being murdered and Joseph Lemay about a suspicious stranger he saw who could have been the murderer.

He interrogated Sarah Hart regarding a stranger she remembered as standing near the Borden front gate, undertaker James C. Renwick on whether Andrew was buried with a ring that had been a gift from Lizzie, and seamstress Mary Raymond, who confirmed that she had made the dress Lizzie Borden burned and that it had been stained with paint almost immediately after Borden first wore it.

Robinson's greatest contribution, however, had little to do with these witnesses or the ideas he brought out for the benefit of the jurors. His effect on the trial's outcome was strongest in the testimony he got excluded from the jury's consideration, evidence the prosecution desperately needed to gain a conviction.

When official stenographer Annie M. White was called to read parts of Lizzie Borden's incriminating and conflicting inquest testimony before the jury, Robinson objected. He argued that Borden's inquest testimony was inadmissible because it was not voluntary; she had been technically under arrest at the time. Although many legal scholars both then and now believe that the court's ruling was in error, the testimony was excluded, which most likely contributed to the jury's decision that evidence proving that Lizzie Borden had killed her father and stepmother was weak (see John William Coughlin).

An equally important ruling by the judges was the exclusion of all information pertaining to Lizzie Borden's attempt to purchase prussic acid the day before the murders. Robinson successfully argued that since neither Borden was killed by acid poisoning, the evidence and testimony mentioning this highly toxic substance should be excluded (see Eli Bence). The prosecution was so upset over this decision that shortly after the court ruled against them, the prosecution rested its case and allowed the defense arguments to begin.

As a lawyer, Robinson spoke in an emotional and melodramatic style. The show of his arguments usually outweighed their substance. In the Borden case however, his courtroom manner turned out to be successful, for Lizzie Borden was acquitted. If his arguments against allowing Lizzie's inquest testimony and prussic acid evidence to be heard by the jury were effective, his concluding summation was, most likely, crucial in persuading the jury to bring back a verdict of "not guilty."

In *Goodbye Lizzie Borden* (1974), Borden expert Robert Sullivan, himself a justice of the Massachusetts Superior Court, criticizes Robinson's style yet admits that it probably made the difference in the Borden trial. Robinson, according to Sullivan, was emotional in speech and purposely confused the jurors. He frequently gave erroneous interpretations of evidence to suit his own purpose—the acquittal of his client—and he distorted the facts or used inaccurate information to support his arguments. Sullivan described Governor Robinson's final appeal to the jury as:

lengthy...disjointed, imaginative, illogical, laced with histrionics with a dash of deception...a dramatic performance...confiding in (the juror's love for)...patriotism, God, motherhood, the protection of woman-hood—especially from the hangman's noose—the sanctity of home and, incidentally, the acquittal of Lizzie Borden...by using the tools of rhetoric, poetry, bombast, threats, pleas and a gross distortion of... damaging evidence...(p. 165)

George Dexter Robinson was born in Lexington, Massachusetts, and educated in the Lexington public school system. He attended college preparatory school in Cambridge, Massachusetts, and graduated from Harvard University in 1856. He became principal of Chicopee High School in Chicopee, Massachusetts, and began studying law in 1865 in the office of his brother Charles. He was elected to the Massachusetts House of Representatives, the Massachusetts Senate and the United States House of Representatives before winning three yearly elections to serve as the governor of Massachusetts from 1884 to 1886.

Robinson received honorary Doctor of Laws degrees from Amherst College (1884) and Harvard (1886). After leaving the governor's chair he practiced law in Chicopee and Boston. He was busy enough to de-cline numerous presidential appointments because of his growing busi-ness. Robinson died in Chicopee in 1896.

Robsart, Amy

Amy Robsart was the pen name of a woman known as Mrs. Wor-swick. Robsart represented the *Boston Post* at the Borden trial, which she covered with *Post* staff artist Norman Ritchie. She also wrote an interview of Lizzie Borden that Lizzie had given to her friend and sup-porter Mary Ashton Livermore, who in turn gave the information to Robsart for publication.

Rogers, Carrie E. Brown (1870-1954)

Carrie E. Brown Rogers was on District Attorney Hosea M. Knowlton's handwritten list of witnesses as part of a group of names under the heading, "As to escape." This probably referred to people in the vicinity of the Borden residence at the time the murders occurred who saw no one enter or leave the Borden property.

Rogers worked in the Troy Dry Goods store as a salesperson or a bookkeeper. The *New Bedford Evening Standard* of November 17, 1892 reported that Rogers had "novel testimony" to offer the grand jury. There was no hint as to the nature of her statement but Knowlton's notes indicate people under the heading "As to escape" claimed to be near the Borden home on the day of the murders.

Rogers testified before the grand jury and was summoned to appear at Lizzie Borden's trial in New Bedford. The prosecution, however, did not call upon Rogers to take the stand and testify.

Carrie E. Brown Rogers was born in Fall River to George H. and Sophia S.L. (Brown) Rogers. She married Walter Everette Peckham, a dealer in dairy products, in 1898. Rogers was a member of the Mayflower Descendents and was directly related to colonial settler John Alden of "Speak for yourself, John" fame. Rogers also belonged to the Daughters of Colonial Wars and the Daughters of the American Republic. She lived her whole life in Fall River and died there at the age of eighty-four.

Ronald, Mrs. Gustave F.

Mrs. G. Ronald was one of the witnesses mentioned in the *Boston Globe* article published on October 10, 1892 and written by reporter Henry G. Trickey. This article, proven to be a complete lie soon after its publication, has been known ever after as the "Trickey-McHenry" hoax (see Edwin D. McHenry and Henry G. Trickey).

According to the article, Ronald was standing near 92 Second Street with Peter Mahaney at 9:40 A.M. on the morning of the murders and heard a "terrible cry or groan." She and Mahaney glanced at the Borden guest room window and saw Lizzie Borden in plain sight with her head covered by a rubber hood. Most of the sensational witnesses named in the story never existed. In all probability, Mrs. Ronald was a product of the fertile imaginations of Edwin D. McHenry.

Rooks, John C.

John C. Rooks was a policeman in New Bedford, Massachusetts. He and fellow officers Milton A. Brownell and Daniel J. Humphrey dispersed a crowd of curious onlookers at the New Bedford courthouse who were trying to enter the courtroom and view the Borden trial on its first day, June 5, 1893. Unfortunately for those in the crowd, there was no space for observers in the court because the room was filled with potential jurors awaiting questioning by lawyers for the prosecution and the defense.

Rose, Eugene

Eugene Rose of Dighton, Massachusetts, was present for possible jury duty in the Borden murder case. The jurors had already been picked before Rose got a chance to answer questions. He was sent home and did not serve on the Borden jury.

Rosenfeld, John J. (1868-?)

John J. Rosenfeld was a reporter with the *Providence Dispatch* and the *Providence Telegram*. He, accompanied by staff artist W.H. Loomis, covered the trial for his newspaper. In 1904 he became city editor at the *Providence Journal*.

Ross, Florence D.

Florence D. Ross of Boston was an official type writer at the Borden trial along with Mrs. William H.M. Dollard and Florence W. Cushing. Their job was to type the official stenographic notes that Annie M. White took during trial testimony. These notes, dictated to the typists, contained the statements of the lawyers, judges and witnesses.

Rounds, Orrin

Orrin Rounds was a horsecar conductor in Fall River. He told police officer Patrick Doherty on August 11, 1892 that he saw a stranger conversing with Andrew Borden on the morning he was murdered. Rounds said that it looked like Borden and the stranger were having an argument when Borden suddenly turned from the stranger and began walking away. The police did not follow up on Rounds' statement and nothing came from this lead to affect the Borden investigation.

Rounseville, Cyrus Cole (1852-1919)

Cyrus Cole Rounseville was summoned to the court as a witness for the prosecution, although he was never called to the stand. Rounseville claimed that he asked Andrew if he was going to his farm to escape the summer heat and Andrew told him he would probably stay in town because of trouble in his family. Some interpreted the statement as referring to the anger Lizzie and Emma felt over Andrew giving Abby's half-sister shares in a house on Fourth Street (see Abby Borden Whitehead).

Rounseville was born in Acushnet, Massachusetts, to Cyrus Cole and Irene P. Rounseville. He moved to East Freetown with his widowed mother at an early age and received his education in the East Freetown public school system. Rounseville attended Bryant and Stratton Business College in Boston and following graduation in 1869 moved to Fall River.

Rounseville worked as a clerk in Fall River for the Narragansett Steamship Company. He was later employed as an administrator in some of Fall River's many textile firms. He invested his money in local businesses, mainly banks, and became vice president of both the Union Savings Bank and the Troy Co-operative Bank. He married Miss Mary Pittman of Fall River in 1893 and was active in both church and civic affairs at the time of his death in 1919.

Rubinsky, Hiram

See Lubinsky, Hyman. His name was simply misspelled by the *New Bedford Evening Standard*.

Russell, Alice Manley (1852-1941)

Alice Manley Russell was a close friend of both Emma and Lizzie Borden. She had known the Bordens for twelve years before the murders of Andrew and Abby and had lived next door to them at 96 Second Street until the family of Dr. Michael Kelly purchased the house shortly before the murders occurred.

Russell moved to a smaller house on Borden Street between Second and Third Streets, just around the corner from the Borden residence. She still kept in touch with the Borden sisters and they all remained friends. With the exception of Dr. Seabury Bowen, the Borden family doctor and neighbor directly across the street, Alice Russell was the first

Miss Alice M. Russell.

person Lizzie sent for after she discovered the body of her father in the sitting room.

Russell was a witness at all four legal hearings concerning the crimes: the inquest during the second week in August 1892, the preliminary hearing at the end of August, the grand jury proceedings in November of that year and the final trial in June 1893, where she was a witness for the prosecution. Alice Russell's testimony, especially before the grand jury, destroyed the friendship between her and the Borden sisters. After the trial, Russell was never again a guest of either Borden. At the grand jury hearing, Alice Russell brought up for the first time information concerning the suspicious burning of a dress by Lizzie Borden the Sunday after the murders.

When Lizzie Borden first discovered the disfigured corpse of her father on the sitting room couch she sent the maid, Bridget Sullivan, across the street to fetch Dr. Bowen. After Sullivan returned to the house a few minutes later, Lizzie sent her around the corner to get Alice Russell.

Later that day, when Assistant City Marshal John Fleet was interviewing Lizzie in her bedroom, Alice was present and urged Lizzie to tell Fleet of certain incidents Lizzie had not yet mentioned. Specifically, Russell suggested that Lizzie tell Fleet of an argument Lizzie said she had overheard between her father and a prospective tenant two weeks earlier concerning the use the tenant wanted to make of a retail space in the Borden Building. Alice also wanted Fleet to know that just the day before, Lizzie had confided to her that she believed enemies might want to harm Andrew.

Alice Russell slept in the elder Bordens' bedroom that night and stayed through that weekend to comfort and support Emma and Lizzie. On Saturday, August 6 she was one of the few mourners allowed to attend the funeral of the Bordens at 92 Second Street. Lizzie and Emma, Dr. and Mrs. Bowen, Mr. and Mrs. Charles J. Holmes, Frank Almy, Adelaide Churchill, John Vinnicum Morse and ministers Edwin A. Buck and Dr. Thomas Adams were also present.

On Sunday, August 7 Russell made breakfast for the others who stayed in the house. After the dishes were cleared that morning, Alice saw Lizzie with a dark dress in her hands near the kitchen stove. She said nothing as Lizzie began ripping the garment apart. Alice then left the kitchen and Lizzie fed the dress into the stove. Alice shortly re-entered the kitchen and warned Lizzie not to let anyone see her burning the dress. Later that day, Alice was interviewed by Pinkerton Agency detective O.M. Hanscom of Boston but neglected to tell him of the dress-burning incident.

The next day, Monday, August 8, Alice told Lizzie that she had remembered her omission, felt guilty, and told Hanscom about the dress. Then Alice said to Lizzie, "It was the worst thing that could be done." Lizzie replied to her, "Why didn't you tell me? Why did you let me do it?"

Alice Russell's most important testimony was that which she gave before the grand jury in special session on December 1, 1892. After the grand jury concluded its duties, Alice requested an extra day to tell about the dress. Before Russell's testimony, the grand jury might have concluded that there was not enough evidence against Lizzie Borden to warrant a trial. After her statement about the burning of the dress, however, the grand jury voted 20-1 for the indictment of Lizzie Borden on December 2, 1892.

The information that Russell disclosed about the dress had not previously been heard at the inquest or the preliminary hearing. Her testimony probably destroyed the close personal relationship that she had with Emma and Lizzie.

Alice Russell was one of the most important weapons that the prosecution had in its arsenal against Lizzie Borden. She took the stand in New Bedford on June 8, 1893. Russell described Lizzie's premonitions the day before the murders of harm that might come to the elder Bordens. She also related to the jurors that Lizzie had told her she feared the family bread and milk may have been poisoned by one of her father's enemies, and how sick the Bordens were on the Wednesday morning before the killings.

Russell told the jury about the robbery and disappearance of Abby's jewelry in a bold daylight burglary two weeks prior to the murders and how Andrew protested when Abby went to see Dr. Bowen out of fear she had been poisoned the day before the crimes occurred. Alice also stated that Lizzie told her she was in the barn seeking some tin to repair a screen while Andrew was being attacked. She also said that after the bodies were discovered, Lizzie changed her clothes from a dark dress to a pink and white stripped wrapper.

Alice Russell's testimony serves as proof to those who believe Lizzie Borden guilty of the murders that she had planned the deed well in advance. Lizzie mentioned threats from non-existent enemies that were carried out on August 4 by someone who was not a member of the Borden household. She changed from a bloodstained dress to a clean one and later burned the evidence in the kitchen stove. She concocted the story of why she had gone to the barn and set up friends, especially Alice Russell, so that they would have to tell of incidents on the witness stand that were supportive of Lizzie's innocence.

Lizzie could not have foreseen, however, that Alice would see her burn the dress which possibly was worn, bloodstained, during the murders and later speak of the incident to a detective. To those who are convinced Lizzie was a murderess, Russell's testimony is proof of her guilt.

Russell was cross-examined by defense team leader George Dexter Robinson. Robinson was able to get her to admit that she never saw any blood on the dress Lizzie burned. Russell also noticed no blood on Lizzie's skin or hair when she and Adelaide Churchill were comforting and fanning Lizzie in the kitchen soon after Andrew's body was found.

Russell was then asked about a message that Lizzie said Abby received from a sick friend. She answered that this caused Lizzie to believe Abby had left the house instead of going upstairs to the guestroom where she met her death. Russell stated that she herself never saw a note. She did admit, however, she heard Lizzie tell Dr. Bowen that Abby probably threw it into the kitchen stove before she left the house.

Alice Manley Russell is remembered through photographs and interviews with those who knew her as not particularly attractive but with a "gentility about her," in the words of Borden chronicler Frank Spiering. She was awkward with a thin, long neck, thick, curved eyebrows and a sharp nose, much like the New England females contemporary columnist Joe Howard often ridiculed in his articles about the Borden trial (see Joe Howard).

Alice Russell was born in New Bedford to Frederick W. and Judith (Manley) Russell. She was employed as a clerk in Fall River for several years and later in life taught sewing in the local public school system. Russell was promoted to supervisor of sewing in 1908 and retired from that position in 1913. She never married and lived in Fall River for the rest of her life. Russell was also related by marriage to defense witness Delia S. Manley.

Russell, Augustus S.

Augustus S. Russell of Dartmouth, Massachusetts, was summoned for jury duty in the Borden trial. He was not questioned or picked to serve.

Russell, C.C.

A photograph labeled "C.C. Russell" appears in Edwin S. Porter's 1893 book about the Borden murders, *The Fall River Tragedy*. He is not mentioned in the text of that work. Neither is he listed in the *Fall River City Directory*. His name does not appear in any Fall River, New Bedford or New York City newspaper and no other book on the Borden crimes mentions him. Both his significance in the Borden case and the reason Porter chose to put Russell's picture in his book elude this author.

Russell, Charles Edward (1860-1941)

Charles Edward Russell covered the Borden trial for the *New York Herald*. He later became one of the most successful of the crusading journalists of the early 1900s known as the "muckrakers," a group of writers who exposed corruption and evil in all facets of American life during the first decade of the twentieth century.

Charles Edward Russell was born in Davenport, Iowa and worked for his father's pro-Republican *Davenport Gazette*, packing the freshly printed newspaper as it came off the press. He soon developed an interest in writing news articles, an interest which was fostered by a streak of rebelliousness he had shown since youth.

Russell eventually wrote exposé stories about the plight of midwestern farmers, tenement poverty among New York City's immigrant population, meatpacking conditions and the unspeakable living conditions found in Georgia's prisons. His articles helped expose many of these hidden horrors and contributed to the growing reform movement of the day known as "Progressivism."

Russell, Mary U. (1829-1904)

Mary U. Russell, a widow, was one of the two female matrons employed at the Fall River jail. The other was Hannah Reagan, who became embroiled in a controversy over whether or not Lizzie Borden, a prisoner at the time, had an argument with her sister Emma at the jail.

Although Mary Russell shared the watch over Lizzie with Reagan during the time she was awaiting her preliminary hearing scheduled to begin on August 25, 1892, Russell did not hear any argument between the sisters and had little to do with Lizzie Borden or the murder trial. The same cannot be said of Hannah Reagan (see Hannah Reagan).

Ryan, ??

Mr. Ryan, mentioned only by his last name in the *Fall River Herald*, was a tenant at one of Andrew Jackson Borden's properties. He occupied an upper floor and was either so obnoxious or such a bad tenant that Borden evicted him.

According to the *Herald* story, the other tenants in the building strongly disliked Ryan and his family, and Borden ordered him to move out. Ryan then became so verbally abusive that Borden had to use an alternate exit to leave the house.

After the Bordens were killed, a rumor circulated that before Ryan left, he stated that he would like to see Andrew dead. The story of Ryan was printed in the *Herald* the day after the Bordens died but nothing resulted from a police investigation of the incident. Ryan, if he ever existed, was never located.

Ryder, J.

J. Ryder was a police inspector in Boston's Station One. He and fellow police officer Lawrence Cain helped Fall River policeman William H. Medley search for Samuel Robinsky, who wrote an intriguing letter to Emma Borden from Waltham, Massachusetts, dated August 17, 1892. Ryder and Cain looked for Robinsky in the Boston-Needham-Chestnut Hill area. Robinsky was never located and to this day, his identity and the light he could have thrown on the Borden mystery remains open to speculation (see Samuel Robinsky, Emma Borden, George L. Mayberry, and Lawrence Cain).

S

St. Amant, Exentive

Exentive St. Amant was interviewed at the same time as her husband Romuald by policeman Joseph M. Heap about an incident involving Romuald St. Amant and a stranger who begged him for a ride from Fall River to New Bedford (see Romuald St. Amant, Jean St. Laurant, Joseph Michaud, Alexander Côté, Francois Charrete and Joseph M. Heap).

St. Amant, Romuald

Romuald St. Amant was a coal truck (wagon) operator in Fall River. He told police officer Joseph M. Heap on August 14, 1892 that he was driving his wagon on the day of the murders when a man approached him in a panic and asked him for a ride. St. Amant allowed him to board the wagon. The stranger offered St. Amant ten dollars, not a small sum of money in 1892, to transport him to New Bedford. St. Amant's wife, Exentive, did not want her husband to make such a long journey, even for the $10 fee. The stranger continued to insist on being taken into New Bedford until St. Amant finally kicked him off of the wagon (see Joseph M. Heap, Exentive St. Amant, Jean St. Laurant, Alexander Côté, Joseph Michaud and Francois Charrete).

St. Laurant, Jean H.

Jean St. Laurent was a grocer who resided at 59 Jencks Street in Fall River. He was interviewed by police officer Joseph M. Heap on August 14, 1892. St. Laurant told Heap that a stranger had asked him where the nearest livery stable could be found. He also gave the policeman a physical description of the stranger.

No clues to the Borden crimes resulted from this interview. Could this stranger have been the same man who asked Romauld St. Amant for a ride to New Bedford in front of four other witnesses—Exentive St. Amant, Alexander Côté, Francois Charette and Joseph Michaud? (See also Romauld St. Amant and Joseph M. Heap.)

Sawyer, Charles S. (1843-1907)

Charles S. Sawyer was a house painter. He was deputized and put on guard duty at the Borden home by Fall River police officer George A. Allen after Andrew's body was discovered. Sawyer gave statements at the inquest, preliminary hearing and final trial. He commented on the observations he had made while standing at the door on the north side of the Borden home.

Charles S. Sawyer testified that he was at the machine shop of Augustus C. Rich at 81 Second Street, located just north of the Borden home on the opposite side of the street. It was there that he heard of the murders and began walking south towards 92 Second Street. In the meantime, Officer Allen, the first policeman on the scene, was already in the house. Allen looked around the first floor, saw Andrew's body on the sitting room couch, then ran out of the house to report back to the police station.

Meanwhile, walking towards the Borden home, Sawyer ran into Alice Russell, who was also going to the house of her friend Lizzie Borden. The two talked while walking. As they approached the Borden house, Sawyer apparently thought better of actually entering the residence. As he was turning around near the gate of Adelaide Churchill, the Bordens' neighbor directly to the north at 90 Second Street, Allen stopped him. The two men returned to the Borden house where Allen deputized Sawyer and had him guard the side door at about 11:20 A.M. Allen then sprinted to the police station, about four hundred yards away, to get more help.

In the frantic hours that followed, the police and everyone else forgot about temporary deputy Sawyer, who remained at his post until 6:00

P.M. that evening. After he complained that he was getting hungry, Sawyer was replaced by a Fall River policeman and sent home. Sawyer must have felt relief at being replaced, for not only could he now eat, but also because, as he said at the trial, he was nervous that the killer might come up from behind and dispatch him as he had the Bordens.

At the final trial in New Bedford, Sawyer took the stand on June 16, 1893. He described how he became a temporary guard as well as other things that he remembered. It was Sawyer who locked the bolt to the Bordens' cellar door from the inside. He also saw Lizzie Borden sitting in the kitchen in a rocking chair being aided by Alice Russell and Adelaide Churchill. He recalled seeing no blood on Lizzie's clothes, skin or hair and said he was, at times, within three feet of her. Therefore, had she been bloody, Sawyer would have noticed it.

Sawyer also saw John Vinnicum Morse return from the Daniel Emery home and informed Morse of the murders. Morse listened to Sawyer, then entered the house. Sawyer was on guard when a group of youngsters, including Thomas Barlow, Everett Brown and the son of Augustus C. Rich entered the yard. Brown and Barlow, the "Me and Brownie" who claimed to be in the loft making footprints before Officer William Medley inspected it, entered the barn. He remembered seeing Alfred Clarkson, who was also in the barn and later a witness at the trial, but could not say when Clarkson was there.

Sawyer, as a defense witness, was most likely put on the stand to support Clarkson's claim that he was in the barn at 11:38 A.M. that morning, before Medley arrived. Sawyer however, could remember few specifics as to what had occurred while guarding the house and contributed little of real value to the defense argument.

Sawyer was a large man who wore a red plaid shirt while on guard duty. He was born in Portland, Maine, and educated in New York. His desire was to be a portrait painter, but that dream never materialized. He fought in the Civil War with the New York Volunteer Infantry and became a prisoner of war when captured by the Confederate army.

After the war ended, he moved to Fall River and tried to become a scenic artist. He married Mary A. Negus in 1872. By 1897, after the Borden trial had become a part of history, Sawyer had given up hope of succeeding as an artist and founded Charles A. Sawyer and Company, House and Sign Painter. He operated that business until forced into retirement by ill health. He was a boarder at the home of widow Phoebe Warner at the 78 Second Street in 1892, not far from the Borden house. Sawyer died in Fall River in 1907 at the age of sixty-four.

Sawyer, Stephen P.

Stephen P. Sawyer worked in the stove business in New Bedford, according to the *New Bedford City Directory* of 1892. He told Officer William Medley, who travelled to New Bedford to interview Sawyer, that he was in William H. Drummond's New Bedford drug store and noticed a man there acting strangely. Sawyer's lead turned out to be worthless and the Fall River authorities did not persue it any further.

Schofield, Mrs. William

See Scholick, Sarah.

Scholick, Sarah

Stenographer Annie M. White referred to Scholick in her stenographic record as "Sarah Scholick(?)" There is no listing in the *Fall River City Directory* of 1892 for the family name "Scholick." The closest to that name is Mrs. William Schofield of 9 Cook Street.

On August 8, four days after the Bordens were killed, Scholick told police officers Patrick Doherty and Philip Harrington that Janice Duckworth told her two young girls had heard screams from the Borden home at the time the murders were said to have taken place (see Janice Duckworth, Mamie Smith and Annie Connelly).

Scott, Anna Page

Anna Page Scott was a reporter for the *New York World*, the flagship newspaper of Joseph Pulitzer. She and reporter Elizabeth G. Jordan covered the Borden trial for readers of the *World*.

Searles, Mortimer

Searles was called to the New Bedford courthouse as a potential juror in the Borden trial. He was a dealer in rubber stamps from New Bedford. Searles stated while being questioned that he had no interest in the case, but did have an opinion which he believed nothing could change. He was excused and did not serve on the Borden jury.

Seaver, Charles L.

Charles L. Seaver of Mansfield, Massachusetts, was questioned by both the defense and the prosecution as a potential juror in the Borden murder trial. He was challenged by Lizzie Borden and excused.

Seaver, George F.

George F. Seaver was a Massachusetts state policeman from Taunton who arrived in Fall River at 5:00 P.M. on the day of the murders to help local authorities search for clues. He questioned members of the Fall River police force and visited the Borden house. The search in which he participated however, did not happen until two days later, on Saturday, August 6 (most accounts give this date as the Saturday after the murders, August 6. At the trial, Seaver gave the date as the 13th).

On that day Seaver, a veteran of fifteen years as a Massachusetts state police officer, along with Deputy Marshal John Fleet, medical examiner William A. Dolan and policeman Dennis Desmond (all under the supervision of City Marshal Rufus B. Hilliard) began tearing the house apart and looking behind furniture, searching through closets and opening every box and storage trunk they could find. The most important item they discovered was forever after called the "handleless hatchet."

After Lizzie's inquest in Fall River on August 9-11, 1892, where presiding judge Josiah C. Blaisdell declared her "probably guilty," Lizzie was transferred to the jail in Taunton to await her preliminary hearing, scheduled for August 25. To avoid a possible scene with an ugly or over-curious crowd, Lizzie was spirited out of the Fall River jail at

3:00 P.M. on August 12 to the railroad station to board the train to Taunton.

Lizzie, accompanied by Seaver, Hilliard and the Reverend Edwin A. Buck, sneaked out the jail's side entrance and took a round-about route to the station. The train departed with a shaken Lizzie Borden and her escorts. By the time the train arrived in Taunton at 4:20 P.M., the news of Lizzie's presence had preceded it and a large crowd awaited her at the Taunton station. To fool the crowd, Seaver ran up along the cars at the north part of the station and Lizzie and the others detrained at the south end.

George Seaver took the stand as a witness for the prosecution at the trial of Lizzie Borden on June 10, 1893. There he described the search of the Borden house on August 13 and in so doing, proved that the search was a thorough one, not the haphazard tour that John Fleet had earlier remembered on the stand. Not only was everything searched that could be searched, but Seaver had noted and measured over a hundred bloodstains in the areas where Abby and Andrew had met their deaths, including spattered blood on the frame and glass of pictures hanging over the sofa where Andrew had died and on the wall above his head.

Probably the most interesting part of Seaver's testimony was when he was asked in cross-examination by George Dexter Robinson several questions about the wood in the handleless hatchet. Seaver stated that before he joined the police he was a carpenter. When Robinson asked him if he had much experience with wood, Seaver answered, "Yes, sir, I think I have had considerable." Yet, he could not tell what kind of wood was in the eye of the handleless hatchet, whether the wood was fresh or rotten or whether the break in the wood was recent or had been done some time ago.

Soon after, still on the stand, when asked about the types of fabric he saw on the dresses in closets in the Borden home, he stated that he could not say because he was not an expert on fabric. Thus ended George F. Seaver's participation in the Borden mystery.

Shaw, Bartholomew

See Shea, Bartholomew.

Shay, Bartholomew

See Shea, Bartholomew.

Shea, Bartholomew

There was no Bartholomew Shay or Shaw listed in the *Fall River City Directory* for 1892. Researcher Neilson Caplain, however, discovered a Bartholomew Shea with the same job local newspapers and later Borden writers have ascribed to Shay or Shaw.

Shea was the chief city detective of the Fall River Police Department. In May 1892 Lizzie Borden reported that someone had broken into the Borden barn and stolen pigeons she had been keeping there. Writer Victoria Lincoln related that after the Bordens sold a horse they kept in the barn, youths twice broke in to steal Lizzie's pigeons. Andrew Borden killed the birds with a hatchet, Lincoln continued, to prevent future thefts or break-ins. It was at about this time that Lizzie Borden spoke to Shea.

No one knew the subject of conversation between the detective and the youngest daughter of Andrew Borden. Shea was not called to testify at Lizzie's trial. While dressmaker Mary A. Raymond was testifying on the stand for the defense, she mentioned that while she was at the Borden house making dresses, Shea visited Lizzie. Before Raymond could discuss this matter further, the defense attorney changed the subject, and the prosecution did not question her about it in cross-examination.

Shea, Mark

Mark Shea was a Fall River patrolman who, according to author Leonard Rebello, helped keep crowds away from the Borden home, 92 Second Street, after word of their brutal killings spread around town.

Sherman, Isaac C.

Isaac C. Sherman of Freetown, Massachusetts,s was listed in the *New Bedford City Directory* as being in the fruit and produce business. He was summoned to New Bedford for possible duty on the Borden jury but was neither questioned nor picked to serve.

Sherman, Mary W.

Mary Sherman was a matron at the New Bedford House of Correction. As such, she oversaw New Bedford's most famous contemporary prisoner, Lizzie Borden, while her trial was in session.

Shortsleeves, Joseph (1846-1915)

Joseph Shortsleeves was a carpenter who was remodeling a store in the Borden Building the day the Bordens were killed. He was one of a number of witnesses, including Abraham G. Hart, John T. Burrell, Everett M. Cook and the two men present with Shortsleeves, Jonathan Clegg and James Mather, who testified at the trial of Lizzie Borden as to Andrew Borden's movements in downtown Fall River before he returned to his home for the last time. Shortsleeves also was a witness at the preliminary hearing ten months before the trial. There, he was called upon to give the same information that he gave later at the trial in the New Bedford courthouse.

Shortsleeves was working in a store that Andrew Borden was planning to lease to hatter Jonathan Clegg in the Borden Building located in downtown Fall River. He was in the process of lowering a front window to meet Clegg's specifications (see Johnathan Clegg). Andrew entered the store at about 10:30 A.M. and, as he inspected Shortsleeve's work, stooped over to pick up and examine a broken lock he saw on the floor. He then dropped the lock, went upstairs, came back down a few minutes later, picked up the lock again, put it in his pocket and left the building about 10:40 A.M. Shortsleeves related the story of Andrew's visit on the witness stand at Lizzie Borden's trial.

Joseph Shortsleeves was born in Canada and immigrated to the United States in 1854. The first record of his presence in Fall River was in the *City Directory* of 1892. He was listed in future directories under his name, as well as under the names "Short" and even the French version, "Courtemanche." Writer Frank Spiering called him Joseph "Shirtsleeves" in his book *Lizzie* (1984).

Shortsleeves was a veteran of the Civil War. He fought with the 4th Regiment, Heavy Artillery of New York. He later became a member of the Grand Army of the Republic (GAR) and married Mary Ann Sloan. He died in his adopted city of Fall River at the age of sixty-nine.

Silvia, Joseph

Joseph Silvia was a butcher who lived on a farm owned by John S. Brayton near Gardner's Neck. He was interviewed by police officer William H. Medley at the suggestion of Peleg P. Brightman. Brightman had reported seeing a bloody ax near the house where Silvia and his family resided. Since neither Silvia nor any member of his family was near Fall River on the day of the murders, He was not considered a suspect after his talk with Officer Medley on August 9, 1892.

Authors Edwin S. Porter and Victoria Lincoln claim that Brightman himself was considered a suspect and that the police believed the bloody ax belonged to him rather than to Silvia. In any case, neither Brightman nor Silvia was found to be connected to the Borden slayings in any way (see Peleg P. Brightman and John S. Brayton).

Sisson, Mrs. George

Mrs. George Sisson was one of the many witnesses named in the *Boston Globe* article of October 10, 1892, later referred to as the "Trickey-McHenry Hoax." She and several other "witnesses" were reported to have sensational first-hand information that would prove Lizzie Borden had killed her father and stepmother. Soon after the article was published the *Globe* was forced to issue an embarrassing retraction because all of the claims and most of information proved false (see Edwin D. McHenry and Henry G. Trickey).

Mrs. Sisson, reporter Trickey wrote, was present at the funeral of the Bordens and overheard a conversation between Lizzie Borden and maid Bridget Sullivan. During the discussion Mrs. Sisson heard Lizzie call Sullivan a fool and asked Sullivan how much money she wanted to keep quiet about a certain subject. Trickey also wrote that Andrew told Sisson he had made a will and left $25,000 to his daughter Emma and a similar amount to Lizzie. All else would go to his wife Abby. If true, a jury would have certainly considered that a motive for murder.

Trickey, in addition, claimed that Lizzie offered to sell Mrs. Sisson a watch for ten dollars that was supposedly the one stolen from the Borden house in a daring daylight robbery two weeks earlier. None of these claims made in the story could be supported when held under scrutiny and Mrs. Sisson, whose address was given as 189 Rock Street, probably never existed.

Slocum, Walter C.

Walter C. Slocum was described as a young man from Dartmouth, Massachusetts, who was questioned at the Borden trial as to his fitness to serve on the jury. He said he had formed no definite opinion about the case and was not against capital punishment. Lizzie Borden, however, did not like his appearance and challenged him. Slocum was therefore excused and did not serve on the Borden trial jury.

Smalley, Orrick (1829-1894)

"Captain" Orrick Smalley, a resident of New Bedford, was called as a witness by the grand jury which met November 7-21, 1892. He claimed to have knowledge that Lizzie Borden had been angry at her father shortly before the murders.

Smalley claimed that after the murders occurred, while he was vacationing in Craigville, Massachusetts, he had a conversation with a stranger later identified as George W. Hathaway. Hathaway said he had a friend who told him Andrew Borden mentioned there was trouble in his family and that Lizzie had told her father she wished to see him dead. This friend was probably Martin Blaine, executive treasurer of the Globe Yarn Mill Company, or Cyrus Rounseville, depending on whether you believe author Frank Spiering or an article in the November 11, 1892 issue of the *New York Times*.

Smalley was born in Dartmouth, Massachusetts, and spent most of his life at sea. He began working on a fishing boat at the age of eight and later became captain of a whaling vessel. He also held office in both civic and private organizations. Smalley was at one time city marshal in New Bedford and a customs house inspector. He was also the chairman of the Overseers of the Poor and an active member of the North Christian Church in New Bedford. He had a son who also became a prominent member of New Bedford society.

Smith, A.J.

A.J. Smith was described as a "Special Officer" in the *New Bedford Evening Standard* of June 9, 1893. He was on guard with officers George Gendron and Washington A. Eldridge at the front entrance of the New Bedford courthouse during the Borden trial to keep the crowds away. There were so many people who desired to view the proceedings that there was no room in the buiding where the trial was taking place, so Smith, Gendron and Eldridge stood at the front door to keep order. Smith found himself doing the same duty, keeping a group of about one hundred people quiet, two days later with officers Charles H.H. Gifford and Joseph Mather.

Smith, Addie B.

Addie B. Smith was a salesperson who worked at the Tilden-Thurber art gallery in Providence, Rhode Island. In 1897, four years after she had been found "not guilty" in the murders of her father and stepmother, Lizzie Borden went to Providence to shop. At the art gallery Smith showed Lizzie a vase. Lizzie inspected it and soon left without making a purchase. Later that day, Smith noticed that two porcelain pieces were missing from their display and reported the disappearance to Henry Tilden, one of the owners.

Five months later a lady whom Smith did not recognize entered the store to return the larger of the two missing pieces saying that it was damaged and needed to be repaired. Smith recognized the piece and asked the lady where she had gotten it. The stranger said it was a present from Lizzie Borden.

Smith told Tilden of the lady, and he in turn asked Smith to get the woman's name and address. He then called Detective Patrick H. Parker of the Providence police. Parker interviewed Lizzie Borden in Fall River, and Borden denied stealing the objects. After reporting the results of the interview to Henry Tilden, Tilden swore out a warrant for the arrest of Lizzie Borden on a charge of theft. The end result was a controversial confession to the murders of Abby and Andrew Borden that Lizzie supposedly signed to avoid prosecution (see Henry Tilden, William G. Thurber, Stephen O. Metcalf and Morris House).

Smith, Alfred A. (1877-?)

Alfred A. Smith claimed that on the day the Bordens were murdered he picked up a bloody hatchet and a pair of bloody kid gloves on the Borden property near the Buffinton home, where Adelaide Churchill lived. He made a formal statement of his experience to one C. Hammond of Philadelphia. Also present when Smith told his story was Massachusetts Reformatory Deputy Superintendant Charles Hart and Fall River City Marshal Rufus B. Hilliard. Hammond described the interview with Smith in a letter to District Attorney Hosea M. Knowlton.

At the time he talked to Hammond, Hart and Hilliard, Smith, sixteen years old, was serving jail time at the Massachusetts Reformatory in Concord, Massachusetts for breaking-and-entering and larceny. The letter was dated January 9, 1893 and the statement was made between December 8, 1892 and the date of Hammond's letter, which is a part of the collected papers of District Attorney Knowlton.

In his statement, Smith said that after he left work at the Globe Street Railway Company at about 10:00 A.M. he travelled by horse car to City Hall. There, he got off the car and walked down South Main Street where he stopped and bought a pair of shoes at Stanton Bros. Boot and Shoe store on South Main, just south of Spring Street. He then walked a short distance to John Robertson's candy store on Second Street, located opposite St. Mary's Church just past Spring Street, which crossed Second Street to the south of the Borden home. After buying some candy Smith then turned north up Second Street towards City Hall once again.

Smith said that as he passed the Borden home before the murders were discovered, he saw a lady with bangs on her forehead looking out of a window. He continued walking north but turned around and was in front of the Borden house again. This time he saw a woman untying a bundle that contained a wooden handle about eighteen inches long. She then backed away from the window and Smith returned to Robertson's to purchase more candy.

As he walked north past the Borden home a second time, Smith continued, he saw a small pile containing a pair of kid gloves and a hatchet covered with blood inside the Borden fence near Adelaide Churchill's property line. He took the gloves and hatchet and noticed a woman looking at him from the side door of the Borden house. As he watched her, she withdrew into the house. He told Hammond that he thought the gloves and hatchet belonged to a carpenter who had cut himself, for he had not yet heard about the murders.

He decided to keep the hatchet even after he knew of the killings and stated that he sold it three weeks later to storekeeper Thomas Connors for ten cents worth of candy. Since the gloves were too small for him to wear he threw one away and kept the other at his home. He said he never mentioned the incident because he was afraid, although he was not sure exactly what he feared.

The statement was witnessed and signed by "C. Hammond, Phila. Cast Steel." Even though Hammond's transcription of the interview had City Marshal Hilliard asking Smith four short questions, Hilliard never followed up on this lead and Smith and his bloody hatchet were never again mentioned in investigations into the Borden murders.

Alfred A. Smith was the son of Robert and Ann (Greenwood) Smith of Fall River. He lived with his father, a foreman and later a baker on

Suffolk Street. Smith was employed by the Globe Street Railway Company in 1892 as a driver and laborer. There are no other details of his life on record after he was sent to the Massachusetts Reformatory on December 28, 1892.

Smith, David R. (?-1923)

D.R. Smith owned a drugstore at 135 South Main Street in Fall River. It was established about 1878 and Smith ran the store until his death. Eli Bence was a clerk at Smith's drug store and claimed that on August 3, 1892, the day before Abby and Andrew Borden were murdered, Andrew's daughter Lizzie came into the store and attempted to buy ten cents worth of the highly toxic poison prussic acid (see Eli Bence).

At her inquest, Lizzie Borden denied ever entering Smith's store in her life or even knowing of its location. Bence's story of Lizzie's presence in Smith's store was, however, supported by store clerk Frederick Hart and customer Frank H. Kilroy. Unfortunately for the prosecution at Lizzie Borden's trial, no evidence concerning the prussic acid was allowed to reach the jurors.

Smith, Elijah

Elijah Smith was from Easton, Massachusetts. He was summoned to appear at the trial of Lizzie Borden in New Bedford for possible jury duty. He stated that he was against capital punishment and was excused from the courtroom.

Smith, George E.

George E. Smith, from Norton, Massachusetts, was excused from jury duty in the Borden case because he stated on the stand that he was against the use of capital punishment.

Smith, Harry C.

Harry C. Smith replaced reporter Amy Robsart for the *Boston Post* at the Borden trial. Smith was also a "stringer" for five of New York City's major newspapers: the *World, Herald, Recorder, Sun* and *Press*.

Smith, Mamie (1882-?)

Ten year-old Mamie Smith and her eight year-old playmate Annie Connelly were reported by Janice Duckworth to have claimed that they heard screams coming from the Borden home at the time the Bordens were murdered. Duckworth also said that the two girls had seen a man leaving the Borden property wiping his hands with a handkerchief.

Fall River police authorities Philip Harrington and Patrick Doherty spoke with Mamie Smith at her home, 37 John Street. Mamie denied ever making the statements attributed to her by Duckworth and said that at the time of the murders, both she and Annie were at the home of Mamie's cousin in the area of Second and Rodman Streets.

Speer, V.

V. Speer attended the trial of Lizzie Borden as a reporter for the *New York Sun*.

Spooner, Walter D.

Walter D. Spooner was a deputy sheriff in New Bedford, Massachusetts. He was stationed at the bottom of the New Bedford courthouse steps at the rear of a corridor which led to the court room on the second floor of the building. His duty was to make sure that only authorized people and those with the proper tickets entered the room where the Lizzie Borden murder trial was taking place.

Springer, Otis S.

Otis S. Springer was from the Massachusetts town of North Attleboro and worked for the Thompson and Springer Company there. He was summoned to New Bedford for jury duty but excused because his name was not properly handed to the court after being drawn from the official box, according to the *New Bedford Evening Standard*.

Stafford, James Coggeshall (1817-1895)

James Coggeshall Stafford was questioned by Moulton Batchelder in a "sanity survey" Batchelder conducted at the request of District Attorney Hosea M. Knowlton (see Moulton Batchelder). He was living on North Street in New Bedford. When he lived in Fall River, he knew Sarah Morse Borden, Andrew Borden's first wife.

Stafford recalled that Sarah Morse Borden was, in his words, "very peculiar" and had a bad temper. She also strongly stated her likes and dislikes. Stafford said, however, that he never heard of any insanity in the Morse family.

His mother-in-law, Mrs. Ann Howard, was a neighbor of the Bordens when they lived at 12 Ferry Street in 1857; Ann Howard had lived at number 9. That was Stafford's only connection to the Bordens and probably the reason Batchelder interviewed him.

James Coggeshall Stafford was born in Tiverton, Rhode Island, to Peleg and Prudence (Coggeshall) Stafford. He married Esther A. Howard of New Bedford and was recorded as living in Fall River for the first time in that city's 1859 edition of the *City Directory*. His occupation was listed as "sea captain."

While in Fall River, he and his wife shared a house with the family of his brother-in-law, Captain Nathaniel P. Gray and his wife, the sister of Esther Stafford. Stafford was last listed as living in Fall River in the *City Directory* of 1864. He was known to be residing in New Bedford by 1892 in a house near the Grays, who had moved there in 1870. His mother-in-law, Elizabeth Ann Gray, became a widow in 1879 and it was likely that the Staffords relocated to New Bedford around that time to be of aid to Mrs. Gray.

Staples, John F.

John F. Staples of Berkley, Massachusetts, was called to the New Bedford courthouse to be questioned as to his fitness to serve on the Borden jury. He said he had already formed an opinion about the case and could not render a fair judgement. Staples was excused and did not serve on the jury.

Stevens, Frank Shaw (1827-1898)

Frank S. Stevens contributed to the posting of a $60,000 bond for Emma Borden after she applied to be the administratrix of the estate of her late father, Andrew Jackson Borden. Others who contributed to the bond posting were Joseph A. Borden, Jerome C. Borden, Franklin L. Almy and Andrew Borden, a namesake of the deceased.

Stevens was a successful Fall River businessman. He was born on August 6, 1827 and began his professional life as a clerk in Westfield, New York. Stevens travelled west to California in 1849 in search of gold but returned east in 1866, making his home in Swansea, Massachusetts. He later moved to Fall River and was president of the Globe Street Railway Company, the Metacomet National Bank and other local corporations.

He was elected to the state senate in 1884 and was a delegate to the Republican national nominating convention in 1884, 1888, 1892 and 1896. Stevens died in Swansea, Massachusetts, on April 25, 1898.

Stevens, Walter P.

Walter P. Stevens was a reporter and editor for the *Fall River Daily News*. He testified for the defense at the Borden trial on June 15, 1893. His testimony concerned his investigation of the Borden property the morning of the murders and especially his presence in the Borden barn. Stevens' testimony was used by the defense to counter that of Fall River police officer William Medley, who said he inspected the barn loft and saw no footprints there. If Medley's observations were accurate, Lizzie Borden had to have lied when she said she was in the loft as her father was being murdered in the sitting room of the Borden house.

Stevens testified that he was at the police station when Officer George A. Allen arrived from his initial inspection of the Borden home after the murders were reported. Allen had been sent there by City Marshal Rufus B. Hilliard after the murders were called in to the police. Allen saw the bodies and quickly returned to the station house for instructions and reinforcements. Stevens, who happened to be at the station at the time, rushed to 92 Second Street. He and Officer Michael Mullaly arrived at the same time.

Stevens, and fellow reporter John J. Manning of the Associated Press examined the premises, walking through the yard and around the Borden fence, circling the house from the front door on the west side of the house, moving up the south end, along the east side and finishing up by the cellar door. They inspected the area around the cellar entrance looking for footprints the murderer might have left in his escape. Stevens noticed that the cellar door was locked from the inside.

Stevens next decided to enter the barn, and this act most interested both the prosecution and the defense at the trial. Stevens said he entered the barn at about noon. Officer Medley on the stand stated that he went into the barn between noon and 12:15 P.M. Stevens said that he did not ascend to the loft himself, but heard three people walking around in the loft before Medley went up. The defense argued that there had to be footprints in the loft when Medley arrived there, so either the policeman was careless, incompetent or lying.

After Stevens finished his testimony, steam engineer Alfred Clarkson said he was one of the three in the loft Stevens had referred to, and the other two were the young boys known as "Me and Brownie." Under Moody's cross-examination of Clarkson, however, the engineer admitted Medley might have been up in the loft while he was there and simply did not see him. He also said that he was unsure just when he was in the loft and that the time he gave as 11:38 A.M. was only an estimate. This weakened the testimony of both Clarkson and Stevens and re-enforced the value of Medley's statements. The issue of footprints in the barn, then, was never completely resolved at the trial.

Stokes, H.K.

H.K. Stokes reported the Borden trial for the *Providence News*. In addition, he was a "stringer" for the New England newspapers the *Pawtucket Times*, the *Portland Times*, the *Portland Arfus*, the *Woonsocket Call*, the *Springfield News*, the *Hartford Times* and the *New Haven Register*. He was also a sketch artist for the *Providence Journal*, the *Providence News* and the *Eastern Associated Press*.

Strassman, A.

Reprter A. Strassman was sent by his newspaper, the *New York Recorder*, to cover the Borden trial.

Sturdy, Herbert K.

Herbert K. Sturdy of North Attleboro worked for the firm of J.F. Sturdy and Sons in that city. He was called to New Bedford for jury duty in the Borden case. He was never examined, most likely because the required number of jurors had already been reached. Sturdy, therefore, did not serve on the Borden jury.

Sullivan, Bridget Margaret (1864-1948)

Bridget Sullivan was the only known person in the Borden house, besides Lizzie Borden herself, who survived the harrowing morning of Thursday, August 4, 1892. The other two residents there, Andrew Jackson Borden and his wife Abby, were hacked to death. Sullivan, the Borden maid, testified at the inquest and preliminary hearing and was a star witness for the prosecution at the final trial.

Bridget was called "Maggie" by the Bordens, either because they had recently had a maid by that name before Sullivan came to work for them, as writer Robert Sullivan suggests, or because the Bordens called all of their domestics by that name, as mentioned in Glossary A of the

Bridget Sullivan, c.1892.

Fall River Society's *The Commonwealth of Massachusetts vs. Lizzie A. Borden: The Knowlton Papers, 1892-1893* (1994).

Her major tasks were cooking, cleaning and ironing, all of which she did on the morning of the murders. Her duties were restricted to the outside of the house and the downstairs area. She had no upstairs tasks except those concerning her own room which was located in the attic area at the rear of the house.

On the witness stand, Bridget told in detail what occurred in the Borden home the morning of the double killings. First Abby, then Andrew came down from their bedroom between 6:30 A.M. and 6:45 A.M. Then visiting Uncle John Vinnicum Morse came from the guestroom, then Lizzie. Emma was not home. Indeed, she was not in Fall River, but in Fairhaven, Massachusetts, visiting friends.

Bridget remembered seeing Abby using a feather duster to clean at about 9:00 A.M. and Abby ordered Bridget to begin washing the first floor windows. Sullivan went into the barn to get her window washing tools and proceeded to clean all of the outside windows on the first floor, then rinsed them and came back in the house to wash the inside portions of the windows. On the stand at the trial, Bridget stated that she never saw anyone in the rooms she looked into while washing the outside windows.

While washing the inside windows of the sitting room, Bridget heard Andrew Borden fumble with the front door locks. He was returning from his walk and inspections downtown and had trouble opening one of the bolts. Bridget walked to the door and began opening the locks from inside. She had trouble with one and uttered a mild curse. From in back of her on the stairs leading up to the second floor landing, Lizzie laughed at the scene.

Sullivan saw Andrew enter the house and heard Lizzie tell him that Abby had received a note that someone was ill and had left the house. Although there is no way of knowing, Andrew probably assumed the person in need was Abby's younger half-sister, Sarah Whitehead, the daughter of Abby's father Oliver Gray and his second wife Jane.

Andrew then went to his bedroom, but came down again shortly after, at about 10:50 A.M. He went to the sitting room to take a nap, and Lizzie helped make him comfortable while Bridget began washing the dining room windows. Lizzie told her to be sure to lock all the doors and said that Abby had gone out to help a sick acquaintance, although Lizzie was not sure who the ill party was.

After Bridget finished the windows, Lizzie mentioned a sale at Sargent's, a local dry goods establishment, and Bridget said she might go there after taking a short rest in her room. She then went to her attic bedroom at almost exactly 11:00 A.M. Bridget remembered hearing the City Hall clock strike the hour, and thus knew the time.

About ten minutes later, Bridget was awakened by Lizzie loudly calling up to her from the rear door, telling her that, "Father's dead! Somebody's come in and killed him!" Bridget came down and went into the house. The only way in from her attic room was to leave the house at the side door and walk outside to the front entrance.

When Bridget arrived in the main part of the house, Lizzie told her to run across the street and get Dr. Seabury Bowen, the family physician. She went but soon returned. Dr. Bowen was not in but his wife expected him shortly. Lizzie next told her to run up the street and inform her friend Alice Russell. She left, and when she returned to the house, Bowen and next door neighbor Adelaide Churchill were already there.

Bridget then said that if she knew where Abby's sister lived, she would go there to inform Abby of the tragedy. Lizzie answered that she thought she had heard Abby enter the house earlier and the maid should check upstairs. Voicing fear of going up to the second floor alone, Mrs. Churchill volunteered to go with her. On the landing leading to the guest room, they discovered the bludgeoned and bloody body of Mrs. Borden.

After the police were notified, they began searching the house for clues that afternoon, one of many searches they made over the next nine days. Bridget led two policemen, Officers Michael Mullaly and John Devine into the cellar. They were shortly followed by Assistant City Marshal John Fleet. Bridget showed them a box that contained two axes and two hatchets. All four tools were confiscated by the police and eventually sent to Harvard chemist Dr. Edward S. Wood for analysis. On a second trip down to the cellar that day, the police found the "handleless hatchet," presented at the trial as the true murder weapon, but Bridget was not with them when that hatchet was discovered.

After the murders, Bridget refused to stay in the Borden home and temporarily moved into a neighbor's home where she was friends with the maid. By the time of the trial, Bridget Sullivan was working in New Bedford, Massachusetts, for jailkeeper Joshua Hunt and his wife, perhaps to assure that the maid would be available as a witness and would not leave the area before the trial began.

Bridget told of all the events she witnessed on the day of the murder at Lizzie Borden's trial. Much of what modern historians know about what occurred that day comes from her statements. In cross-examination by defense attorney George Dexter Robinson, Bridget described the now-infamous breakfast of day-old mutton broth, johnnycakes and coffee with cookies, butter, bananas and other fruit. She also said that though she did not think Emma and Lizzie liked Abby Borden, relations between Andrew's wife and his two daughters were civil and there was no trouble at all on the fatal morning.

Both the prosecution and the defense argued that Bridget's statements helped their case. The attorneys for the Commonwealth said that

Bridget proved Lizzie disliked Abby and that she was alone in the house when she and Andrew were killed. Only Lizzie had the opportunity to kill the Bordens at that particular time. Also, the prosecution claimed that the note Lizzie mentioned to Bridget to explain Abby's absence from the house was never found because it never existed. At the very time Lizzie was explaining her stepmother's absence to Bridget, Abby was lying dead on the guest room floor.

The defense stressed the facts that Bridget never heard anything or saw any blood on Lizzie after she was awakened at 11:10 A.M. and that Bridget worked for the Bordens for two and one-half years and never witnessed a fight between the daughters and their stepmother.

Bridget Sullivan never returned to Fall River after the trial ended with Lizzie's acquittal. She had relocated west to Anaconda, Montana, by 1897 because she had friends and relatives living there. She made her living in Anaconda as a domestic doing basically what she had done in Fall River. She met and married John E. Sullivan (no relation), a smeltman in the Anaconda mining industry, in 1905 and remained married until his death in 1939.

While married and as a widow, Bridget continued working as a servant and few in Montana knew of her connection to America's most famous unsolved murder case. She moved to Butte, Montana, in 1942 in poor health. There, she lived with a niece, and her health got worse.

That year, when she developed pneumonia and believed she was going to die, she contacted her friend Minnie Green who was living in Anaconda and said she had a dark secret to tell before she passed away. While Green was travelling to Butte, however, Bridget recovered and her confession, if that was what it was going to be, never happened (see Minnie Green). Bridget Sullivan died in Butte, Montana, on March 26, 1948 at the age of 84 and was buried with her husband in Mount Olivet Cemetery in Anaconda, Montana.

Bridget Sullivan was born one of 13 children in Billerough, County Cork, Ireland, in 1864 to Eugene and Margaret (Leary) Sullivan. She emigrated to the United States in 1883 and gained employment as a scullery maid at the Perry House in Newport, Rhode Island. Bridget stayed there for one year, then moved to South Bethlehem, Pennsylvania, to live with relatives. While there, she was employed as a domestic by the Smiley family.

Bridget left Pennsylvania in 1888 and made her way to Fall River, Massachusetts. She worked for the families of William Reed and Clinton V.S. Remington until hired by the Bordens in November 1889. She was described as tall and well-developed with hair braided tightly to her head. She was also remembered as being pretty, a hard worker, intelligent, articulate, willing to learn new skills and submissive in taking orders. Yet, as the Borden affair showed, she could also occasionally be emotional. She will always be remembered for the crucial role she played in one of America's most intriguing mysteries.

Sullivan, Dennis F.

Dennis F. Sullivan's name was on District Attorney Hosea M. Knowlton's handwritten list of potential witnesses under the heading "As to not seeing prisoner escape." Sullivan lived at 86 Third Street in Fall River. He had stopped while walking on Second Street near the Borden house to talk to Mrs. John Gormley at about the time of the murders and said that neither he nor Mrs. Gormley saw any suspicious-looking characters near the Borden property. This would further the case for the prosecution, which claimed that the only people near the Borden house at the time of the killings were those who belonged in the house and no stranger had the opportunity to commit murder there that morning.

Sullivan was a clerk for the firm of Slades and Company, merchants and grocers. He was summoned to appear at the trial of Lizzie Borden in New Bedford in June 1893 but was not called to the stand as a witness (see Elizabeth A. Gormley).

Sullivan, James F.

James F. Sullivan was a physician who was in attendance at the trial of Lizzie Borden. His chief responsibility was to revive witnesses, jurors and observers of the trial who fainted due to the excessive heat in the courtroom. Dr. Sullivan lived in New Bedford.

Sullivan, Michael

Michael Sullivan, a laborer in Fall River, was interviewed by police officers Philip Harrington and Patrick Doherty on August 23, 1892. He had no pertinent information related to the crimes at the Borden house, and there is no record of what he said to his interviewers.

Sullivan, Timothy A.

Timothy Sullivan was a conductor for the Globe Street Railway Company. He told authorities that while he was on duty the morning of August 4, 1892, he remembered seeing Andrew J. Borden walking downtown. His statement helped the police trace Andrew's movements before he was killed later that morning. Because Sullivan simply rode past Andrew and did not talk to him, he was not called as a witness at any of the formal investigatory meetings concerning his murder.

Swift, Augustus (1831-1906)

Augustus Swift was one of the twelve jurors picked to judge the guilt or innocence of Lizzie Borden at her trial in New Bedford, Massachusetts, which took place between June 5 and June 20, 1893. On the last day of the trial, Swift and the other eleven jurors found Lizzie Borden "not guilty" of the murders of her father and stepmother, Andrew and Abby Borden.

Augustus Swift was born in Falmouth, Massachusetts, to Nathan D. and Pamela C. (Cowen) Swift. He and his family moved to New Bedford when Augustus was young. There, he learned his trade as an iron moulder. Swift left the New England area for a few years. Upon his return he was was employed at the Fairhaven Iron Foundry. Swift married Nancy S. Jenney of Providence, Rhode Island, in 1854 and later established the Acushnet Iron Foundry in New Bedford. He lived there the rest of his life and died at the age of seventy-five.

Swift, Ezra J. (1841-?)

Ezra J. Swift of New Bedford was in the compressed yeast business. He was called to the courthouse on June 5, 1893 as a potential juror in the Lizzie Borden trial. When questioned however, Swift said he was against capital punishment. Swift was excused from jury duty in the Borden case.

Swift was born in Falmouth, Massachusetts, on August 6, 1841 and was a sailor much of his life. He then worked as an agent for the Fleischman Yeast Company. Swift was also active in the New Bedford YMCA and was its director at one time.

Swift, Marcus George Barker (1848-?)

Marcus George Barker Swift was the the personal lawyer of Alice Russell who was a friend of Lizzie Borden and a witness before the grand jury and at the final trial. Russell planned to give damaging testimony against Borden concerning a suspicious act she saw Lizzie complete on August 7, three days after the murders of Andrew and Abby Borden.

Russell was suffering from insomnia when she appeared before the grand jury in Taunton, Massachusetts, on November 15-20, 1892. Swift advised Russell to return home to Fall River until her insomnia passed (see Alice Russell).

When Russell realized that she had neglected to tell the grand jury that she saw Lizzie Borden burn a dress in the kitchen stove the Sunday after the murders, Swift advised her to contact District Attorney Hosea M. Knowlton and tell him. As a result, the grand jury reconvened in special session on December 1, 1892 and after hearing Alice Russell's testimony voted 20-1 for a trial.

Swift studied law at the University of Michigan and arrived in Fall River in December, 1874. He was a successful partner in the law firm of Swift and Grime and a member of the First Congregational Church.

T

Taber, Charles H.

New Bedford policeman Charles Taber was on duty at the front entrance of the New Bedford courthouse on June 7, 1893 with Officer Thomas F. Callanan. Their job that day was to keep the crowd of onlookers out of the room where the trial was being held. Officer Daniel J. Humphrey was at the rear entrance at that time performing the same service. The crowds at both entrances were reported as being quiet and co-operative.

Taber, Edward S. (1826-?)

Edward S. Taber of New Bedford was president and treasurer of the Morse Trust, Drill and Machine Company. He was called to the courthouse for jury duty at the Borden trial.

On the stand answering questions, Taber said that he was not related to any of the Bordens. He also stated that although he had opinions about the case, he was not prejudiced.

Taber felt that he could reach a fair decision based on the evidence presented, but asked the court to excuse him due to old age. Taber was sixty-seven years old. The court granted his wish, and Taber did not serve on the Borden jury. It is possible Taber was the younger brother of John H. Taber (see John H. Taber).

Taber, John H. (1823-?)

John H. Taber of New Bedford was listed in the *New Bedford City Directory* but there was no mention of his occupation. At seventy years of age at the time of the Borden trial, it is likely that Taber had retired from active employment. Taber asked to be relieved from the duties of serving on the Borden jury because of his age, and he was excused. It is not known if John H. Taber was any relation to Edward S. Taber who was also from New Bedford and also excused from service on the jury in consideration of his age.

Talford, John

John Talford was a New Bedford policeman, who along with an Officer McBay, blocked crowds as Lizzie arrived from her jail cell in Taunton for her arraignment before Judge John Wilkes Hammond in superior court on May 8, 1893 for the murders of her father and stepmother. After a trial date of June 5, 1893 was set Lizzie was returned to her cell in Taunton. Talford's name was misspelled as "Telford" in newspaper reports.

Taylor, Charles H.

Charles H. Taylor was the editor of the *Boston Globe* at the time the story known as the "Trickey-McHenry Affair" was published in that paper. This hoax greatly embarrassed the prestigious *Globe* when the story was published on October 10, 1892 (see Edwin D. McHenry and Henry G. Trickey).

Taylor, H.C.

H.C. Taylor covered the Borden trial for the *New York World*. Leonard Rebello lists him as "H.C. Tyler" in *Lizzie Borden Past and Present*.

Tebbitts, Joseph E.

Joseph Tebbitts of Mansfield, Massachusetts, was a member of the grand jury that decided Lizzie Borden must stand trial for the murders of her father and stepmother. That decision was rendered by the grand jury on December 2, 1892.

Terry, Carl A.

Carl A. Terry affixed his signature to Lizzie Borden's will as a witness on January 30, 1926. The two other witnesses were Ellen R. Nottingham and Charles L. Baker. Terry was a law partner of Baker in Fall River firm of Baker, Seagrave and Terry.

Terry, Ernest Alden (1885-1955)

Ernest Alden Terry was Lizzie Borden's chauffeur during the latter part of Miss Borden's life. He must have been an extremely loyal employee for Lizzie Borden remembered him and his family in her will. Terry received $2,000 in cash and a piece of property Lizzie owned that was adjacent to her home in Fall River, called "Maplecroft." Terry's wife Ellen and their daughter Grace also received the sum of $2,000 each. He was a pallbearer at Lizzie's funeral.

Tetrault, Joseph H. (1863-?)

Joseph Tetrault was the coachman for the Borden sisters when both lived at Maplecroft. Emma developed a strong dislike for him for reasons now forgotten, and fired him, even though Lizzie wanted the coach driver to stay. Tetrault went back to his old profession of barber until later rehired by Lizzie Borden.

It is possible that hard feelings over Tetrault contributed to Emma's decision to leave Maplecroft in 1904. Tetrault left Fall River for the final time in 1908. He moved to Providence, Rhode Island, the city of his birth.

Tetro, Joseph

See Tetrault, Joseph.

Thomas, Philip H.

Philip H. Thomas, a jeweler from North Attleboro, was called for jury duty to the New Bedford courtroom where Lizzie Borden was tried for the murders of her father and stepmother. Thomas was neither questioned nor picked for the jury, probably because the full number of jurors had already been reached.

Thomas, Titia (Tish)

Tish Thomas, a manicurist in Madame Rosilla Butler's beauty shop on Tremont Avenue in Boston, was mentioned in a letter from L. Apthorp of Wilton, New Hampshire, dated June 14, 1893. In the letter Apthorp said Thomas told one of her customers that a friend of hers mentioned a story about Lizzie Borden and a cat.

According to the letter, Jim Wilder was in the Borden home as a guest on July 7, 1890 when a cat owned by the Bordens suddenly jumped into Wilder's lap, startling him. Lizzie Borden, in the room at the time, apparently became upset and took the cat outside. She returned a few minutes later and assured Wilder that the cat would not bother him again. Lizzie had chopped off the cat's head with a hatchet.

Wilder related the incident to his sister Susy, who told Tish Thomas. The authorities in Fall River did not follow up on this lead after the Bordens were murdered. A description of this incident is in the Knowlton papers (HK329) as an undated manuscript under the title "OUIJA."

Thompson, Charles P.

Charles P. Thompson was a superior court judge who came from Gloucester, Massachusetts. He presided at the grand jury hearing December 2, 1892 in Taunton that resulted in the indictment of Lizzie Borden for the murders of her father Andrew and her stepmother Abby.

Thurber, William G.

William G. Thurber was co-owner of the Tilden-Thurber art gallery in Providence, Rhode Island, where Lizzie was accused of stealing two porcelain art objects in 1897, four years after she had been acquitted of the murders of her father and stepmother. Lizzie denied she ever took anything. The incident was far from over.

Thurber notified Lizzie Borden that he would press charges against her and greatly embarrass Lizzie unless she signed a document in front of witnesses confessing to the crime of August 4, 1892 in Fall River, Massachusetts. According to a story that first surfaced in 1952, Lizzie signed the confession in the presence of Tilden, Thurber and three other witnesses: employee Morris House, newspaper reporter Stephen O. Metcalf and detective Patrick H. Parker. Some Borden writers, especially Edwin D. Radin in *Lizzie Borden: The Untold Story* (1961), have pronounced the confession a hoax.

Thurston, Frank

Frank Thurston was Assistant Superintendent of Streets in Fall River. He backed up the statement of Abner Coggeshall that Coggeshall was at work the morning of the Borden murders and, therefore, could not have heard screams coming from the Borden home at 92 Second Street (see Abner Coggeshall).

Thurston, Thatcher T.

Thurston was a reporter for the *Fall River Globe*. He and Edwin H. Porter covered the Borden trial for the *Globe*. Thurston was well-respected by his fellow reporters and considered one of the best reporters in the Fall River area.

Tilden, Henry

Henry Tilden was a co-owner in the Tilden-Thurber Art Gallery in Providence, Rhode Island. He was involved in the shoplifting incident that elicited the so-called confession of Lizzie Borden to the 1892 murders of her father and stepmother (for more information see William C. Thurber, Morris House, Strephen O. Metcalf and Patrick H. Parker).

Tilghman, Hiram

Hiram Tilghman was employed in New Bedford as a driver for the firm of Kirby and Hicks. Lizzie Borden and Taunton Sheriff Andrew Robeson Wright arrived in New Bedford by rail from Taunton on June 3, 1893 to prepare for the upcoming trial. Upon leaving the train they boarded Tilghman's rig and immediately headed for the New Bedford jail on Court Street.

Her arrival at the jail was noticed by the nervous maid of Josiah A. Hunt, the jailkeeper. The maid was Bridget Sullivan, now in the employ of Keeper Hunt and his wife.

Tillson, Henry H.

New Bedford businessman Henry H. Tillson had been a packer and preserver of furs for thirty years and was considered an expert on their care. He was called to the witness stand by the prosecution at the Borden trial and questioned about the use of prussic acid for the cleaning of fur, specifically a sealskin cape that Lizzie Borden claimed needed attention.

Tillson, pharmicist Charles H. Lawton and analytical chemist Nathaniel Hathaway attempted to answer questions put to them by the prosecution but could not completely address the queries. Defense lawyer George Dexter Robinson objected to every question put to Tillson, Lawton and Hathaway. Tillson did manage to say, however, that he never heard of the use of prussic acid to clean fur.

Eventually the court declared all evidence relating to prussic acid inadmissible at the trial. Soon after the court reached its decision concerning the admissibility of the prussic acid evidence, the prosecution rested its case.

Tingley, Leon H.

Leon H.Tingley of Attleboro was called for jury duty in the Borden trial. He was a farmer, according to the *Attleboro City Directory*. Tingley was challenged by Lizzie Borden and did not sit on the jury.

The *New Bedford Evening Standard* mentions Leon H. Tingley in its June 5, 1893 edition. In the June 6th issue, however, it mentions instead one James Tingley. James Tingley is also listed in the *Attleboro City Directory* as a produce dealer. Leon is used instead of James as the Tingley who appeared at the trial mainly because his name was used by Marilynne K. Roach in her description of the jurors in the courtroom in the *Lizzie Borden Quarterly* (October 1999) and she claims to have used the official trial transcript.

This highlights one major problem for researchers seeking information from original sources: the newspapers of the day were notorious for getting facts wrong, especially names. Many names were either misspelled beyond recognition or simply confused with a person whose name was similar to that of the subject of the news story.

Tinkham, David P.

David P. Tinkham from Easton, Massachusetts, was considered for jury duty in the Borden trial until he stated that he was against the use of capital punishment. Tinkham was then excused.

Tinkham, Otis

Otis Tinkham of New Bedford was listed in the *New Bedford City Directory* as an edge trimmer. He was called for jury duty in the Borden murder trial but did not appear in court when his name was called. He did not serve on the jury.

Tourtellot, John Quincy Adams

J.Q.A. Tourtellot, a physician in Fall River, was a member of the first autopsy team that examined the bodies of Andrew and Abby Borden on their dining room table at 3:00 P.M. the day of the murders. The others present at this first autopsy were Drs. John W. Coughlin (also Mayor of Fall River at the time), William A. Dolan, Albert C. Dedrick, John H. Leary, Thomas Gunning, Emmanuel Dutra, Anson C. Peckham and Borden family physician Seabury W. Bowen.

Towle, George W.

Dr. George W. Towle was the physician of Emma Borden while she was living in New Hampshire during the last few years of her life. On the night of June 1, 1927, Towle gave Emma a sedative because she had trouble falling asleep. Although Emma did not yet know it, earlier that very evening, her sister Lizzie had died.

Emma awoke early the next morning, June 2 and fell down a flight of stairs leading from her bedroom to the kitchen of her home. She shattered her hip and died on June 10, 1927. On her death certificate Towle wrote that a contributing cause to the death of Emma Lenora Borden was "...senility. Duration-unknown."

Trickey, Henry G. (1862-1892)

Henry G. Trickey was a famed crime reporter who worked for the *Boston Globe*. He wrote the exposé story concerning the murders of Andrew and Abby Borden that became known as the "Trickey-McHenry Affair." The article, published on October 10, 1892, captured the attention of the entire nation and is a prime example of what modern historians call "yellow journalism." It was almost entirely false and remains to this day an embarrassment to those who believe reporting the news is an important and honorable profession.

Trickey was the star crime reporter on the *Globe* and arrived in Fall River the day after the Borden murders to cover that affair for his newspaper. Reporters from all over the nation came to Fall River in the ensuing months but because Trickey worked for a Massachusetts paper, he had an inside advantage with the Fall River police investigators. He became close to policemen Michael Mullaly, William Medley and Assistant City Marshal John Fleet.

The *Globe* reporter also had a strong professional relationship with Providence, Rhode Island private detective Edwin D. McHenry, who had been hired by the Fall River police to aid in the criminal investigation. The two men had previously worked together on cases covered by Trickey and investigated by McHenry. The detective approached Trickey in early October 1892 and said he was willing to sell the reporter all of the information the police had against Lizzie Borden, by then the prime suspect in the case, for the sum of $1,000.

McHenry claimed City Marshal Rufus B. Hilliard had handed him a list of twenty-five suspects and the testimony they would give at any future trial. Trickey, like any avid reporter, was interested in scooping the competition and accepted his proposition. He gave the detective thirty dollars, all the cash he had at the time, and rushed back to Boston on the next available train to get the rest of the money from his editor.

After he returned to Fall River the following afternoon, McHenry tried to stall the excited reporter. Fearing McHenry would try to sell the same information to a reporter from the rival Boston *Herald,* Trickey offered the detective $400 on the spot, a deal McHenry accepted.

Still fearful of being scooped by the *Herald*, Trickey, now back in Boston, pressured his editor into publishing the sensational story without first checking the facts. The front-page news item was published on October 10, 1892. Almost immediately, problems arose. People named as important witnesses could not be found, nor was there anyone in Fall River who had ever heard of them. Many of the addresses of these witnesses were either vacant property or did not exist at all.

Those few mentioned in the article who did exist, including Borden family lawyer Andrew Jennings, Rev. E.A. Buck, Emma Borden and Hannah Reagan, immediately denied the truth of the *Globe's* claims.

Some sent angry telegrams to the paper. Others threatened to sue the paper for libel, especially about one part of the story that strongly hinted Lizzie was pregnant at the time of the murders and the father was none other than her uncle, John Vinnicum Morse.

At first, the *Globe* defended the truth of the story. By the next day however, as the protests against the story mounted, its editors began to retreat from a full defense of the piece. They now blamed McHenry for giving out false information about the names and addresses of the "witnesses." McHenry explained that there was an obvious need to keep their real identities secret. Finally, in Tuesday evening's edition of the *Globe*, the paper offered a full front-page retraction and apology.

Adding to the *Globe's* embarrassment, Trickey apparently offered Borden maid Bridget Sullivan $1,000 to leave the country. Bridget reported the offer to District Attorney Hosea M. Knowlton, and as a result the same grand jury that indicted Lizzie Borden for the murders of her father and stepmother also indicted Henry G. Trickey for tampering with a government witness and had a warrant issued for his arrest. Trickey fled to Canada two days after the indictment.

On December 3, 1892, he died there while trying to jump aboard a moving train. Knowlton sent a representative of the Commonwealth of Massachusetts to Canada to view the body and it was indeed the corpse of the *Boston Globe* reporter (see Edwin D. McHenry).

Trickey's death was not the only result of this unfortunate hoax. McHenry's detective business and reputation were ruined. Also public opinion, which had been leaning towards blaming Lizzie Borden for the murders, now saw her as an unjustly dishonored victim of the *Boston Globe's* prejudice against the well-to-do. Thus, Lizzie gained invaluable sympathy from people not only around the nation but, perhaps more importantly, from the residents of Bristol County, Massacahusetts, where the jurors who would decide Lizzie's fate at trial were to be chosen.

Henry G. Trickey was born in Dover, New Hampshire, to John W. and Betsey E. Trickey. As a youth Trickey and his family moved to Belmont, Massachusetts, and he graduated from the local high school with honors. He moved to Boston to study law but decided against becoming an attorney after a year.

He landed a job as a reporter for the *Tribune* in Cambridge, Massachusetts, at the age of seventeen and was soon hired by the *Boston Globe*. His beat was the Lexington-Belmont-Arlington area outside of Boston until he was assigned to the Boston city desk.

Trickey was an enthusiastic, successful reporter and wrote colorful pieces on Boston's opium dens in 1885, conducted an exclusive interview with ex-Confederate leader Jefferson Davis the following year and reported on some of Boston's more notorious murder cases. He married Mary Gertrude Melzar of Wakefield, Massachusetts, in 1890 and enjoyed membership in the Boston Press Club and the Press Cycle Club.

After his writing on the Borden murders was exposed as a hoax, Trickey left his home in Dorchester, Massachusetts, and went to the house of a relative in Evanston, Illinois. From there he travelled to Hamilton, Ontario, Canada where he registered at a hotel under the name Henry Melzar. It was there on December 3, 1892 that Trickey fell under the wheels of a westbound train in Hamilton.

Tripp, Mrs. A.B.

Described as a neighbor of the Bordens, Mrs. Tripp operated a restaurant at 80 Second Street, three houses north of Lizzie's home. Tripp was mentioned briefly in the *Fall River Herald's* August 12 edition. She was questioned by police officer William H. Medley and later at the inquest of Lizzie Borden as to the relationship between Lizzie and the two elder Bordens. The record of the actual questions asked Mrs. Tripp or her answers to them has yet to be made available to Borden scholars.

Tripp, Augusta D.

Augusta D. Tripp, wife of Cyrus W. Tripp, resided in Westport, Massachusetts. She was the daughter of a Mrs. Poole and the sister of Carrie M. Poole of 20 Madison Street, New Bedford.

On July 21, 1892, Lizzie Borden and her sister Emma travelled to New Bedford together. Emma, after dropping Lizzie off, continued on to Fairhaven, Massachusetts. Later that week, Lizzie and the Pooles went to Westport to visit Augusta Tripp, a dear friend of Lizzie Borden from their school days.

Mrs. Tripp was interviewed by policeman William Medley in Westport on August 8, four days after Andrew and Abby Borden were murdered. Tripp told Medley Lizzie hated Abby and Lizzie said that her stepmother was "deceitful, being one thing to her face and another to her back" (see Carrie M. Poole, Mrs. ? Poole and Emma Borden).

Tripp, Carrie

Journalist Carrie Tripp reported on the Borden murder trial for the *New Bedford Evening Standard.*

Turner, Edward

On the witness stand at Lizzie Borden's trial on June 9, 1893 in New Bedford, Massachusetts, police officer Philip Harrington was asked how he first heard about the Borden murders. He stated that he was told of the crimes by "a young man named Turner." No other description or name was given. The *Fall River City Directory* for 1892 lists several Turners as living in Fall River but only one, Edward, who was listed as a "student" seems to fit the description as being youthful.

Turner, Vida Louise Pearson

Vida Pearson sang Lizzie Borden's favorite hymn, "My Ain Countrie," at Lizzie's funeral which was held at Maplecroft, the deceased's home. When Mrs. Turner entered the living room, she was surprised to find herself alone. Even Lizzie's body was absent. She had been buried secretly the previous night. Turner sang her song to an empty room, quickly left the house and was paid by the undertaker in charge of the funeral.

Vida Turner sang in the choir of the Fall River Congregational Church on Rock Street. As Vida Pearson, she married Alfred G. Turner.

On July 6, 1979, Turner gave an interview published in *Lizzie Borden: A Case Book of Family and Crime in the 1890s* (1980) edited by Joyce G. Williams, J. Eric Smithburn and M. Jeanne Peterson. Turner was described by Joyce Williams as having a "rich contralto voice." She was frequently asked to sing at local funerals.

Tyler, H.C.

H.C. Tyler wrote about the Borden trial for the *New York World*, for which he was both a reporter and a member of the editorial staff. Author Kent refers to Tyler as "H.C. Taylor" in *The Lizzie Borden Sourcebook*.

V

VanWyke, Theo

Theo VanWyke of Mount Vernon, New York, wrote a crank letter to Fall River City Marshal Rufus B. Hilliard, one of scores Hilliard received concerning the murders of Andrew and Abby Borden in the weeks after the crime. VanWyke wrote that he was an expert in the art of palmistry and if Hilliard could send him a clear photograph of Lizzie Borden's hand he could tell if she were guilty of innocent of the murders. There is no record that Hilliard sent VanWyke the requested photograph.

Vincent, Mark T.

Mark T. Vincent worked for DeWolf and Vincent on Union Street in New Bedford, Massachusetts. His business is listed in the *New Bedford City Directory* of 1892 as "hardware, etc." Fall River policeman William H. Medley travelled to New Bedford and interviewed Vincent on September 12, 1892. His report, as recorded by stenographer Annie M. White, said that Vincent owned the hardware store of Hillman and Vincent.

Vincent told Medley that he sold an ax to a Portuguese man on August 2, two days before the Bordens were brutally dispatched with a similar type of tool. Medley then took Vincent to observe a Portuguese who worked in the slaughterhouse on the farm of William and Isaac Davis. The Davises, father and son, were known to be friends with John Vinnicum Morse, the uncle of Lizzie and Emma Borden and at one time a suspect in the murders. After seeing the suspect at the farm, Vincent said that he was not the man who purchased the ax from his store.

Vinnicum, William

William Vinnicum of South Swansea, Massachusetts, owned a farm in nearby Swansea. John Vinnicum Morse, most likely a relative given the name common to both men, visited Vinnicum's farm on Wednesday, August 3, 1892, the day before the murders of Andrew and Abby Borden. Morse then returned to the Borden home where he had been staying later that evening.

On Friday, August 5, the day after the murders, Morse left the Borden house and walked to the post office. There he wrote out a card to William Vinnicvum and mailed it. He then was chased by a mob as he walked back to 92 Second Street and was saved from harm by the quick actions of either policeman John Minnehan or John Devine, one of whom had been shadowing Morse since he left the Borden residence (see John Vinnicum Morse and John Minnehan).

W

W., D. ??

This sketch artist, who is remembered today only by his initials, was present at the Borden trial. Listed among the reporters and sketch artists in Leonard Rebello's *Lizzie Borden Past and Present*, he worked for one of New Bedford's evening newspapers. However, it is unclear which journal employed him.

Wade, Frank C.

Frank C. Wade was interviewed by Fall River policemen Patrick Doherty and Philip Harrington on August 12, 1892. Wade reported that he saw a strange man near a pond acting suspiciously soon after the Borden murders. Officers Harrington, Doherty and William Medley dragged the pond but found nothing connected to the Borden case.

Wade, John T.

John T. Wade was a poultry farmer from Taunton, Massachusetts. He was summoned to New Bedford to appear in court as a potential member of the jury. On the stand Wade declared that he was not biased in the case and that he believed that he could come to a fair decision based on the evidence presented. He was challenged by Lizzie Borden however, and did not serve on the Borden jury.

Wade, Vernon

Vernon Wade owned a grocery store at 98 Second Street, two houses south of the Borden residence. George Pettey, a witness for the prosecution at the trial, stated that he passed the Borden home at 10:00 A.M. the day of the murders and saw Borden maid Bridget Sullivan washing the outside windows. He heard of the murders about one hour later while in Wade's store.

Pettey then walked north from Wade's grocery store to the Borden house. While there, Borden family physician Dr. Seabury Bowen offered to show Pettey the corpse of Andrew Borden. Pettey accepted Bowen's offer and saw Andrew's body on the sitting room couch (see George Ambrose Pettey).

Above Vernon Wade's store on the second story, according to both the *Fall River Daily Herald* and the *New Bedford Evening Standard*, lived Mary P. Chace and her husband Nathan. Mrs. Chace said she observed a man in the Borden yard stealing pears the day of the murders. Instead of the murderer, Mrs. Chace had seen mason's helper Patrick McDonald, who was working in John Crowe's stone yard, just east of the Borden property, on Third Street (see Patrick McDonald).

Walker, Nathan O.

Nathan O. Walker, a resident of Dighton, Massachusetts, was called for jury duty in the Lizzie Borden murder case. He claimed that he was prejudiced and was excused.

Walker, Thomas H.

Thomas Walker, a known local alcoholic, was an early suspect in the Borden killings. Police officers Philip Harrington and Patrick Doherty were sent to find and arrest him. When they located Walker and questioned him at the police station they asked where he was at the time of the murders.

Walker was a tailor by trade and worked for Peter Carey at Carey's shop at 98 South Main Street. Walker had recently married and moved into a house owned by Andrew Borden on Fourth Street. Because a rumor was circulating that the killer might have been a tenant or former of Borden, Walker became a suspect (see ?? Ryan).

One of the many rumors abounding in Fall River after the murders involved Walker. He supposedly fought constantly with his new wife and after each incident became drunk. He also was always behind on his rent to Andrew Borden, and Andrew and Walker had a confrontation at Carey's tailor shop three weeks before the murders. Borden was supposed to have threatened to evict Walker and Walker became upset.

Walker claimed that he was nowhere near 92 Second Street when the murders occurred. In fact, he was at work at Peter Carey's South Main Street tailor shop. When the police interviewed Carey, the tailor supported Walker's alibi that he had actually shown up for work at the time of the murders, a rare event when Walker became drunk. The police quickly eliminated Walker as a potential suspect (see Peter Carey).

Walsh, James A.

James A. Walsh of Fall River was the official photographer at the Borden murder scene. He was hired by Fall River Medical Examiner Dr. William A. Dolan to photograph the house, inside and out, as well

Mr. Walsh who photographed the bodies.

as take pictures of the mutilated corpses of Andrew and Abby Borden. All of the gruesome pictures of the murder scene as well as the photographs of the house and yard over the ensuing months found in the many books written about the Borden killings were the work of James A. Walsh.

Walsh testified at the trial of Lizzie Borden about the accuracy of the photographs he took when they were introduced by the prosecution as evidence and labeled as exhibits. When cross-examined on the witness stand by defense attorney George Dexter Robinson, Walsh stated that he took all of the interior pictures himself on August 4, 1892.

Waltrons, A.E.

Waltrons covered the Borden trial for the *New York Press*. He was also a member of the *Press* editorial staff. His specialty was covering political events in Albany, New York, and Washington, D.C.

Warner, Phoebe

Phoebe Warner was the widow of Sumner Warner and resided at 30 Second Street, a block or two north of the Borden home. Police officers Philip Harrington and Patrick Doherty interviewed Mrs. Warner on August 17, 1892 in an attempt to investigate every lead.

Phoebe Warner knew Andrew and Abby Borden as well as their two daughters, who came to call on her at her home during an illness. Warner told the investigators that she had heard rumors but knew nothing that would help the authorities in their efforts to solve the murders.

Warren, John Collins (1842-1927)

John Collins Warren was a noted physician, editor and Harvard University professor. He was recommended by Dr. George Gay to Attorney General Albert E. Pillsbury as a medical expert for the prosecution. Pillsbury, and later District Attorney Hosea M. Knowlton, decided not to make use of Warren's expertise.

John C. Warren was born in Boston to Jonathan Mason and Annie (Crowninshield) Warren. He attended private schools in Boston and went on to Harvard where he received a Bachelor of Arts degree in 1863. Later that year, he entered Harvard Medical School and graduated with a Doctor of Medicine degree in 1866. He then had a private practice until 1871 when he was appointed instructor of surgery at Harvard.

Warren also became the editor of the *Boston Medical and Surgical Journal*, a post he held from 1873-1881. He was associated with Dr. Henry H.A. Beach, who was also recommended as an expert for the prosecution.

Warren was promoted at Harvard to assistant professor of surgery in 1882, associate professor in 1887 and finally a full professor in 1893. He received several honorary degrees of Doctor of Laws and belonged to many professional associations in the United States and in Europe. Warren authored many books on surgery and medicine before dying in Boston at the age of eighty-five.

Washburn, Cyrus (1824-?)

Cyrus Washburn of Raynham, Massachusetts, was called to serve on the jury at the Borden trial. He pleaded the court to be excused because of old age. The court consented to his request and Washburn was allowed to return to his home. At the time, he was sixty-nine years old.

Weaver, Thomas H.

Thomas Weaver, a carpenter from New Bedford, was called to the courthouse for jury duty. He was not questioned, however, and was sent home without serving on the jury that eventually acquitted Lizzie Borden.

Wells, J. Henry

Henry J. Wells was a successful Fall River businessman. He was a financier, property owner and a partner in Aldrich and Wells, a local hardware store.

Wells was also a business acquaintance of Andrew Jackson Borden. He attended the funeral of Andrew and Abby Borden on Saturday, August 6, 1892 and helped carry Abby's casket at Oak Grove Cemetery to the Borden family plot. The other pallbearers for Abby Borden were Frank L. Almy, Simeon B. Chace, Henry S. Buffinton, James C. Eddy and John H. Boone.

Westcott, William (1845-1921)

William Westcott was one of the twelve men chosen to sit on the jury that heard the evidence against Lizzie Borden and found her "not guilty." He was from Seekonk, Massachusetts, and was a farmer his whole life.

Westcott was born in Seekonk to Valorus and Charlotte (Perry) Westcott. He lived in a house on Pine Street in Seekonk which his ancestors had built and remained a resident there until he died. He married Helen M. Perry in 1869 and upon her death in 1876, married Catherine Amelia Turner.

In his notes concerning potential jurors, Hosea M. Knowlton wrote that Westcott had no interest in religion, although he was listed as attending the local Congregational Church, was married to his second wife (the phrase "second wife" was underlined) and had not talked about the case to anyone. State policeman George Seaver called Westcott, according to Knowlton's notes, "a good, practical man."

Whalon, Daniel

Daniel Whalon of Westport, Massachusetts, was summoned to New Bedford for jury duty. Whalon admitted while being questioned that he did harbor opinions about the murder case but felt that he was not prejudiced and could render a fair judgement. He stated however, that he did not support capital punishment and thus was unacceptable to the prosecution. Whalon was excused and did not serve on the Borden jury.

Wheeler, George H.

There were two George H. Wheelers listed in the *Taunton City Directory*. He earned his living either as a machinist and engineer or as a manufacturer of brick moulds. Wheeler was summoned from Taunton New Bedford to serve jury duty in the trial of Lizzie Borden but stated that he was against capital punishment and excused.

Wheeler, Simeon A.

Simeon A. Wheeler was from Taunton, Massachusetts, and quite possibly a relative of the George H. Wheeler mentioned above. Like George H. Wheeler, Simeon was called to serve on the Borden jury but during questioning said that he was prejudiced and was excused. Wheeler was listed in the *Taunton City Directory* as the proprietor of the Leonard Ice Cream Company.

White, Annie M.

Annie M. White was an official court stenographer for Bristol County, Massachusetts, at the time of the trial of Lizzie Borden. She was listed as a resident in the *New Bedford City Directory* for the years 1887-1894.

In her capacity as official stenographer, White recorded the testimony of witnesses at both the inquest of Lizzie Borden in Fall River, August 9-11, 1892, and at the preliminary hearing in the same city, August 25-September 1, 1892. Miss White was also called by the defense to quote from the inquest testimony of Bridget Sullivan, who had stated that Lizzie was crying when she first realized her father was dead. The defense hoped to convince the jury that Lizzie was not cold

Miss White reads the evidence of the first trial.

and uncaring, but simply a woman with strong feelings and a great love for her father who, like most women of the period, expressed their most intimate emotions far from the public eye.

White was also called by the defense as its last witness to read from the testimony of Alfred Clarkson. Clarkson had been a defense witness who claimed to be in the Borden barn and saw people milling around in the loft before Officer William Medley arrived there and claimed that he saw no footprints where Lizzie said she had stepped as her father was being murdered.

The most dramatic courtroom incident that involved Annie White occurred on June 10 when she was called to the stand by the prosecution to read from the inquest testimony of Lizzie Borden. When Borden answered questions at her inquest, the only people present were Lizzie herself, Judge Josiah C. Blaisdell and stenographer White.

Lizzie's answers at the inquest were confusing, contradictory and, in the opinion of many, incriminating. Lawyer and Massachusetts Superior Court Justice Robert Sullivan, in *Goodbye Lizzie Borden* (1974), believes that it was Lizzie's inquest testimony that convinced Judge Blaisdell to believe Lizzie Borden "probably guilty" of the murders of Andrew and Abby Borden and send the case to the grand jury.

Defense attorney George Dexter Robinson objected to the inclusion of Lizzie Borden's inquest testimony as evidence in the trial, saying that it had been obtained illegally (see John William Coughlin and George Dexter Robinson). The court supported the defense objection and the only statements Lizzie Borden made concerning the murders were not allowed to be heard by the jury. Eventually her inquest testimony was published in the *Providence Journal* and the *New Bedford Evening Standard*, but by then the jury was sequestered and had no knowledge of Lizzie's inquest statements.

White, Isaac B.

Isaac B. White was called as a witness for the defense at the Borden trial on June 16, 1893. When his name was announced, however, he was not present in the courtroom and never gave testimony at the trial.

Whitehead, Abby Borden (1884-1974)

Abby Borden Whitehead was the daughter of Abby Borden's half-sister Sarah (Gray) Whitehead and the niece of her namesake, Abby Durfee Gray Borden. Neither she nor her brother George, Jr. played a direct role in the Borden murder case, but that might have been simply the result of chance.

Sarah Whitehead had planned to attend the policemen's picnic at Rocky Point on the day the Borden murders occurred. She intended that her daughter Abby spend the day at her Aunt Abby Borden's house on Second Street. George was to go to another aunt, Lucy, who lived in another section of Fall River near the home of City Marshal Rufus B. Hilliard. There was a late change in plans however, and both Abby and George went to the home of their Aunt Lucy.

Marshal Hilliard told their aunt of the deaths of the Bordens while standing in Lucy's front yard. At the time, Abby was helping her aunt wash some windows. Shocked by the news of Abby's death, Lucy dropped the window she was washing on Abby's hand. Later that week, young Abby attended the funerals of her Aunt Abby and Uncle Andrew Borden accompanied by her mother Sarah and her grandmother Jane E.D. Gray.

Seventy years later in 1972, Abby Whitehead, by then Abby Potter, gave an exclusive and extensive interview to Judge Robert Sullivan, whom she knew was writing a book on the Borden tragedy. She had relocated to Providence, Rhode Island, but returned to Fall River with Judge Sullivan to give him both a tour of the area and the personal interview described in his book *Goodbye Lizzie Borden* (1974). In his well respected work, Sullivan wrote that it was Abby Whitehead Potter who first related the story of Lizzie decapitating a cat at 92 Second Street (see Titia Thomas).

Whitehead, George O. (1887-?)

George O. Whitehead was the young son of Sarah (Gray) and George W. Whitehead and a nephew of Abby Borden. His sister was Abby Borden Whitehead, Mrs. Borden's namesake (see Abby Borden Whitehead).

Whitehead, George W., Sr. (1861-1898)

George Whitehead, a teamster who lived at 45 Fourth Street, was the husband of Sarah (Gray) Whitehead, the half-sister of Abby Borden.

Whitehead, Sarah Bertha (Gray) (1864-1932)

Sarah Bertha (Gray) Whitehead was the younger half-sister (by thirty-six years) of Abby Borden. She was the daughter of Oliver Gray and his second wife Jane. She lived in a house at 45 Fourth Street, sharing the property with her widowed mother.

Scholars of the Borden murder case have speculated that if, when Andrew Borden died and his wife inherited Andrew's fortune, Lizzie and Emma feared that Abby would use the family money and property to help her family, mainly Sarah, and leave Andrew's two daughters with little or nothing. This, they contended, could have been the motive for the brutal murders of the Bordens on August 4, 1892.

Sarah was called "Bertie" by her older sister Abby, who was more a mother than a sibling to her. Abby felt especially close to her younger sister and lavished a great deal of her attention on her. Abby had no children of her own, and she knew that her husband's daughters Lizzie and Emma despised her. Sarah was Abby Borden's friend and confidant.

Immediately after the murders, no one in the Borden home thought to inform Sarah of the double tragedy until Borden maid Bridget Sullivan mentioned it as an afterthought. Some Borden scholars believe that Sarah was the only person who would have sent Abby a note of distress such as the one Lizzie said Abby received the day of the murders. Sarah, however, was not ill that day.

Sarah Whitehead did not own the property on Fourth Street that she and her family shared with her mother. She owned a one-fourth share as did Andrew Borden, who had purchased it from the widow Mrs. Gray and given it to his wife, Abby. This act of rare charity on the part of the elder Borden angered his two daughters, even after Andrew tried to mollify them by giving each a share of their late grandfather Abraham Borden's home on Ferry Street in Fall River (see Jane E.D. Gray).

At her sister's trial, Emma Borden testified that Andrew's gift to his daughters did not end the daughters' anger. Andrew actually bought the Ferry Street property back from Lizzie and Emma for cash a few weeks before the murders.

Sarah Whitehead was also interviewed in the "sanity survey" that Moulton Batchelder conducted at the request of District Attorney Hosea M. Knowlton (see Moulton Batchelder). In it Sarah said that she never heard of any insanity in the Morse family, but did say they were "ugly."

Sarah Bertha Whitehead was born in Fall River to Oliver and Jane E.D. (Baker) Eldridge Gray. She married George W. Whitehead, a teamster and later a produce salesman in Fall River. She relocated to New York City in 1912 and died in Winnipeg, Canada. After the Bordens were murdered Andrew's daughters inherited all of Andrew's estate. Sarah and her other sister, Priscilla, split only the meager estate of Abby, which amounted to $1,626.05 in savings and $90 in cash.

Whittaker, William

Whittaker was a "spare" or substitute trolley conductor in Fall River for the Globe Street Railway Company. He carried John Vinnicum Morse and six priests in his trolley car when the Bordens were murdered, thus confirming Morse's alibi that he was not near 92 Second Street when Abby and Andrew Borden were slain. Morse's claim was substantiated by a conductor named Kennedy who, as the conductor of a passing street car, remembered seeing the six priests in Whittaker's trolley.

Wilbar, Frederick C.

See Wilbur, Frederick Copeland.

Wilber, Lemuel K.

See Wilbur, Lemuel Keith.

Wilbur, Frederick Copeland (1857-1928)

Frederick Copeland Wilbur was mistakenly called Frederick Wilbar by the *New Bedford Evening Standard*. He was listed as a potential juror and was one of twelve men who were chosen to sit on the jury that decided on June 20, 1893 that Lizzie Borden was not guilty of murdering her father and stepmother.

Wilbur resided in Raynham, Massachusetts, at the time of the murders and trial and earned his living as a cabinet maker. He was the son of William and Jeminah (Tracy) Wilbur and was married to Elvira Caswell.

At the time of the trial, Wilbur was a prominent and respected citizen of Raynham. He was described in the personal notes of District Attorney Hosea M. Knowlton as a Republican and a member of the

Juror Frederick C. Wilbur.

Congregational Church, although not very interested in religion. According to Knowlton's notes, Wilbur believed that Lizzie was guilty of the crime.

One of Knowlton's advisors on the possible jury members, state detective George Seaver, described Wilbur as a "Good, fair man." Yet another advisor, listed only as "Gilmore" in Knowlton's notes, described him as "Uncertain." For Knowlton and the prosecution Gilmore's assessment turned out to be the more precise of the two.

Wilbur, John (1833-1915)

John Wilbur, no relation to juror Frederick Copeland Wilbur, above, was also one of the twelve men who sat on the Borden jury that acquitted Lizzie Borden. District Attorney Hosea M. Knowlton's adviser George Seaver, a state detective who also believed Frederick Wilbur was likely to decide in favor of the prosecution, called John Wilbur a "Good, square man for jury (sic)." Another prosecution advisor known only as "Gilmore" was more accurate, as he was in his description of Frederick Wilbur. Gilmore called John Wilbur "Doubtful."

John Wilbur was born in Somerset, Massachusetts, to Daniel Whitman and Welthy (Hall) Wilbur. He was a farmer in Somerset and also made a living as a road surveyor and housewright. Wilbur also had a local reputation as a breeder of fancy poultry. He married Esther D. Mosher of Warren, Rhode Island, in 1853 and spent his final years in Worcester, Massachusetts.

In notes published in *The Commonwealth of Massachusetts vs. Lizzie A. Borden: The Knowlton Papers, 1892-1893* (1994) Wilbur was listed as being an American, a Republican, a Methodist not interested in church affairs and one who had previously served on a grand jury. He also had not spoken of the Borden case to anyone else. Knowlton must have felt John Wilbur would be open to the prosecution's arguments but he and the other eleven jurors were convinced by the defense attorneys that Lizzie Andrew Borden did not commit the crimes for which she was charged.

Wilbur, Lemuel Keith (1837-1912)

Lemuel Keith Wilbur, a juror at the Borden trial, was not related to either Frederick Copeland Wilbur or John Wilbur. Lemuel was born in Norton, Massachusetts, to Oren and Polly (Eldridge) Wilbur and married Elizabeth Hudson Fuller of Easton, Massachusetts.

Wilbur was a respected resident of Easton at the time of the Borden trial who counted seven farms among his extensive agricultural holdings. He also possessed several hundred acres of woodland and potential farmland and at one time was involved in the lumber and coal business.

The *New Bedford Evening Standard* of June 5, 1893 described Wilbur as a handsome man of fine complexion with a face "betokening intelligence." District Attorney Hosea M. Knowlton's notes said that he was possibly a supporter of the Democratic Party, a family man with a wife and three children and that he had previous experience as a juror.

Although he was known to be against capital punishment, Knowlton's notes stated that his wife Elizabeth believed Lizzie was guilty of the double murders. The district attorney must have gambled that his wife's opinion might sway him, for he approved of Wilbur as a member of the Borden jury. Elizabeth's opinion notwithstanding, Wilbur agreed with the other eleven jurors and found Lizzie Borden "not guilty" on June 20, 1893.

Wilcox, Albert M.

Albert M. Wilcox, listed in the *New Bedford City Directory* of 1892 as an employee of the P.M. Company, was a resident of Fairhaven, Massachusetts. As a potential juror in the Borden trial he appeared before the prosecution and defense lawyers at the New Bedford courthouse on June 5, 1893. He stated that he was against capital punishment and was excused from jury duty.

Wilcox, William B.

William Wilcox and his wife were present at the funerals of Andrew and Abby Borden on Saturday, August 6, 1892. He worked as a clerk and received a brief mention as one of the mourners at the funeral in the *Fall River Herald*.

Wilder, James

There was a story circulating in Fall River after the Borden murders that sometime before the Bordens were killed, Lizzie chopped off the head of a family cat for jumping onto the lap of a guest. The story was attributed to both hairdresser Tish Thomas and Abby Borden Whitehead, a niece of Lizzie's stepmother Abby. James Wilder was supposedly the guest who was surprised by the Bordens' enthusiastic feline. There was no listing for a James Wilder in the *Fall River City Directory*.

Wiley, George T.

The *Fall River City Directory* of 1892 lists George Wiley as a bookkeeper at the Richard Borden Manufacturing Company. He, along with Ms. Dimon(d), was interviewed by private detective Edwin D. McHenry, who reported that Wiley was a clerk at the Troy Mill.

McHenry claimed that Wiley told him Adelaide Churchill, the Bordens' next door neighbor, told Wiley she saw something so unspeakable at the Borden home that she would never tell anyone what she had witnessed, "even if they tore her tongue out" (Annie M. White's quote of McHenry in her stenographic notes).

Wilkinson, Charles A.

Charles A. Wilkinson was the boss of Hyman Lubinsky, the Jewish ice cream peddler who claimed to have seen a woman at 92 Second Street come out of the barn and go into the house at about the time the murders of the Bordens occurred. At Lizzie's trial Lubinsky testified that he told his story of the woman on the Borden property to Wilkinson as well as to police officer Michael Mullaly and others. Wilkinson is listed in the *Fall River City Directory* as a maker or seller of "confectionery tools." He did not testify at any of the hearings or trials involving Lizzie Borden.

Williams, John T.

John T. Williams was summoned to the courthouse in New Bedford, Massachusetts, as a possible juror in the trial of Lizzie Borden. He lived in Taunton, Massachusetts, at the time and sold confectionery goods and periodicals for the company of Wood and Williams. He stated on the stand that he did not believe in capital punishment and was excused from serving on the Borden jury.

Willis, William H.

William H. Willis of New Bedford was a retired harness maker. When summoned to the New Bedford courthouse to appear for jury duty, Willis stated that he was eager to serve at the trial. He said that when the murders occurred, he was out of town on business and had heard nothing of the murders.

At this point, defense attorney Andrew Jackson Jennings gave the presiding judges a document which said Willis had stated he wanted to serve on the jury to convict Lizzie Borden of the murders of her father and stepmother. Willis heatedly denied this statement and the prosecution accepted him as a juror. He was, however, challenged by Lizzie Borden and did not serve on the jury.

Wilson, Charles H.

Charles H. Wilson, a Fall River policeman, was one of the first officers City Marshal Rufus B. Hilliard sent to 92 Second Street after the murders of the Bordens were reported to the authorities. Wilson testified for the prosecution at the Borden trial in New Bedford in June 1893.

Soon after Hilliard sent Officer George A. Allen to investigate a possible murder at the Borden home, Allen returned to the station house with a description of what he saw and a request for further instructions. Hilliard then sent Deputy Sheriff Frank H. Wixon, Officers Patrick Doherty, Michael Mullaly and William O. Medley, and Assistant City Marshal John Fleet to the Borden residence, followed almost immediately by Officers Philip Harrington and Charles Wilson. While Fleet went to talk to Lizzie Borden in her bedroom, Wilson and Harrington performed what was to be the first of several searches of the premises, including Lizzie's bedroom and some closets and drawers in other parts of the house.

Wilson, a witness for the prosecution, took the stand on June 9, 1893. He said that he heard Fleet interrogating Lizzie Borden when he, Wilson, first arrived at the house. Wilson also testified that he overheard Lizzie tell Fleet that the last time she saw her stepmother was at 9:00 A.M., when Abby was making up the bed in the guestroom where John Vinnicum Morse had slept the night before. Lizzie then said Abby received a note about a sick friend and, she thought, left the house. Wilson also remembered that Lizzie told Fleet she had been in the barn between twenty minutes and half an hour while Andrew was attacked and killed in the sitting room.

When District Attorney Hosea M. Knowlton asked Wilson on the stand if he had any further comments, Wilson added that Lizzie had said it was not necessary to search her room because it had been locked and Assistant Marshal Fleet then told his men to search the room quickly as Lizzie might be sick. This contradicted the statement given the previous day by Fleet who had claimed that the search was thorough. Officer Wilson had no more to do with the Borden case after his testimony.

Wilson, Mary J.

Mary J. Wilson was a dressmaker mentioned in the notorious *Boston Globe* article of October 10, 1892 now known as the "Trickey-McHenry Affair." According to the story, Wilson lived at 110 Rodman Street in Fall River and would testify as a witness for the prosecution that Lizzie once offered to sell her a gold watch for ten dollars. This watch closely resembled the one that belonged to Abby Borden which Andrew Borden reported stolen two weeks before the murders.

Wilson also supposedly agreed to testify that Lizzie frequently was insolent to Mrs. Borden and treated her badly. Based upon attempts to locate other "witnesses" mentioned in the newspaper article, Mary J. Wilson probably did not exist and was instead a creation of detective Edwin D. McHenry's fertile mind (see Henry G. Trickey and Edwin D. McHenry).

Wilson, Minnie C.

Minnie C. Wilson was mentioned in the same "Trickey-McHenry Affair" article reprinted in the *New Bedford Evening Standard* from the *Boston Globe* as was Mary J. Wilson. Reporter Henry G. Trickey also referred to her as a dressmaker. They were probably the same person, neither of whom was proven to have actually existed (see Mary J. Wilson).

Wing, Anjeanette Wilbur (1849-1924)

Anjeanette Wing was summoned as a witness in the Borden trial but was not called to the witness stand. She lived with her husband Joseph at 86 Middle Street in Fall River. There is no record as to what her testimony would have covered.

Anjeanette Wing was born in Tiverton, Rhode Island, to David and Hannah (Rounds) Wilbur. She married Joseph Wing, a clerk for the Fall River grocery firm of Cobb, Bates and Yerxa Company. She and her husband lived in Fall River at the time of the Borden murders. After her husband died in 1909, Anjeanette left Fall River for Cranston, Rhode Island, where she lived for the rest of her life.

Winslow, George (1848-?)

George Winslow was a farmer from Mansfield, Massachusetts. He was called to New Bedford as a potential juror in the trial of Lizzie Borden. On the stand Winslow stated that he had no opinion concerning the case and that he was ready to serve. He sported a "fierce moustache," according to the *New Bedford Evening Standard*. Although Winslow was acceptable to the lawyers for the prosecution, he was challenged by Lizzie Borden and did not serve on the jury.

Winslow, Leander A. (1859-1929)

Leander A. Winslow was on District Attorney Hosea M. Knowlton's handwritten list of potential witnesses under the heading "As to escape." This most likely meant that he was in a position to see anyone entering or leaving the property of Andrew J. Borden about the time of the murders. Winslow was summoned to court but never called at the trial as a witness.

Winslow was born in Fall River, the son of James and Elizabeth Winslow. He married Mary Jane Durfee of Fall River in 1881 and was a business partner of Edmund J. Sokoll in the firm of Sokoll, Winslow and Co., Confectioners. He later held a position as a clerk in the Fall River Electric Light Company. Winslow lived in Fall River his whole life and was active in several fraternal organizations.

Winward, James E. (1848-?)

James E. Winward's business interests were listed in the 1893 *Fall River City Directory* as "carpets and furniture; also undertaker." Winward's Undertaking Rooms was the preferred undertaking establishment of Fall River's upper class and the one Lizzie Borden chose to be in charge of the funerals of Andrew and Abby Borden after they were brutally murdered on August 4, 1892.

Although James C. Renwick was the undertaker who actually prepared the bodies for burial and testified at the trial, it was James E. Winward who escorted Lizzie from the Borden home, where the funerals were held, to a carriage waiting to transport the mourners to Oak Grove Cemetery for the burial services.

Soon after the body of Andrew Borden was discovered in the sitting room (and before Abby's corpse was found in the second floor guest room), Alice Russell and Adelaide Churchill, friends of Lizzie, were calming her down and attempting to make her comfortable in the kitchen area. Lizzie left the kitchen and went up to her room. When she returned to the kitchen after changing her dress to a pink wrapper, she told Russell, "When it is necessary, I should like to have Undertaker Winward."

At 9:00 A.M. on the day of the double funeral, Winward was notified by one of the city officials that after the graveside services the bodies would not immediately be buried, but instead put in a holding vault until a second autopsy was performed. After that autopsy the skulls of the Bordens were removed and prepared as an exhibit for a trial, should one take place. The family was not told of the second autopsy or cleaning of the skulls until they were displayed at the trial.

Wixon, Frank H. (1841-1908)

Frank H. Wixon was a Bristol County deputy sheriff from Fall River. He was paying a friendly visit to friends at the Central Police Station when a telephone call to City Marshal Rufus B. Hilliard informed him that something unusual had occurred at the Borden house at 92 Second Street. Wixon was one of the first to arrive on the murder scene. He testified at the preliminary hearing and the final trial as to what he observed at the Borden home the morning of the murders.

Wixon arrived at the Borden residence at approximately 11:35 A.M. and was followed almost immediately by Assistant City Marshal John

Officer Wixon.

Fleet and Officers William Medley, Charles H. Wilson and Philip Harrington. He observed the bodies of both victims that morning and then walked about the back yard.

Wixon testified as a witness for the prosecution at the Borden trial on June 9, 1893. He said that the wounds on Andrew Borden's body appeared fresh and that the blood was bright with no signs of coagulation; it reminded him of fresh wounds he had seen in battle on Roanoke Island during the Civil War. Abby's blood, in contrast, was hardening and of a "dark maroon color. It had thickened up."

Wixon was then allowed to give his opinion that Abby died before Andrew. If true, this meant that Andrew's survivors, Emma and Lizzie Borden, and not Abby's heirs, the Whiteheads, would inherit Andrew's fortune.

Wixon told the jury that after examining the bodies he went out into the Borden rear yard and climbed a six foot high wire fence by standing on a pile of lumber. He said he was able stand on the fence and see over to the other side, the property used by John Crowe's stone yard. There Wixon saw three men, John Dennie, Joseph Desrosiers and

Patrick McGowan, at work. This statement was important to the defense for it showed the jury that a murderer could have left the Borden property by climbing the fence and escaping down Third Street.

Frank H. Wixon was born in Dennisport, Massachusetts, to Captain James and Bertha Wixon. The Wixon family moved to Fall River and Wixon entered the pharmacy trade in 1857. He enlisted in C Co. of the 5th Massachusetts Regiment under General Ambrose Burnside during the Civil War. After the war Wixon returned to Fall River.

Wixon's father died in 1872 after serving as a deputy sheriff in Bristol County for thirty years. Wixon was appointed to succeed his father and served in that position until his death in Fall River in 1908. He married Anna D. Estes in 1875 and was a member of the Grand Army of the Republic (GAR) and other fraternal organizations at the time of his death.

Wood, Edward Stickney (1846-1905)

Edward Stickney Wood, a physician and chemist at Harvard Medical School, testified at the trial of Lizzie Borden on June 13, 1893 as a witness for the prosecution. He also headed the forensic team at Harvard that examined evidence sent there from the Borden murder scene by Fall River authorities.

At Harvard, Wood received four jars of physical evidence taken from the home and from the bodies of murder victims Andrew and Abby Borden. The jars contained samples of milk delivered to 92 Second Street on the day of the murders, milk from the following day, the stomach and stomach contents of Andrew Borden the day he died and similar contents from his wife Abby. After testing these samples, Wood formed opinions as to whether or not poison was involved in the deaths of the Bordens and which victim died first. Wood also received and analyzed some clothing of Lizzie Borden and hatchets found by the Fall River police in the Borden home.

Wood was called to the stand as an expert witness for the prosecution, but his testimony seemed to aid the defense team at least as much as it did the Commonwealth. Until Dr. Wood was called as a witness most of the prosecution's questioning was handled by William Moody.

With Wood on the stand however, District Attorney Hosea M. Knowlton took over the interrogation.

Knowlton questioned the Harvard chemist on his background as an expert on poison and bloodstains, the study of which in the nineteenth century was called "physiological chemistry." He questioned Dr. Wood about his analysis of the stomach contents of the victims and of the milk they consumed the day they died. Knowlton then asked about his examination of one of Lizzie Borden's dresses and his results from the testing of several hatchets sent from the Borden home.

On the witness stand Wood claimed first of all that there was absolutely no evidence of poison, specifically prussic acid, in the stomach contents of either victim. Secondly, Wood strongly stated that, given the assumption both Bordens sat down to eat breakfast at the same time, Abby Borden preceded her husband in death by one and one-half hours. This was determined by an analysis of the state of the undigested and partially absorbed contents of each victim's stomach.

When asked about the "handleless hatchet" that the prosecution believed was the actual murder weapon, Wood said that it was possible, though far from certain, that the hatchet in question was the tool that dispatched the Bordens. That would have depended upon when the handle had been separated from the hatchet head.

There was no evidence of blood on the hatchet head with the piece of wood in its eye that was sent to Dr. Wood for analysis. If the handle had been broken after the tool was cleaned, then it could have been used to kill the Bordens and still show no signs of blood. There would have been no blood caught in the cracks of the broken handle.

If, on the other hand, the handle had been broken and disposed of before it was cleaned, then there would have been blood in the break. So it was possibly used as the death weapon. But, without the knowledge of when it was cleaned, nothing concerning the hatchet as the murder weapon could be stated with absolute certainty.

When Knowlton asked Wood about blood and hair on the hatchets, the forensic expert said he saw no blood on the hatchets and tests as to whether the hair was human or animal were inconclusive. One sample was definitely animal hair, and the other sample was lost during the shipping between Fall River and Cambridge. He also could not tell if a spot of blood on one of Lizzie Borden's skirts was from her or one of the victims.

In cross-examination by defense attorney Melvin Adams, Wood was questioned further about a dark spot on Lizzie's white skirt which was about the size of the head of a small pin. Wood said that the spot, at the rear of the skirt towards the center near the bottom, was blood. But whose blood, Dr. Wood could not tell. Perhaps it was from one of the victims. But, Wood stated, it could have been Lizzie Borden's menstrual blood.

Next, Wood's testimony turned to the spattering of the victims' blood onto the body or clothes of the murderer as he attacked his victims. In cross-examination Wood stated that blood from an attack such as the two Bordens experienced could spatter everywhere or almost nowhere. If the killer attacked Andrew from behind, he or she could have been showered with Andrew's blood from his waist up. In killing Abby the spray would be from his waist down towards his feet.

Edward S. Wood was not a strong witness for the prosecution. In stating that the killer most likely would have been covered in his or her victims' blood, he aided the defense since no one had observed any blood on the skin, hair or clothing of Lizzie Borden.

Defense attorney George Dexter Robinson used Wood's statements about the prussic acid to argue successfully that all evidence related to poison should be excluded from the trial. Wood had also given opinions about the handleless hatchet that the defense could have used to argue that the prosecution did not have any murder weapon that, without a shadow of a doubt, could be connected to the accused.

In appearance Wood was described as red-faced and gray haired. Some saw him as handsome. Borden writer David Kent stated that he looked like "an army officer browned by long duty on the plains."

Wood was born in Cambridge, Massachusetts, and received his Bachelor of Arts degree from Harvard in 1867. He entered Harvard Medical School the following year and received the degree of Doctor of Medicine in 1872. He then went to Europe where he studied physiology and medical chemistry in Berlin and Vienna.

Wood was appointed assistant professor of chemistry at Harvard in 1871 and a full professor five years later, a position he kept until his death. He married Elizabeth Richardson of Cambridge, Massachusetts, in 1883 and was under the care of Dr. Maurice H. Richardson at the time of his death at the age of fifty-nine.

Wood, George A.

George A. Wood of Taunton was summoned to court in New Bedford to serve as a juror at the Borden trial. He worked as a seller of periodicals and confectionery and was a partner of John T. Williams in the firm of Wood and Williams (see John T. Williams). Wood stated that he was against capital punishment and was excused from serving on the jury that eventually acquitted Lizzie Borden.

Wood, Henrick

Fall River policemen Philip Harrington and Patrick Doherty attempted to interview Henrick Wood at his house at 19 Oxford Street on August 11, 1892. Wood was not at home when the two officers called. Some Fall River authorities suspected Wood of being Dr. Benjamin J. Handy's "wild-eyed man," but a picture of Wood eliminated him as soon as Handy saw his picture; Handy said Wood looked nothing like the stranger he saw (see Benjamin Jones Handy).

Wood, John

See Mahr, Henry.

Wordell, Allen H. (1848-1920)

Allen H. Wordell was a member of the jury that found Lizzie Borden "not guilty" of the murders of her father and stepmother, Andrew Jackson and Abby Durfee Gray Borden. He had never served on a jury before and had not mentioned the Borden murders to anyone previous to being chosen to sit on this jury, according to the handwritten notes made by District Attorney Hosea M. Knowlton before the trial began.

Wordell had a reputation as being devoted to his wife and children and as a good businessman. Wordell was born in Fall River but was living in North Dartmouth, Massachusetts, at the time of the trial. He married three times and in 1893 made his living as a retailer of agricultural tools and seed for the firm of Wilson and Wordell, located in New Bedford.

Wordell, Isaac B. (1856-1894)

Isaac B. Wordell was a member of the Fall River Police Department. Although he had no active role in the investigation of the Borden murders, his name appeared on official witness summons forms as a constable. He was promoted to inspector with the rank of lieutenant when the police department was reorganized in 1893, and in this capacity he signed the summonses ordering witnesses to appear at the Borden trial.

Isaac Wordell was born in Providence, Rhode Island, to William and Rebecca (Luther) Wordell and was appointed a patrolman in the Fall River Police Department in 1883. On the force, he was a partner of William Medley and was a member of the Fall River police at the time of his death.

Worswick, Mary A.

See Robsart, Amy.

Wright, Andrew Robeson

Andrew Robeson Wright was Sheriff of Bristol County and also a bailiff at the trial of Lizzie Borden. Wright had at one time lived in Fall River and served as city marshal, the position held by Rufus B. Hilliard during the Borden murders and trial. His wife Mary Jane

Sheriff Andrew Wright.

Wright was a matron at the Taunton jail and thus was with Lizzie Borden while she awaited trial. The Wrights' daughter Isabel was a childhood friend of Lizzie's while both were growing up in Fall River.

Sheriff Wright accompanied Lizzie Borden on the train that took her from Taunton to New Bedford on the morning of Saturday, June 3, 1893. He took a seat directly behind Lizzie and reporters said that she appeared unconcerned about the destination and reason for the trip. After Lizzie and Sheriff Wright arrived at the Old Colony railroad station, they entered a waiting carriage driven by Hiram Tighman and proceeded to the county jail.

On June 20 the jury found Lizzie "not guilty." At the announcement of the verdict, the courtroom burst into cheers. Andrew Wright had the responsibility of keeping order in the court. Frank Spiering, describing the scene in *Lizzie* (1984), says that as the spectators began cheering Wright did not even make an attempt at keeping order and actually broke into tears of joy himself. A contemporary account in the *New Bedford Evening Standard*, in contrast, has Wright pounding his desk for order, yelling for the standing crowd to sit down and actually pushing some viewers out of the aisle.

Wright, Edward E. (1862-1931)

Edward E. Wright was a druggist in New Bedford. He and fellow New Bedford druggist William R. Martin believed that Lizzie Borden had entered their drug stores and attempted to buy hydrocyanic, also called prussic, acid from them before the murders of the Bordens. Wright and Martin both testified before the grand jury in Taunton on November 17, 1892.

Wright was employed by I.H. Shurtleff, Apothecary in New Bedford until he opened his own business, the Wright Drug Company, in 1889. The last year Wright was listed in the *New Bedford City Directory* as running his firm was 1907. Wright claimed that while Lizzie was travelling with her sister Emma to visit friends in New Bedford, Lizzie came into his drug store to purchase the prussic acid. Neither Wright nor Martin testified at the Borden trial because the court declared all evidence concerning the prussic acid inadmissible.

Wright, Isabel Mathewson

Isabel Wright was the daughter of Bristol County sheriff and bailiff Andrew Robeson Wright and his wife Mary Jane, female matron of the Taunton jail. Isabel Wright was a childhood friend of Lizzie Borden when both families lived on Ferry Street in Fall River. While Lizzie was in the Taunton jail for ten days awaiting her preliminary hearing, Mrs. Wright recognized the old playmate of her own daughter and the two had a tearful reunion.

Wright, Mary Jane (Irving) (1832-1905)

Mary Jane Wright was the wife of Bristol County Sheriff Andrew Robeson Wright. While her husband was Bristol County Sheriff between 1886 and 1896, she was the female matron of the Taunton jail. Lizzie Borden stayed at the jail in Taunton while awaiting her preliminary hearing because it was the only one in the Fall River area which had accommodations for female prisoners. The Taunton jail had fifty-six cells for male prisoners and nine for women. Each jail cell was 9

1/2' long and 7 1/2' wide. Lizzie's cell had a bed, a chair and a wash-bowl.

Years earlier when the Wright family had lived on Ferry Street in Fall River, Lizzie Borden was a friend of the Wrights' daughter Isabel. Initially, Mrs. Wright did not realize that the murder victims were their Ferry Street neighbors. After Wright realized the connection, she asked Lizzie if she was the childhood friend of her daughter. When Lizzie answered in the affirmative, Mrs. Wright left Lizzie's cell in tears.

Lizzie remained a prisoner in Taunton for ten days after which time she was transferred to Fall River for her preliminary hearing. There, she stayed in the room of jail matron Hannah Reagan at the Fall River police station. Apparently Mrs. Wright was a comfort to her famous prisoner. After Lizzie was acquitted and took a vacation, she returned to Taunton and personally thanked Mrs. Wright for her kindness while she was Lizzie's matron and keeper. Mary Jane Wright died in Fall River at the age of seventy-three.

Wright, William B.

William B. Wright of Boston was the assistant to Norfolk County court reporter Frank Hunt Burt. William H. Haskell and C.E. Barnes were Burt's two other assistants. They were in charge of the official type writers who wrote down the stenographic notes taken at the Borden trial by Annie M. White. Those employed as type writers were A.M. Dollard, Florence W. Cushing, Florence D. Ross and Mrs. William H. Haskell. All were from Boston.

Wyatt, George

George Wyatt was known around Fall River simply as "George." Even though he was a respected and visible citizen in his capacity as clerk of the court, few apparently knew his last name. His job was to formally announce judges and any others who appeared for any trial as a witness, plaintiff or defendant.

He had an acerbic though lovable personality. When Lizzie arrived in the Fall River police station's courtroom for her preliminary hearing, her seat was occupied by observers. Many of them were from the Christian Endeavour Society. He gruffly hustled them elsewhere in a quick and efficient manner. The *New Bedford Evening Standard's* reporter noted Wyatt's stern demeanor and remembered that Wyatt, so serious about his responsibilities, "sometimes even dictates to Judge (Josiah Coleman) Blaisdell."

Wyatt, Mary B. (1852-?)

Mary B. Wyatt's name appeared on a handwritten list of witnesses written by District Attorney Hosea M. Knowlton. She was one of eleven people listed under the heading, "As to escape." Wyatt was a widow living with Dr. and Mrs. Seabury Bowen at 91 Second Street. Knowlton probably wanted to know if Wyatt had seen anyone enter or leave the Borden residence at the time the murders had taken place.

Mrs. Wyatt was first mentioned in the *Fall River City Directory* in 1892 and was last listed here in 1921. She was questioned by the Fall River police after the murders of the Bordens. Wyatt most likely had nothing of value to add to the investigation, for though she was summoned to appear at the Borden trial, she was not called to the stand as a witness.

Bibliography

Adilz, Fritz. "An Armchair Solution To The Borden Mystery," *Lizzie Borden Quarterly* 3:1 (January 1996): 7-10.

Attleboro City Directory, 1888.

Bertolet, Maynard F. "John Vinnicum Morse," *Lizzie Borden Quarterly* 5:1 (January 1998): 3.

Binette, Dennis A. "The Edmund Lester Pearson/Frank Warren Knowlton Correspondence," *Lizzie Borden Quarterly* 4:4 (October 1997): 7-11.

Boston City Directory, 1892.

Brown, Arnold R. *Lizzie Borden: The Legend, The Truth, The Final Chapter*. Nashville, Tennessee: Rutledge Hill Press, 1991.

Caplain, Neilson. "Lizbits (Chronology of the Lizzie Borden Murder Case)," *Lizzie Borden Quarterly* 4:2 (April 1997): 5-7.

———. "Lizbits (The Enigmatic Miss Sullivan)," *Lizzie Borden Quarterly* 2:6 (Winter 1995): 9.

———. "Lizbits (One Fact-One Book)," *Lizzie Borden Quarterly* 3:3 (July 1996): 5.

———. "Lizbits (Victoria Trivia)," *Lizzie Borden Quarterly* 2:6 (Winter 1995): 9.

———. "Lizbits (A Walk Along Second Street)," *Lizzie Borden Quarterly* 5:3 (July 1998): 5.

———. "Lizbits (The West Side of Second Street)," *Lizzie Borden Quarterly* 5:4 (October 1998): 1, 5, 17.

Curry, Judy P. "A Closer Look At Actress Nance O'Neil," *Lizzie Borden Quarterly* 2:3 (Summer 1994): 4-5.

Fairhaven City Directory, 1893.

Fall River City Directory, 1892, 1893, 1894, 1926, and 1927.

Fall River Daily Globe, 1892-1893.

"INTENSE EXCITEMENT," *Fall River Daily Globe*, 6 August 1892. Reprinted in *Lizzie Borden Quarterly* 4:3 (July 1997): 15.

Flynn, Robert A. *Lizzie Borden and the Mysterious Axe*. Portland, Maine: King Philip Publishing Company, 1992.

Gloucester City Directory, 1879.

Golden, Eve. "Vamp: The Rise and Fall of Theda Bara," excerpted in *Lizzie Borden Quarterly* 5:3 (April 1998).

Kent, David. *Forty Whacks: New Evidence in the Life and Legend of Lizzie Borden*. Emmaus, Pennsylvania: Yankee Books, 1992.

————, ed. *The Lizzie Borden Sourcebook*. Boston: Branden Publishing Company, 1992.

Lincoln, Victoria. *A Private Disgrace: Lizzie Borden by Daylight*. New York: Pyramid, 1969.

Lyons, Louis M. *100 Years of the* Boston Globe. Cambridge, Massachusetts: The Belknap Press of Harvard University, 1971.

Martins, Michael and Dennis A. Binette, eds. *The Commonwealth of Massachusetts vs. Lizzie A. Borden: The Knowlton Papers, 1892-1893*. Fall River, Massachusetts: The Fall River Historical Society, 1994.

New Bedford City Directory, 1893.

New Bedford Evening Standard, 1892-1893.

New York Times, 1892-1893.

New York Times Index, 1890-1893. New York: R.R. Bowker Company, 1966.

Oak Grove Cemetery, Fall River, Massachusetts. Cemetery records, 1892-1900.

O'Dwyer, Riobard and Maynard F. Bertolet. "Bridget Sullivan Before and After," *Lizzie Borden Quarterly* 3:2 (April 1996): 1, 11-12.

Our County and Its People: A Descriptive and Biographical Record of Bristol County, Massachusetts. Boston: Boston History, 1899. Found in the Cox microfilm file of the Family History Center of the Church of Jesus Christ of Latter Day Saints, Tucson, Arizona.

Pagano, Anthony J. *Images of America: Melrose.* Dover, New Hampshire: Arcadia Press, 1998.

Pearson, Edmund. *Studies In Murder.* New York: Random House, 1938.

Porter, Edwin H. *The Fall River Tragedy.* Fall River, 1893.

Providence, City of. *City Directory,* 1893-1894.

Radin, Edward D. *Lizzie Borden, The Untold Story.* New York: Dell Publishing Company, 1961.

Rebello, Leonard. *Lizzie Borden Past and Present.* Fall River, Massachusetts: Al-Zach Press, 1999.

————. "The Elusive Alice M. Russell," *Lizzie Borden Quarterly* 1:3 (July 1993): 2.

Representative Men and Old Families of Southeastern Massachusetts. Chicago: J.H. Beers and Co., 1912.

Roach, Marilynne K. "Choosing the Borden Trial Jury," *Lizzie Borden Quarterly* 6:3 (October 1999): 1, 18-22.

Spiering, Frank. *Lizzie.* New York: Random House, 1984.

Sullivan, Robert. *Goodbye, Lizzie Borden.* Brattleboro, Vermont: The Stephen Greene Press, 1974.

Taunton City Directory, 1874, 1879, 1882, and 1902.

Trow's New York City Directory, 1892-1893.

White, Annie M., Stenographer's Minutes (unpublished), copy in private collection of Jules Ryckebusch).

Williams, Joyce, J. Eric Smithburn, and Jeanne M. Peterson, eds. *Lizzie Borden: A Case Book of Family and Crime in the 1890s.* Bloomington, Indiana: T.I.S. Publications, 1980.

Subject Index

About the Author

Paul Dennis Hoffman is the author of several magazine articles on the Borden murders as well as on topics as diverse as the history of rock and roll music, silent movies, racism in American history, and education. He received his B.A. in American history from the State University of New York at Albany and an M.A. in American history and a Ph.D. in education, both from the University of Arizona.

Dr. Hoffman has been interested in the Borden case for over 40 years and has spoken widely on the subject. He was born in New York City and currently lives with his wife and daughters in Tucson, Arizona. His son, daughter-in-law, and two grandchildren reside in Virginia.

p3 interment